Social and Economic History of England

EDITED BY ASA BRIGGS

W9-BTP-463

The Age of Plunder
King Henry's England
1500–1547

W. G. HOSKINS

FORMERLY READER IN ECONOMIC HISTORY
IN THE UNIVERSITY OF OXFORD

LONGMAN
London and New York

Longman Group Limited London

*Associated companies, branches and representatives
throughout the world*

*Published in the United States of America
by Longman Inc., New York*

© Longman Group Limited 1976

First published 1976

Library of Congress Cataloging in Publication Data

Hoskins, William George, 1908–
　　The age of plunder.

　　(Social and economic history of England)
　　Bibliography: p.
　　Includes index.
　　1. Great Britain – Economic conditions.
2. Great Britain – Social conditions.
3. Great Britain – History – Henry VIII, 1509–1547.
I. Title. II. Series.
HC254.4.H67　1976　330.9'42'052　75–43647
ISBN 0 582 48544 4 paper
ISBN 0 582 48273 9 cased

Set in IBM Journal 10 on 12pt
and printed in Great Britain by
Lowe & Brydone (Printers) Ltd,
Thetford, Norfolk

Contents

94783

List of Figures and Tables

Introductory Note

Interest in economic history has grown enormously in recent years. In part, the interest is a by-product of twentieth-century preoccupation with economic issues and problems. In part, it is a facet of the revolution in the study of history. The scope of the subject has been immensely enlarged, and with the enlargement has come increasing specialization. Economic history is one of the most thriving of the specialisms. Few universities are without an economic historian. New research is being completed each year both in history and economics departments. There are enough varieties of approach to make for frequent controversy, enough excitement in the controversy to stimulate new writing.

This series, of which Professor Hoskins's volume if the fourth, is designed to set out the main conclusions of economic historians about England's past. It rests on the substantial foundations of recent historical scholarship. At the same time, it seeks to avoid narrow specialization. Economic history is not lifted out of its social context, nor are the contentious borderlands of economics and politics neglected. The series is described as 'a social and economic history of England'.

The bracketing together of the two adjectives is deliberate. Social history has received far less scholarly attention than economic history. A child of the same revolt against the limited outlook of the political historian, it has grown less sturdily. Its future depends on the application of greater discipline and more persistent probing. Developments in recent years are encouraging, and many of them will be reflected in these volumes. So too will developments in historical geography and, where they are illuminating, in demography and sociology. There is hope that just as the economist has provided useful tools for the study of economic history, so the sociologist may be able to provide useful tools for the study of social history and the demographer valuable quantitative data. There is no need, however, for economic and social historians to work in separate workshops. Most of the problems with which they are concerned demand cooperative effort.

However refined the analysis of the problems may be or may become, however precise the statistics, something more than accuracy and discipline are needed in the study of social and economic history. Many of the most lively economic historians of this century have been singularly undisciplined, and their hunches and insights have often proved invaluable. Behind the abstractions of economist or sociologist is the experience of real people, who demand sympathetic understanding as well as searching analysis. One of the dangers of economic history is that it can be written far too easily in impersonal terms: real people seem to play little part in it. One of the dangers of social history is that it concentrates on categories rather than on flesh and blood human beings. This series is designed to avoid both dangers, at least as far as they can be avoided in the light of available evidence. Quantitative evidence is used where it is available, but it is not the only kind of evidence which is taken into the reckoning.

Within this framework each author has complete freedom to describe the period covered by his volume along lines of his own choice. No attempt has been made to secure general uniformity of style or treatment. The volumes will necessarily overlap. Social and economic history seldom moves within generally accepted periods, and each author has had the freedom to decide where the limits of his chosen period are set. It has been for him to decide of what the 'unity' of his period consists.

It has also been his task to decide how far it is necessary in his volume to take into account the experience of other countries as well as England in order to understand English economic and social history. The term 'England' itself has been employed generally in relation to the series as a whole not because Scotland, Wales or Ireland are thought to be less important or less interesting than England, but because their historical experience at various times was separate from or diverged from that of England: where problems and endeavours were common or where issues arose when the different societies confronted each other, these problems, endeavours and issues find a place in this series. In certain periods Europe, America, Asia, Africa and Australia must find a place also. One of the last volumes in the series will be called 'Britain in the World Economy'.

The variety of approaches to the different periods will be determined, of course, not only by the values, background or special interests of the authors but by the nature of the surviving sources and the extent to which economic and social factors can be separated out from other factors in the past. For many of the periods described in this series it is extremely difficult to disentangle law or religion from economic and social structure and change. Facts about 'economic and social aspects' of life must be supplemented by accounts of how successive generations thought about 'economy and society'. The very terms themselves must be dated.

Where the facts are missing or the thoughts impossible to recover, it is the duty of the historian to say so. Many of the crucial problems in English social and economic history remain mysterious or only partially explored. This series must point, therefore, to what is not known as well as what is known, to what is a matter of argument as well as what is agreed upon. At the same time, it is one of the particular excitements of the economic and social historian to be able, as G. M. Trevelyan has written, 'to know more in some respects than the dweller in the past himself knew about the conditions that enveloped and controlled his life'.

ASA BRIGGS

Preface

Few dates in English economic history can compare with that of the death of Henry VIII in 1547. It was the end of an age in more ways than one, with the brief and pathetic aftermath of Edward VI's reign before the outburst of the Elizabethan Age.

It is curious that the social and economic history of Henry's reign has never before been studied as a whole. The immense literature of his reign has been mainly concerned with Henry's marital and political disasters and his religious manoeuvrings; but on the social and economic side nearly every important book and essay begins at 1540, an odd date in many ways which is mainly attributable to the great Tawney, though he never intended it so. Thus Henry's reign, all but the last seven years, has been relatively neglected. Yet it is Tawney's magisterial work, *The Agrarian Problem in the Sixteenth Century*, published in 1912, that stands as the one great exception to this statement.

The choice of the title *The Age of Plunder* may seem to call for some explanation. In one sense the whole of English history, certainly since 1066, has been a history of plunder by the governing class and its officials and other hangers-on. The Norman Conquest was itself a plunder of the whole country by adventurers from across the Channel and resulted in the almost complete turnover of landed property in the country from English to foreign landlords. The sixteenth century was the greatest act of plunder since that time, carried out by the native governing class: it produced the biggest changeover in land-ownership for nearly five hundred years, mainly arising from the systematic plunder of the Church at all levels and later the plunder of the Crown itself by the magnates of the realm.

It is difficult to define plunder, and even more so the word 'corruption'. Some historians, especially biographers of Tudor notabilities, naively conclude that it scarcely existed since absolute proof is rarely to be found. The problems of definition have best been stated by Professor Joel Hurstfield in his *Freedom, Corruption, and Government in Elizabethan England* (1973) and I do not propose to traverse the same ground. Corruption had always existed in the background: years before the open plunder of the Church in the 1530s that great man whose life redeems the squalid reign of Henry VIII, had already observed in his *Utopia*: 'So God help me, I can perceive nothing but a certain conspiracy of rich men procuring their own commodities under the name and title of a Commonwealth.' Thomas More wrote this when he was well under forty years old, and some twenty years before the naked plunder of the monasteries, where there was little or no attempt at concealment. But he was well acquainted with the inner workings of the City of London and the private conversational schemings of its rich men. His father had been an eminent judge, and he himself was a brilliant lawyer in his twenties. He moved in high legal and other circles and knew how they worked, whatever the public smokescreen might conceal. More put his finger on the heart of the matter well before the populace at large could see the plunder openly at work, the rich enriching themselves regardless of the common weal. So it is today.

The sixteenth century, then, was a century of more or less open plunder of the resources of the State, more open in the reigns of Henry VIII and Edward VI, less so under Elizabeth. But it never ceased. Most monarchs were aware of it and did little about it provided it was kept within a small circle. There has been no lack of apologists for this enrichment of the rich at the expense of the rest of the community. I have read them all and am not impressed by the argument. The most common defence is that the historian must not judge the doings of those in power, the Establishment, in the sixteenth century by the standards of the twentieth. I do not accept this argument. The plunderers under Henry VIII well knew what they were doing. It was the naked use of power.

History is written almost invariably from the standpoint of the socially dominant class, just as one of the prizes of military victory is the privilege of writing the military history of the time, true or false. My own ancestors in Henry VIII's time were generally in the middle of the social spectrum, typical of their time in being yeomen who made no money out of the Great Plunder, and husbandmen, and a few craftsmen and labourers among them. Then, too, I grew up in a part of England which was still basically a pre-industrial society. There was virtually no industry in the modern sense, people all knew each other, and more often than not had been born in the place where they worked; and there was also much ragged poverty, low wages, and whole streets of bad housing put up in the sixteenth century and leaning precariously, held together one felt only by the dirt of ages. It was a leisurely world, and there was a great deal of talking done on street corners or from the tops of hedgebanks, when time stood still as if clocks had not been invented.

Such a world still exists for me sixty years later: I now recognize how much of sixteenth-century England has lived on into an age of huge towns and anonymous armies of wage-earners. Historians necessarily chop history into 'periods', but older human societies often remain encapsulated in a later and an alien age. I therefore write with sympathy of the kind of world I have known and can still see in places, without supposing it was a golden age. Like that great French social historian Georges Lefebvre, I can say 'j'ai travaillé à mon rang dans la communauté'. The rich and powerful ones of the past have, some would say, been neglected in this book (except Henry himself) but they were political beings for the most part and have all been copiously treated by other historians. I have written deliberately about the mass of people who constituted the commonwealth of King Henry's England: only about the magnates in so far as they manipulated, or employed, the acquiescent majority.

Apart from this personal and inherited background, my approach to the social and economic history of this period of practically fifty years from the 1490s to 1547 has as far as possible been solidly based on statistics. I am aware that this does not make for the easiest of reading, but no matter. It was Georges Lefebvre who also said that in social history one must study large groups of the population and not merely the dominant class, that the statistical method should be used wherever possible. Not all history can be treated so: there will always be the unique and the imponderable. But, he says, 'pour faire de l'histoire il faut savoir compter': one must count or vast problems are overlooked and unexplored. Yet even when calculating our statistical tables, we must always see the social classes behind them, and behind them again the ordinary men and women of the time. History is far from being merely applied statistics.

Yet it is in the 1520s that we get such a comprehensive valuation of the country, both lands and personal estate, that we are obliged to analyse this magnificent record in detail. Though many of the returns are irretrievably lost, enough survive to enable us to draw a picture of the distribution of wealth, group by group and region by region, for a wide sample of Henrician England. For the first time in English history we are able to measure with a fair amount of exactitude the great inequality in the distribution of worldly goods in representative towns and country areas, and to draw certain conclusions from this picture.

And unless we realize how great was this inequality we cannot properly discuss a great deal of the social and economic history of this century. Not until Gregory King's more tentative estimates in the late seventeenth century do we get anything like a comparable analysis. It must be confessed that though this valuation of all their property was kept secret from the mass of the population, and was therefore a trap into which even the rich (except the wily merchants of London who learnt of the real purpose of the so-called Muster) fell headlong, the returns can be criticized in some ways: but then what historical record in wide use has not at some time been subject to such doubts? The fact remains that this is substantially a sweeping and on the whole accurate return; but because of the vagaries of Tudor arithmetic (especially in totalling figures) and perhaps one's own occasional stumbles in this jungle of figures, I have not tried to apply any elaborate statistical techniques to the bare facts. I leave this to others, without much faith in their elaborations.

On the statistical side, too, I have used the lists of freemen, where they have been published, to arrive at a more detailed picture of the occupational structure of certain towns. These tables, too, are very revealing about a complexity of urban life and trade greater than we had hitherto imagined. We get away thankfully from the flabby generalizations about wool and cloth and see how a town was constituted in fact, with up to a hundred different occupations in the larger towns and sixty or more in the medium-sized. Thus a slump in the exports of the cloth trade on a national scale can easily be exaggerated in the economic fortune of the country as a whole, though it may have had minor and indirect effects. The freemen's lists have been subject to close scrutiny and have in some places been discounted. I hope I have taken sufficient account of such towns where the freedom was more or less severely restricted; but where I have used the lists for a select number of towns they show a remarkable level of agreement when classified by groups of trades, and where they differ the differences are of particular interest to the economic and social historian. I remain unrepentant about the use of these records, taking due account of their obvious imperfections, because they give us a more accurate picture of early sixteenth-century towns than we could get in any other way. Combined with the figures relating to the distribution of personal estate, which could vary considerably as between different towns in the same region without destroying some useful national generalizations, we begin to see the realities of economic life in Henrician England.

I could only wish that I had been able to make a similar contribution to the all-important subject of population in the sixteenth century, but there is no general agreement on this, not least because we do not have even rudimentary record sources before parish registers begin in the autumn of 1538; and the number of those registers that survive intact from that early date is but a fraction of the whole. In some respects, too, I am conscious of shortcomings, especially in the realm of the history of prices. Population and prices are the cornerstones of pure economic history, but I have to leave further research and controversy to others. An army of modern economists are no nearer an agreed answer today than we are for the sixteenth century. Nor indeed can they agree within any tolerable distance about the distribution of wealth in late twentieth-century Britain. Knowing the difficulties of such calculations for the sixteenth century, I hope I may be forgiven much when I survey the estimates of contemporary economists about our own economy.

I have been an unconscionable time in producing this book and have repeatedly been overtaken by the books and articles of others in specialist fields. I hope I have kept abreast of the latest work, but have no doubt failed somewhere. Chiefly, though, I must thank those who have waited patiently so long for the work to be finished, above all the publishers, who over a space of nearly twenty years have suffered quietly and not pressed at all unduly. The same apology must go to my generous benefactors who have waited without fuss, above all the Leverhulme Trustees who elected me as a Research Fellow as long ago as 1961–63 and as an Emeritus Research Fellow in 1970–71. In 1969–70, too, the ever generous Marc Fitch Fund gave me financial assistance with secretarial and research expenses. I am deeply grateful to both these benefactions for their timely help.

For better or worse, this work is now completed. On the personal side I have to thank my friend Dr Joan Thirsk, of St Hilda's College, Oxford, for reading my text and giving me valuable advice. If any faults remain after her patient scrutiny they must be attributed to my own obtuseness and only occasionally to my holding a different opinion. To some of my former research students at Oxford, I also owe thanks for keeping me reasonably up to date, working as I do in isolation. They have already begun to produce their own books and scholarly articles and I am now learning from them. Above all I owe much to Dr David Palliser of the University of Birmingham, and Dr Paul Slack of Exeter College, Oxford. Not least I have to thank Dr Peter Bowden for his ready permission to reproduce certain of his elaborate tables of food-stuff prices which he originally published in his chapter in Volume IV of the *Agrarian History of England and Wales* (ed. J. Thirsk). They did not appear in time for me to use them fruitfully in my own book, but I have printed them (with some modifications) as Appendix III and have no doubt they add considerably to its value for the agrarian history of the reign of Henry VIII. I wish I could have made better use of them, but time must call a halt at some point.

Then, too, I am grateful to Dr John Sheaill of the Nature Conservancy for his ready permission to use his maps of the distribution of wealth and population in the England of the 1520s; and to Mr John Stirling, the University Librarian at Exeter University, for his efficient service in providing me with out-of-the-way books. I also owe a great debt to Mrs Sheila Stirling for her expert labours on the Select Bibliography, which proved to be a much larger task than I had envisaged for her.

Finally, I owe much to my wife whose patience with a naturally difficult author in the throes of a complicated book never failed. I must also gratefully acknowledge her invaluable help in the final stages of the preparation of the typescript for the publishers. If after all this, any errors remain I alone am responsible.

Exeter, 1975   W. G. HOSKINS

List of Abbreviations

A.H.E.W.	*Agrarian History of England and Wales*, ed. Joan Thirsk
A.H.R.	*Agricultural History Review*
A.P.C	Acts of the Privy Council
Cal. S.P. Ven.	Calendar of State Papers Venetian
Econ. H.R.	Economic History Review
L.P.	Letters and Papers of Henry VIII
N.C.H.	Northumberland County History
P.R.O.	Public Record Office
T.E.D.	Tudor Economic Documents, eds. R. H. Tawney and E. Power
T. Leics. A.H.S.	Transactions of the Leicestershire Archaeological and Historical Society
T.R.H.S.	Transactions of the Royal Historical Society

So God help me, I can perceive nothing but a certain conspiracy of rich men procuring their own commodities under the name and title of a Commonwealth.

Sir Thomas More: *Utopia*

We, which talk much of Christ and His Holy Word, have I fear me, used a much contrary way; for we leave fishing for men and fish again in the tempestuous seas of this world for gain and wicked mammon.

Sir William Petre, in a letter to
Sir William Cecil, 1551

CHAPTER ONE

The Face of the Country

THE England to which Henry VIII succeeded in the spring of 1509, two months before his eighteenth birthday, was still medieval in every important respect. The King enjoyed jousting; the archer and the long-bow were objects of national pride and training, and would be for another generation or so despite the cannon and firearms used by foreign armies. Around possibly half the villages of England stretched the hedgeless open fields that had hardly changed, except in detail, for hundreds of years. Even in the enclosed regions of the west and north, the fields were medieval in size and shape. Manors and manor courts were a legal reality almost everywhere in the countryside. Most towns still looked to their medieval walls as their principal protection. Though a few unimportant places had let their walls fall into ruin, others more vulnerable were strengthening them. The incorporated towns were governed by medieval charters, and run by small oligarchies which were generally self-perpetuating and closed to all but a carefully chosen few. Gilds were strong and effective: their pageants were a regular feature of urban life. In larger towns, such as Coventry, there was an elaborate pattern of ritual and ceremonies that was purely medieval in origin and was highly active until the Reformation put a stop to it all.[1] The Church, like its latest buildings — and a high proportion had been rebuilt in the preceding generation and were still being built — was deeply medieval in worship and outlook; and the two ancient universities continued their immemorial and unchanging task of training an élite for the higher offices of Church and State.

[1] See Charles Phythian-Adams, 'Ceremony and the citizen: the communal year at Coventry 1450–1550', in Clark and Stock, eds., *Crisis and Order in English Towns*, pp. 57–85.

1

In town and countryside, the great mass of people lived in aged and decaying medieval houses: only the richer merchants of the towns and, in the country the richer squires and franklins in southern England, had built themselves newer and grander houses in a generation of prosperity before 1500. Erasmus, who had visited England on several occasions between 1499 and 1517, thought English houses were filthy. To this he attributed the prevalence of plague and the 'deadly sweat'. The houses were badly planned, with little or no ventilation; but above all it was the insanitary domestic habits that repelled him, coming from the culturally more advanced Netherlands. Floors were covered with rushes which were occasionally removed, 'but so imperfectly that the bottom layer is left undisturbed, sometimes for twenty years, harbouring expectorations, vomitings, the leakage of dogs and men, ale-droppings, scraps of fish, and other abominations not fit to be mentioned'. And these were the conditions in good-class houses, with large glazed windows (a luxury unknown among the mass of people) which let in light but sealed out any fresh air. Erasmus thought that a few domestic reforms such as giving up the use of rushes and better ventilation all round might well do more to stamp out plague than anything else. But plague and other killer epidemics were accepted philosophically by the English, for even in the 1550s a Venetian observer reported that 'they have some little plague every year, but do nothing about it'.[2] In this respect, too, the country was entirely medieval. Epidemics were the will of God.

Such surplus money as accrued was lavished in nearly every parish on the church: on its rebuilding and repair, or on costly plate, or the coloured images of saints, or rows of vividly coloured windows, or painted rood-screens. All the colour of life lay in the church, not in the home. Monasteries still towered over and ruled many towns, or lay quietly buried in the deep green countryside from Cornwall up to Cumberland,

> Forgotten in a forest-glade,
> And secret from the eyes of all

until Henry's commissioners sought them out however remote, and interrogated them a generation later.

Castles were still being built by old-fashioned men such as the Duke

---

[2] Apart from the quarantine of plague-stricken houses in London and Oxford in 1518, and similar action in a few other towns in the late 1530s, this statement was true. See Slack, 'Some Aspects of Epidemics in England, 1485–1640'.

of Buckingham at Thornbury in Gloucestershire (begun in 1511 and un-completed at his death ten years later), though the note of modernity sounded faintly even here for Thornbury was intended to be a castel-lated palace 'uniting the convenience of a residence with the security of a stronghold'. But elsewhere other magnates were building themselves true country houses, houses for show, with little or no thought of defence. Except along the Anglo—Scottish border there was now a strong central government, and the age of the private army had ended. Bradgate in Leicestershire was begun probably in the 1490s by the Marquis of Dorset and almost finished by the time of his death in 1501. Apethorpe in neighbouring Northamptonshire was begun about 1500; and the lovely brick house of the Mannocks at Giffords Hall in Suffolk was well under way when Henry came to the throne. Yet even these new houses were still being built basically on the medieval plan, with the great open hall occupying most of the centre block and two project-ing wings, one for the private apartments, the other the service block. As late as the mid-1550s William Cecil was building at Burghley in the old fashion. The 'new fashion' did not come flooding into England until Elizabeth I's time.[3]

The country-house civilization was just beginning to emerge, begin-ning its four-hundred-year dominance of English society; but the number of such houses was as yet small. Probably one could not have counted a score in all, completed or in course of being built in the year 1509. Castles were still considered important, though only the Duke of Buckingham was old-fashioned enough to build yet another. The Dukes of Norfolk were building themselves a palace at Kenninghall in the depths of Norfolk, but wisely did not make it look anything like a castle. This great house was apparently begun by the second duke, who reigned from 1514 to 1524, and completed by his son, the third duke, who lived here in splendour in the 1520s.[4] The country houses, and their enlightened and often powerful occupants, were one of the main growing points of English society in its struggle to emerge from the Middle Ages during the sixteenth century; but they were not numerous enough to effect this change until well into the reign of Elizabeth.

England was generally regarded by foreign visitors as a rich and agree-able country, apart from its climate. The reports of the Venetian ambassadors are particularly valuable and detailed, sent in cipher to

---

[3] Summerson, *Architecture in England, 1530—1830*, pp. 19, 23.
[4] Letters were being dated from Kenninghall by the third duke from the spring of 1525.

3

their masters in Venice and now mostly translated in the *Calendars of State Papers Venetian*. One of the earliest of these is now commonly known as *A Relation . . . of the Island of England*, and was written in the last two or three years of the fifteenth century. It speaks of the pleasant hills and beautiful valleys, the delightful woods, the plenty of water everywhere. The writer found England deficient in grain-growing lands (he could never have visited East Anglia or the Midlands) but noted 'an immense profusion of every edible animal' and game-birds of every kind. With its fertile soil, its heavy wool production, and the precious tin of Cornwall and Devon, he thought 'the riches of England are greater than those of any other country in Europe'.

Much of the Venetian's view of England was impressionistic and misleading; but one thing that he (and others) noted in contrast to their native lands was the comparative emptiness of the English countryside. The population seemed to bear no relation to the fertility of the island, and this was not because they were gathered in towns. Probably not one person in twenty lived in anything that a foreigner would have called a town. In the so-called Debate of the Heralds, as late as 1549, the French herald contrasts the populousness of France with the lack of people in England. He thought there were 'more labourers of vines in France than people in England of all estates'. To this the English herald could only reply that the teeming millions of France were mere 'captives and wretches, living in like thraldom as they did to the Romans, and giving tribute for their meat, drink, bread and salt . . . so that I dare let slip a hundred good yeomen of England or Wales to five hundred of such ribaldry'.[5]

These were debating points, but the truth was that England had far fewer people in Henry VIII's reign than she had had in the late thirteenth century or the early fourteenth. It is possible indeed that there were barely half as many people in 1500 as in, say, 1300. Recent work on medieval population before the Black Death has tended to raise our estimates of the size of medieval families and hence of the total population of the country. Russell's figure of 3,700,000 for the year 1348 may well be an underestimate.[6] He also estimates that the population of England reached its lowest point — round about 2,100,000 — in the generation from 1400 to 1430. The muster lists of able-bodied men made in 1524 suggest a probable total of only

[5] Printed in *T.E.D.*, III, 1—11.
[6] Russell, *British Medieval Population*, p. 246.

2,360,000 people for England.[7] In other words, the recovery of population from the repeated blows of plague and other epidemics had scarcely begun. In the hundred years between the 1420s and the 1520s population had only risen by about 12 per cent, or by 3 to 4 per cent per generation, and it seems likely that most of this recovery had been made after 1450 and possibly even after 1470.

The curious fact about the English situation in the early sixteenth century is the enormous contrast it poses with the rapid recovery of some other European countries, notably Germany, a country much more torn by wars and internal troubles than England.[8] Here contemporary writers were speaking of a marked population increase as early as the 1480s and attributing it to the absence of any real pestilence for some twenty years. 'Seldom is there a couple but they have eight, nine or ten children.' Other writers spoke as if people in Germany grew on trees, they were so prolific. In southern Germany a writer in 1538 said that though 100,000 people (so it was said) had perished in the Peasants' Revolt of 1525, 'yet there is no lack of men; rather all villages are so full with people that no one is admitted. The whole of Germany is teeming with children.' The demographic picture was not everywhere the same, but Switzerland's population was also rising rapidly in the same decades. In some Italian cities, too, such as Venice and Siena, there was similar growth, though constant wars elsewhere in Italy confused the picture; and in Flanders the duchies of Brabant and Hainault grew spectacularly in numbers in these years. We know far less about population growth in France at this date, but the French herald in 1549 had no doubt about the contrast between his teeming country and ours.

There is much local evidence in England to suggest that this slow recovery in numbers represents the true picture. In contrast to the rapid growth of many European towns, several statutes were passed in England between 1534 and 1542 for the 're-edifying' of our towns. The preambles to these acts all speak of decayed houses, desolate and vacant ground, pits and cellars left uncovered, and many houses 'feeble' and

[7] The muster totals for 27 counties are given in *L.P.*, IV, pt 1, no. 972. A recent calculation by Cornwall, using a more elaborate method, suggests a population of 2,300,000. The two estimates agree so closely that we may now perhaps regard the figure as settled. See 'English population in the early sixteenth century', *Econ. H.R.*, sec. ser., XXIII, no. 1, 1970.
[8] The substance of these remarks on European population is taken from Rich and Wilson, eds., *Cambridge Economic History of Europe*, IV, esp. p. 20 and following.

likely to fall down. No fewer than seventy-two towns are named besides the Cinque Ports, so nearly eighty English towns in all were regarded as in need of considerable rebuilding. Among these was Great Yarmouth, of which Manship wrote *c.* 1619 in his *History* that

> neither was this town so replenished as then it was, in 220 years after [the Black Death]: for within these forty years last past many void grounds be now builded (and the town is more than a fourth part both in buildings augmented, and in the number of inhabitants increased) which during that time lay waste and in a manner desolate.

It took Yarmouth until the 1570s to begin its slow recovery from the desolation wrought by plague and other disasters. As late as 1590 the Midland town of Stratford-upon-Avon had fewer occupied burgages than it had had in the middle of the thirteenth century. In the countryside, the evidence of a severe decline in population is equally strong: the real recovery in numbers does not come until the 1570s.

England was rightly regarded by Venetian observers as the most fertile and productive part of Britain. As for Wales, it was very mountainous, says the report of *c.* 1500, and the natives only bothered about farming so far as was necessary for their subsistence. 'They take great delight in large herds of cattle, and most of them live upon the produce of their dairies.' Their towns were few and small; most people lived 'separately in the country'. A Scottish farmer, Robert Lindsay of Pitscottie, writing in the 1570s, said that Wales was for the most part barren and unfruitful, lacking tillage, 'for which cause husbandmen live hardly, eating oaten cakes and drinking milk mixed with water'. Yet the Venetian, Barbaro, in 1551, says that the country was very rich in meadow land and one of the most fertile provinces, 'but by so much the worse cultivated, as the inhabitants are more ill-disposed than the rest of the population [of Britain] and they are given to theft'. Here again we must beware of wide generalizations. Wales was a poor country as a whole. In the so-called Benevolence exacted in 1545 she paid only slightly more as a whole than the one English county of Surrey; but the richest Welsh counties (Anglesey and Pembroke) paid about five times as much per thousand acres as the poorest in mid-Wales (Montgomery, Radnor, and Merioneth).

Of Scotland we know even less. Generally poor like Wales, there were nevertheless rich farming districts as well as wild upland pastures and forests. Scotland was, says Barbaro, 'marvellously mountainous, sterile, rugged, and marshy' and had more cause to invade England for booty than England had to attack Scotland. The natives were lazy and delighted more in robbery than in honest work. Half the country was treeless, and the inhabitants burnt coal and peat of which they had plenty. They had wool in plenty also, and gold and silver mines which they knew not how to work. Soranzo, a little later, adds that Scotland was very cold so that the soil produced little grain or fruit 'but abounds in fish and animals for the use of man', above all sheep. Their fine wool was exported mostly to France and Denmark, from which countries they imported most of what they needed. Some of the Scots were 'savages'; the most civilized people of the country resided either at court or near the English border. The Venetian account of *c.* 1500 indeed describes the nobility as residing on their estates 'where they have generally great forests for hunting game. They have excellent houses, built for the most part in the Italian manner, of hewn stone or brick, with magnificent rooms, halls, doors, galleries, and windows'. At the other end of the social scale, most of the country people, according to Robert Lindsay, lived in narrow houses, covered with straw, and reed 'wherein the people and beasts lie together'. These were the 'long houses' which were the commonest type of farmhouse all over the uplands of Britain generally, a type which survived until within living memory in remote parts.

Of Ireland, conquered by the English centuries earlier, the two Venetian ambassadors of the 1550s agree that it had a milder climate than England, and that the soil was very good and would be more productive if it were better cultivated. The merchants were prosperous: the country produced much leather, linen, woollen cloth, metals and good horses. It also produced much wool, but not so fine as that of England. Again we are told that the greater part of the natives were savages, though those subject to the English (within the Pale) were generally more civilized and adapted themselves more readily to English ways. The others were a warlike race, frequently in rebellion against England.

The mean and avaricious Henry VII died on 21 April 1509 at the age of fifty-two. His son succeeded to the throne on the following day, young, handsome, and popular. Even the sagacious Thomas More, in a poem published in 1520, drew a contrast between the old unhappiness of the country and the new age about to dawn. There were, too, powerful material factors at work to encourage the feeling of optimism. The cost of living had been steady for years. If we take the index of food prices as 100 for the period 1451–75, it was still only an average of

103 in the decade 1500—10.[9] But for a low-paid population dependent on the harvest for practically all its food and drink, short-term fluctuations arising from harvest plenty or failure were far more important than long-term trends. The cost of living index rose, for example, to 162 in the dearth of 1482—83 but was thereafter generally low. The harvests of the 1490s were generally bountiful. The next decade, it is true, opened inauspiciously, with two bad harvests and two deficient in 1500—03 inclusive, but after that all went well. The three successive harvests of 1508—10 were magnificent. According to Thorold Rogers the price of wheat in 1509—10 was the lowest recorded for more than two hundred years; and the decade 1510—19 showed only two deficient harvests and none bad. The accession of the new king was therefore welcomed by a people full of 'belly-cheer'.

Then, too, the endemic bubonic plague that could devastate a whole town and kill its trade as well as its people, was relatively quiescent. There had been a bad outbreak in 1499—1500, but on the whole there was nothing general or severe until 1513. Plague had by now become localized, though at intervals it could enlarge into a national epidemic. Thus some towns could be smitten severely (like Exeter in 1503, when the local chronicler says 'the pestilence reigned excessively') but there were no national outbreaks for many years. The new killer known as The Sweat, possibly a virulent form of influenza, had been brought into England in 1485 and broke out again badly in 1508, but on the whole the country escaped lightly from epidemics in the first quarter of the sixteenth century. For the population as a whole, plague or any other killer disease was a disaster comparable with a bad harvest in its human misery and economic consequences. Not until the 1520s did widespread hunger strike again. Yet even then, though the decade started with a great dearth (1520—21), there followed five good harvests in a row (1522—26 inclusive) which must have eased political and social tensions at a time when Henry and Wolsey were engaged in squeezing unparalleled sums in taxation out of all classes for their unpopular French War. But this decade, too, closed with the dearth of 1527—29, in which men were hanged for refusing to starve to death without protest. All this had yet to come, however, when the young Henry VIII came to the throne on a wave of popularity.

[9] Phelps Brown and Hopkins, 'Seven centuries of the prices of consumables, compared with builders' wage-rates', *Economica*, Nov. 1956. For detailed harvest data, see Hoskins, 'Harvest fluctuations and English economic history, 1480—1619', *A.H.R.*, XII, pt 1, 1964, 24—46.

Yet even England, by far the richest of the four countries of Britain, was a backward and underdeveloped economy based almost entirely on agriculture. It had long ceased to be a granary for other countries except in the most favourable years, and even then grain might be exported when inland areas were short. One major cause of this overall deficiency of grain lay in the large-scale conversions from arable to pasture — mostly accomplished before 1485 but still continuing actively under the early Tudors — which had affected the Midlands and Norfolk especially. In grain the country was self-sufficient as a whole in 'normal' years, but was forced to make emergency imports from the Baltic and elsewhere in times of deficiency or total failure of the harvest. Between 1480 and 1549 four harvests in every ten were good to abundant, one in three was about average, and the rest varied from a mild shortage (bad enough, however, in an economy where two people out of three lived on the margin of subsistence) to downright famine. A really bad harvest came once in every six years.[10] Had this occurred with mathematical regularity, it would have been tolerable and capable of alleviation without undue official anxiety; but bad harvests, like good, tended to occur in a row, three or four at a time, and created an explosive situation in the towns above all. Many men were hanged in Henry VIII's England for protesting against a slower death by starvation. William Harrison, quoting from a writer in Edward VI's time, says that Henry hanged no fewer than 72,000 people, mostly 'great thieves, petty thieves, and rogues'. This would be a fearful proportion of the whole population if the figure were true, and that we have no means of knowing. At any rate, hanging must have been one of the major causes of death in King Henry's England. Even in Harrison's day (the 1570s) three or four hundred 'rogues' were 'devoured and eaten up by the gallows in one place and another'. The total of all hangings was probably much higher than this. Thus in Devon alone the Quarter Sessions records show that seventy-four people were hanged in one year (1598) and forty in Somerset in 1596. Even then, a Somerset J.P. deplored 'the foolish lenity of the people' which permitted many crimes to go unpunished. These were, it is true, the years of the greatest famine of the sixteenth century, so the incidence of stealing and other petty crime may well have been abnormal.

---

[10] These figures are based on my essay in *A.H.R.*, XII (see note 9). The Doctor in *The Commonweal of this Realm of England* (1549) expressed the accepted view that a bad harvest came once in every seven years. For a fuller discussion of harvest fluctuations during Henry's reign see, p. 86ff. *et seq.*

England's overseas trade was of relatively little importance in the economy as a whole: the internal market was probably at least ten times as large, possibly as much as twenty times. The export trade was dominated to an overwhelming degree by cloth, growing rapidly at the expense of wool exports, and it paid for a variety of more or less luxury commodities, above all wine, and essential industrial raw materials. Nearly every region of England (we know virtually nothing of the internal trade of the rest of Britain) had its own network of river- or road-traffic and its scores of market towns and river ports; but these were very unevenly distributed. As a whole eastern and south-eastern England dominated the economy, both in the towns and in agricultural wealth (see pp. 13—14), though south-western England was coming up rapidly in the closing decades of the fifteenth century. Economic life was intensely local, with a few notable exceptions along the greater rivers and around the larger towns.

Land was still the paramount source of wealth and employment, and of local prestige and political power. Even the nascent manufactures and mineral workings grew as it were out of the land: coal, tin, lead, and building stone, out of the ground: wool, leather, and grain for brewing, off the surface. Very few industries had no basis in the land. Even ship-building depended on timber from the woods and forests. Indeed, timber played the part in the Tudor economy that is played by coal, steel, and concrete today. It was the most widespread fuel; it was the major material for house-building over at least half the country; and it went to the building of every kind of ship from little coasting vessels to the naval monsters engineered under Henry VIII like the 1,000-ton *Henry Grâce à Dieu.*

RURAL SETTLEMENT AND LANDSCAPES

William Harrison observed, in his *Description of England* (1577), that the landscape was divided into 'champaine ground' and woodland. In the former the houses were 'uniformly builded in every town together, with streets and lanes', whereas in the woodland country, except here and there in the market towns, 'they stand scattered abroad, each one dwelling in the midst of his own occupying'. He reckoned that market towns in his day usually held 300 to 400 families (equivalent to 2,000 communicants or more, he says) and villages, whether woodland or 'champion', might have forty to sixty households, or 200 to 300 communicants. But these figures would have been appreciably smaller in

Henry VIII's time, for from about the 1560s onwards the country had been filling up once more. Most people were 'very poor folks often times without all manner of occupying [employment], since the ground of the parish is gotten up into a few men's hands . . . whereby the rest are compelled, either to be hired servants unto the other, or else to beg their bread in misery from door to door'.

Foreign observers of Tudor England noticed above all that it was a country of woodland and pasture, rather than cornfields, and that it abounded in parks and chases for hunting.[11] In the Debate of the Heralds (1549) the French herald goes so far as to say of England that 'a greate parte of it is waste, desert, and salvaige [i.e. savage or wild] grounde, not inhabyted nor th'erth tylled, but consysteth in forestes, chases, parkes, and enclosures', so that there were as many deer in England as there were people in France. To this the English herald can only reply that the forests, chases and parks were made for the pleasure and pastime of kings, princes, and nobles, and they could be put into tillage if it so pleased the King and government. A German traveller counted upwards of sixty deer-parks in the vicinity of Windsor. The gentry preferred the pleasures of hunting to the hard work of farming their lands. Indeed foreign observers seem agreed that the English of all classes were lazy, only doing as much work as gave them a living, and nowhere near as industrious as the French and Netherlanders.

Apart from the vast areas wasted on the pleasures of the rich, and the equally large areas left relatively wild as common pastures, which nevertheless played an essential part in the cycle of village husbandry, England was primarily a country of pasture and woodland. The two often intermingled. It was a green land, its typical figures were shepherds and neatherds, above all in the north and the west. It harboured enormous numbers of cattle, horses, pigs and sheep. All foreign observers noticed this kind of scene: indeed, even in medieval England there were probably three or four sheep for every man, woman, and child, and there is no reason to suppose that this remarkable balance did not obtain in the time of Henry VIII. In the south and east of England, the lowland side, drier and sunnier, there were large tracts of cornlands, mostly cultivated in open fields and associated with the nucleated villages that William Harrison noticed. Even so, there was no single kind of field system in any one area: the open fields had

---

[11] See Joan Thirsk, Introduction to *A.H.E.W.*, IV, and also her chapter on 'The farming regions of England', on which the following description is largely based.

already developed a variety of forms to suit local needs; the simple
two-field and three-field system was the most common form, but there
were many more complicated variations. Nor was open-field farming
as simple-minded and inefficient as propagandist observers in the
eighteenth century pretended. It was governed in the majority of
villages, especially where two or more manors shared the land, by a
multitude of by-laws laid down by a democratic village-meeting and
periodically altered to meet the need for change. Change may have been
slow, but the possibilities existed. The by-laws collected by Professor
W. O. Ault from the late thirteenth century to the early seventeenth
show the realities of farming life under the deceptively uniform
appearance of the open-field system.[12] Nor was there a single English
county which showed only one kind of agrarian arrangement: even in
East Anglia and the East Midlands there were large regions of wood
pasture with different field patterns and a distinctive social life. Most
counties, too, showed a number of different farming regions by the
early sixteenth century.[13] Commercial farming in some parts near the
larger towns nowhere lay far from backward pockets of peasant-farming
on a subsistence level.

In the countryside many new buildings shone in the intermittent
English sunshine. In some thousands of villages and hamlets the parish
church was being rebuilt in the two generations between about 1480 and
1540; in towns and countryside the monasteries were still adding steadily
to their buildings; and here and there a new kind of grand house was being
built — the English country house — and a new deer park created
around it. The monasteries dominated the building scene down to the
1530s, either in themselves or in the parish churches they were rebuilding, as in the Somerset Levels which were largely owned by Glastonbury Abbey, richest in England outside Westminster. The great days of
the country house were to come after the middle of the century; but on
a lower social level the gentry were building themselves modestly attractive manor houses after the settling-down of the kingdom in the closing
years of the fifteenth century. At an even lower level, that of the
yeomen and husbandmen, the Great Rebuilding did not begin effectively until about 1570, and then it became general throughout the
whole country except in the poorer north and north-west.

[12] W. O. Ault, 'Open-field husbandry and the village community', *Trans. American
Philosophical Society*, new ser., LV, pt 7, 1965.
[13] See the tentative map in *A.H.E.W.*, IV, 4.

TOWNS

Foreign observers serve to correct our ideas about the English countryside and the nature of our farming; but they are valueless on our towns. The so-called *Italian Relation* (1497) says 'there are scarcely any towns of importance in the kingdom excepting these two: Bristol, a seaport to the West, and Boraco, otherwise York, which is on the borders of Scotland; besides London to the South'. Leland is a much more reliable observer, but even he can be impressionistic and misleading. The tax returns of 1524—27 give us the authentic picture, even allowing for the fact that the important town of Newcastle, perhaps the third largest provincial town, was exempted, as were Durham, Chester and Carlisle. Remembering these omissions, the ranking of towns in the 1520s comes out as shown in Table 1.1:[14]

Table 1.1 Tax yield of London and twenty-five leading provincial towns in the subsidy of 1523—27 (to nearest pound)

	£		£
London	16,675	Lavenham	402
Norwich	1,704	York	379
Bristol	1,072	Totnes	*c.* 317
Coventry	974	Worcester	312
Exeter	855	Gloucester	*c.* 307
Salisbury	852	Lincoln	298
Ipswich	657	Hereford	273
Lynn	576	Yarmouth	260
Canterbury	532	Hull	256
Reading	*c.* 470	Boston	*c.* 240
Southwark	455	Southampton	224
Colchester	426	Hadleigh	*c.* 224
Bury St Edmunds	405	Shrewsbury	*c.* 220

The preponderance of eastern England over the rest, so far as urban wealth was concerned, was as marked in Henry VIII's time as it had been two hundred years earlier. Of the twenty-five leading provincial towns in 1334, sixteen lay in the eastern half; the remaining nine were divided equally between the Midlands, the west, and the south. Two hundred years later the balance was substantially the same, though there had been some internal changes of place. If we include Newcastle, then again sixteen of the leading twenty-five provincial towns lay in

[14] Hoskins, 'English provincial towns in the early sixteenth century', *T.R.H.S.*, 5th ser., VI, 1956, 1—19.

13

eastern England. There had, however, been some notable changes during these two hundred years. Most important was the greatly enhanced economic strength of London. In the early fourteenth century London had been just over three times as wealthy as the richest provincial town (Bristol). By the 1520s she was about ten times as wealthy as Norwich, the leading provincial city, and more than fifteen times as rich as Bristol. Then, too, there had been a noticeable tilting of the economic balance towards the west with the rise of Exeter, Totnes, and Worcester. Another remarkable change had been the emergence of Coventry as by far the richest city of the Midlands; and to a lesser degree there was the rise of smaller towns like Canterbury and Reading and Lavenham, all based on the cloth industry.

The dominance of the eastern half of England over the north and west comes out not only in the larger towns but even on a lower level. Thus the heavily battered coastal town of Dunwich in Suffolk was still large enough to pay half as much tax again as Birmingham, where the total subsidy was in any event bumped up by the resident squire, Edward Birmingham, who paid heavily on 'lands'. Despite the metal trades that Leland speaks of, Birmingham had not fully emerged from its feudal background. On the Norfolk coast the busy coastal and fishing port of Cromer paid almost as much tax as Birmingham and Wolverhampton.

By continental standards, it is true, English towns were small. London had between 50,000 and 60,000 people, but after that only three towns had 10,000 or more (Norwich, Bristol and Newcastle), and there were fewer than a dozen towns at the most with 5,000 to 10,000 people. However low we put the population of a 'town' it is safe to say that nine people out of ten lived in undoubted 'country'. By European standards probably not one person in twenty was truly urban, and even for them the country was well within sight.

POPULATION AND WEALTH

For England and Wales together we may estimate a total of about 2,600,000 people. This tiny population still reflected by and large the distribution of medieval times. If we take the absolute totals of the listed men — archers, billmen, and those able to supply harness — and after all this is what the government was interested in, and not in refinements such as the numbers of able-bodied men per square mile, the outstanding fact is that the three eastern counties of Norfolk, Suffolk and

14

Essex were as a whole the most densely peopled part of England. This was the old medieval pattern. They could raise just under 35,000 men, Suffolk being the most populous with 15,099 in all. But what was certainly not medieval was the populousness of the two south-western counties, Devon and Cornwall, which had been of little account in people or wealth in medieval times. Devon even outnumbered Suffolk by the 1520s with a total of 15,486 men of military value; that is including those who were named as able to supply harness though not able to fight.

It is worth noting, however, that there were great variations within the county in the density of population. Large areas could produce only four, five, or six men to every thousand acres, while the rich farmlands of south Devon could summon up twenty-two. The populous parts had nearly six times as many people per thousand acres, a proportion which agrees closely with the range of taxable wealth. These wide variations were to be found in all counties within the Highland Zone of Britain, and to a lesser degree in the lowland counties. They make nonsense of simple county averages, and it is best to stick to absolute totals for our immediate purpose.

In the south-west, too, Somerset had long been a prosperous and populous county. In the 1520s it listed some 12,400 men of military value, and later musters bear this out. Thus south-western England had emerged from the economic backwoods as altogether one of the strongest parts of England. In total population the three counties now slightly outweighed the three eastern counties, for with a revised figure for Cornwall, a land of fishermen and tinners as well as small farmers, we get a total of some 38,000 listed men. In terms of wealth, however, the three eastern counties still led strongly. Slightly smaller in total area, they paid just half as much again as the south-west to the Loan of 1522.

Kent was the most populous county in England at this date, considerably outstripping even Norfolk. The muster figures of 1522 are again a great underestimate, even allowing for the usual omission of the Cinque Ports. They give a total of 8,547 useful men, but a muster for 1560 gives the much more likely total of 15,158 men. The vagaries of Tudor statistics are often beyond explanation, and nowhere more so than in muster returns. We are on safe ground if we take the largest figure out of a sequence, as smaller figures can be plausibly explained away.[15] So Kent comes out first, especially if we allow also for the missing Cinque Ports.

(Note 15 on p. 16.)

15

In eastern England, too, Lincolnshire emerges as populous and wealthy, though less so than the other eastern counties. Early figures are missing, but it could muster over 14,000 men in the late sixteenth century; and in absolute wealth it stood eighth among the counties. The Midland counties that lay behind the rich eastern block were on the whole small and here the figures are somewhat misleading. All we can say is that the counties of the East Midlands were generally populous still, though they had nearly all been the centre of heavy depopulations, of deserted villages, during the preceding century. The five counties of Leicestershire and Rutland, Northamptonshire, Bedfordshire and Cambridgeshire mustered between them only a few hundred men more than Suffolk, across well over twice the area of countryside.

The West Midlands were not so thickly populated in the early sixteenth century, for their industrial districts were as yet unnoticeable, their coal and iron scarcely exploited. Yet even here there are surprises. Thus the relatively poor county of Staffordshire could apparently muster 6,574 men of military value, far more than Gloucestershire of a larger area. This may represent the populousness of a mixed economy of small-scale pastoral farming combined with small-scale metal trades.

When we turn to northern England we are almost completely in the dark. No early musters survive for Yorkshire. All we can say is that in the later musters of 1570—88 the county as a whole could regularly muster some 40,000 men from 3,815,000 acres, roughly ten men from every thousand acres. But again there were wide regional variations, as revealed in the subsidy figures for 1515. In terms of taxable wealth per thousand acres, the East Riding was worth more than twice as much as the West, and three times the North Riding.[16] And within the Ridings themselves there would have been even wider local variations.

By any standards, Lancashire always comes out as a poor county both in people and in wealth. Its great days lay well in the future. Manchester was its biggest town. Leland describes it as the 'fairest, best builded, and quickest' town in the county, chiefly notable for its two market places and its one parish church. Liverpool, with about half a dozen streets at the most, was 'a paved town' according to Leland,

---

[15] One significant explanation is the purely political one. In times of threat from the sea, as in 1539 and 1588, the maritime counties show a heavy muster-roll and the inland counties produce farcically low figures. Thus Northamptonshire drops from 5,544 able-bodied men in 1560 to 1,240 in 1588. See Rich, 'The population of Elizabethan England', *Econ. H.R.*, sec. ser., II, 1950, 254.

[16] Schofield, 'The geographical distribution of wealth in England, 1334—1649', *Econ. H.R.*, sec. ser., XVIII, no. 3, 1965, 504.

much frequented by Irish merchants who landed yarn that was bought by Manchester men. Warrington was a better market than Manchester, while Wigan — 'as big as Warrington, but better builded' — had 'some merchants, some artificers, some farmers', which would have summed up hundreds of English market towns at this date. But it also had a great coal mine only 2 miles away.

The four most northerly counties are poorly documented. They were exempted from the heavy taxation of Henry's reign, probably on the grounds that they had a sufficient burden in keeping the Scots at bay, so we know too little about their economy and its wealth or lack of it. Perhaps the poverty of these extreme northern parts is best brought home to us when we learn that in 1587 the city of London could muster 20,596 men, which was just about as many as the four northern counties between them at that date.

Yet we must not exaggerate the poverty of the far north, especially the eastern side. Newcastle had long been one of the richest towns of the kingdom, and no town can flourish without a populous and rewarding hinterland. In the early fourteenth century she had been third among provincial towns, behind only Bristol and York; and in the 1520s she was still third or fourth. Leland in the 1530s thought 'the strength and magnificence of the walling of this town far passeth all the walls of the cities of England and of most of the towns of Europe', as well they might with the warlike and poverty-stricken Scots so uncomfortably near. But apart from saying that it was a market town, and a casual mention of coal pits half a mile out of town, Leland tells us nothing of the economy of Newcastle. We have to look elsewhere for the explanation of its long-standing wealth, and the fact that it was as populous as Bristol in the untroubled south. Newcastle was one of the largest exporters of wool and cloth in England, and of hides and fells (sheepskins) from the uplands to the west.

The Northumbrian uplands not only nourished great flocks and herds, but their dales were remarkably populous with men, women, and children. As early as 1541 a survey of the eastern and middle Marches of the Anglo—Scottish frontier (i.e. the Northumbrian portions only) speaks of even the remote dales of North Tynedale and Redesdale as overpopulated.[17] The valley of the North Tyne had 'a great number of

---

[17] The survey is printed in full in John Hodgson, *A History of Northumberland*, 1828, pt iii, vol. II, 171—242. Though Hodgson prints '1542' at the heading of the document, it is clearly concluded with the date 2 December 33 Henry VIII, which is 1541.

good grounds both fertile and commodious for tillage, hay, and pasture' but even so was 'overcharged with so great a number of people more than such profits as may be gotten and won out of the ground within the said country are able to sustain and keep'. So great was the pressure that the young men were constrained to steal and rob continually on both sides of the border to get a living. Redesdale had an even worse reputation. The soil was not so rewarding but it was likewise 'over-charged with an excessive number of inhabitants' and they were even bigger cattle-thieves than the men of North Tynedale. Not only was cattle-stealing an economic necessity, but they were always ready to burn and kill for money. Early in the reign of Henry VIII the prior of Tynemouth was accused of bringing a band of more than 500 armed men from the two dales, hired at a wage of sixpence a day, to murder the mayor, aldermen, and principal inhabitants of Newcastle and destroy all the shipping in the port. A muster roll of 1538 enters 391 men, armed and horsed, from North Tynedale alone; and the list is simply headed 'North Tyndell Theiffs'. They fought not only the Scots but the people of the neighbouring valleys and any 'authority' that dared to interfere.[18]

This abnormal pressure of population was directly attributable to the custom of gavelkind or partible inheritance, which prevailed not only in these two dales but also in Coquetdale and possibly elsewhere in the county. A man's property did not go entirely to his eldest son, but was divided equally among all of them at his death. The muster commissioners reported in 1580 that the plenty of able-bodied men was due to the custom that 'if a man have issue 10 sons, 6, 5, or 4 and sits on a holding but of 6s rent, every son shall have a piece of his father's holding'. These fragmented holdings were incapable of yielding a living, but the young men would never leave the wild dales and uplands of their forefathers. They preferred to rob, burn and kill, with the result that nearly every village and hamlet had its fortified *pele* or *barmkin*. At Evistones there was a village large enough to require six or seven strong houses of the pele type, to which all the inhabitants repaired when the young men of the wild North were out for plunder and blood.

In spite of all these local horrors, in most years the countryside poured its wealth of cattle and sheep, hides and fells, into Newcastle. Some of the dales were rich in corn also, as was the more peaceful coastal plain. In the early seventeenth century there were eleven corn mills below the moorlands of Elsdon and Corsenside (reduced to only

[18] *N.C.H.*, XV, 156–60.

one by the 1820s). Yet the threat of war and pillage lay over the Anglo—Scottish border until almost the end of the sixteenth century. The richer Border yeomen and minor gentry were still building their strongholds of stone a century or more after their counterparts were building their comely 'wealden houses' in peaceful Kent, 400 miles to the south.[19]

The pattern of population in England of the 1520s is brought out most clearly in a map prepared from the surviving lay subsidy returns of 1524—25.[20] With all the imperfections of the data, we may assume that it reflects the total population of each region fairly accurately. Perhaps we can hazard the guess that by multiplying the taxpaying population by five, we obtain a good idea of total population. Thus the most populous regions had 100 people or more per square mile, the least populous under 20. The wide variations within a single county (e.g. Devon or Norfolk or the East Riding) come out clearly, but they cannot be pursued here in all their interesting local detail. The overall picture is good enough for our immediate purpose.

As to the wealth of the country, we have abundant evidence from the assessments for subsidies, loans, and benevolences; and though these present the usual statistical pitfalls for the modern historian they give us, nevertheless, an unequivocal picture of the relative wealth of the English economy in the years between 1522 and 1545, both as between different regions and as between the different social classes.

Of the various forms of financial exaction practised on a groaning and restive people by Henry VIII, the so-called Loan of 1522 was the most comprehensive and searching.[21] It was based on a survey made in that year, ostensibly for military purposes. That it also had a financial objective was ordered to be kept strictly secret. Early in 1522 the King, contemplating war with France and Scotland and hard pressed for money, determined on a completely new valuation of the kingdom. Behind the innocent questions about weapons and fitness to serve, it was a fiscal inquiry on a scale hitherto unknown in English society. The

[19] Pevsner, *The Buildings of England: Northumberland*, pp. 46—7, shows that a few castle houses were still being built during the years 1604—11. From then onwards the owners of fortified houses began building ordinary country houses like their counterparts in the Midlands and the south.
[20] See John Sheaill, 'The distribution of taxable population and wealth in England during the early sixteenth century', *Trans. Inst. British Geographers*, 1972, Publication no. 55, pp. 111—26.
[21] A table of the financial yield by counties between 1515 and 1545 is set out in Appendix I.

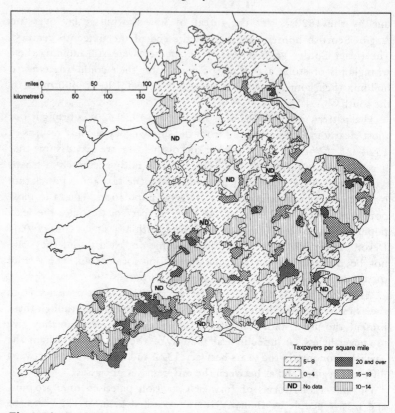

miles 0   50   100
kilometres 0   50   100   150

Taxpayers per square mile

5–9	20 and over
0–4	15–19
ND No data	10–14

Fig. 1 Distribution of population in England, 1524–25 (from Dr John Sheaill).

medieval taxation system was effete and had virtually broken down. It was based on quotas for counties and boroughs fixed two hundred years earlier (in 1334), as modified by extensive reductions granted in 1433 and 1445. Many regions, above all the south-west, were grossly undervalued by the early sixteenth century. All assessments were out of date. There had been a mass of exemptions and evasions even in 1334, and the total yield of 'fifteenths and tenths' was in any event hopelessly inadequate for modern wars.[22] Even the relatively new device of the 'subsidy' was proving a disappointment. In 1522, therefore, the most complete revaluation of the kingdom since Domesday or the Hundred Rolls was set in motion. The constables of every hamlet, village and

---

[22] Nominally the tax took a fifteenth of a man's goods in rural areas and a tenth in the boroughs. Hence its name. It never achieved anything like this level in practice.

parish, and in the towns the appropriate authority, were to certify in writing the names of all men above the age of sixteen and 'whom they belong to'. A breath of the feudal system lingers in that phrase. Also 'who is the lord of every town and hamlet . . . who be parsons of the same towns, and what the benefices be worth by the year . . . also who be the owners of every parcel of land within any town, hamlet, parish, or village . . . with the yearly value of every man's land within the same'. All cattle and farm stock of every kind were to be listed, and the owners thereof; what aliens or strangers dwelt in every town, where they were born and under whose dominion, and what occupation they followed. The return was also to state the value of every man's goods spiritual as well as temporal; and finally 'what pensions goeth forth out of any land there to any religious or spiritual men'. William the Conqueror and his counting of every pig in 1086 was as nothing compared with the magnitude and detail of this inquiry.[23] Unfortunately, most of the original returns have failed to survive, but those that we have are of the utmost value as a picture of the economy.

The major problem of any taxation system at any time is to force the rich to reveal their true resources. The poor have little opportunity for concealment and in any event are scarcely worth the trouble of pursuing. In 1522 the secrecy of the operation was so well guarded that the well-to-do walked into the trap: indeed it was said that many inflated their true worth and credit to enhance their local reputation, so little did they suspect. But the City of London, whose proximity to the seat of power usually results in a leakage of important information, apparently learnt what was afoot. This is suggested by the detailed assessment for London (the Loan Book now preserved in the Public Record Office) in which many assessments are revised in a different hand, implying much undervaluation at the first attempt. Men made their own assessments, but there were certain rudimentary checks. Thus Paul Withypoll, merchant tailor, was put down at £500 in one list but the final assessment puts him at 2,000 marks in goods (£1,333 6s 8d) and £48 per annum in lands. Or there was Ralph Warryn, mercer, whose first assessment was raised from 2,000 marks to £3,000 by a more objective hand. The fact that the City men were too slippery altogether was recognized in the end by fixing the total loan from London at

[23] For the instructions to the local commissioners, see *L.P.*, III, pt 2, no. 2484. 'As these instructions will be sent to many who have not taken an oath to keep secret the practising of the loan, as most of the councillors have done, the collectors of the loan are to be sworn to secrecy till they proceed to their task.'

£20,000, a round sum which was presumably left to the City authorities to apportion and collect. Elsewhere in England the yield of the Loan was worked out to a halfpenny.

The Loan fell on all who possessed personal wealth of £5 and upwards or lands of equivalent value. Those below this level escaped the net until the great subsidy of 1524–25. Those worth £20 and upwards 'lent' to the King the total sum of £105,456 2s 4½d, and a second loan from those worth under £20 produced £57,484 4s 7½d.[24] The grand total from the laity alone was £162,940 to the nearest pound.

The county totals, rearranged in order of magnitude, are shown in Table 1.2:

Table 1.2 Total yield of the Loan by counties: laity only (nearest £)

1	Kent*	13,164
2	Norfolk	11,771
3	Essex	11,207
4	Wiltshire	11,190
5	Devon	10,576
6	Suffolk	10,444
7	Somerset	9,097
8	Lincolnshire	7,417
9	Northamptonshire	6,995
10	Hampshire	6,293
11	Gloucestershire	5,850
12	Sussex*	5,810
13	Berkshire	5,035
14	Dorset	4,630
15	Surrey	3,631
16	Oxfordshire	3,363
17	Cambridgeshire	3,332
18	Warwickshire	3,221
19	Cornwall	3,106
20	Hertfordshire	3,070
21	Leicestershire	2,803
22	Buckinghamshire	2,661
23	Bedfordshire	2,413
24	Huntingdonshire	2,342
25	Worcestershire	2,055
26	Middlesex	1,707
27	Staffordshire	1,500
28	Shropshire	1,249

[24] The totals are given in *L.P.*, IV, pt 1, no. 214, and finally in *L.P. Addenda*, no. 455, dated 1 April 1525.

Table 1.2 — cont.

29	Herefordshire	1,088
30	Nottinghamshire	1,065
31	Derbyshire	953
32	Rutland	712
33	Yorkshire	139†
34	Lancashire	[no figs.]
35	Northumberland	[not assessed]
36	Durham	[not assessed]
37	Cumberland	[not assessed]
38	Westmorland	[not assessed]
39	Cheshire	[not assessed]
40	London	20,000

* Excluding the Cinque Ports.
† Probably only a supplementary payment at the end. The main totals for Yorkshire are missing. In 1515 Yorkshire stood twelfth; in 1524—25, eleventh in order of total tax yield.

The grand total from the Loan was £260,697 6s 10½d, of which the Church contributed £56,252. Bishops and 'prelates of the church' accounted for £38,569 (nearest £) and the general clergy (many thousands of them) yielded £17,683. The Church was divided, like the rest of society, very unequally between the Haves and Have-nots. The other conclusion one can draw from this searching assessment, which spared no one but the very poor, was that the Church owned just about one-fifth of the wealth of England at the time. From the Crown's point of view the county totals are the figures that mattered, so let us accept them for the moment at their face value.

Kent was by far the richest county in England, even more so if we could reckon in the Cinque Ports. Once again the eastern counties proper stand very high, Norfolk in second place, Essex third, and Suffolk sixth. Wiltshire emerges as the fourth richest, Devon as fifth. The ranking of 1524—25 is somewhat different because the tax figures take in the multitude of people assessed at less than £2 in worldly goods and there we find Devon ranking second to Kent, with Norfolk, Essex and Suffolk next in order. The rich textile and farming counties of Somerset and Wiltshire came next, with Lincolnshire not far behind. The balance of wealth was strongly tilted towards the eastern side, from the Humber down to the southern coast of Kent, but a little less strongly than it had been two hundred years earlier.

If the totals are adjusted to take account of the varying acreages of

23

Table 1.3 Yield of the Loan per thousand acres by
counties (1522) in pounds sterling

1	Kent	13.2
2	Wiltshire	12.7
3	Essex	11.4
4	Northamptonshire	10.9
5	Suffolk ⎫ Berkshire ⎬	10.8
7	Huntingdonshire	10.0
8	Middlesex	9.4
9	Norfolk	9.0
10	Somerset	8.6
11	Bedfordshire	8.1
12	Hertfordshire ⎫ Surrey ⎬	7.5
14	Gloucestershire ⎫ Rutland ⎬	7.4
16	Dorset	7.3
17	Oxfordshire	7.0
18	Devon	6.4
19	Sussex	6.2
20	Cambridgeshire	6.1
21	Hampshire	6.0
22	Warwickshire ⎫ Buckinghamshire ⎬	5.6
24	Leicestershire	5.3
25	Lincolnshire ⎫ Worcestershire ⎬	4.4
27	Cornwall	3.6
28	Herefordshire	2.6
29	Nottinghamshire ⎫ Staffordshire ⎬	2.0
31	Shropshire	1.6
32	Derbyshire	1.4
33	*Lancashire	[no fig.]
34	*Yorkshire (East Riding)	[no fig.]
35	*Yorkshire (West Riding)	[no fig.]
36	*Yorkshire (North Riding)	[no fig.]

No figures for Northumberland, Durham, Westmorland,
Cumberland and Cheshire.

* Though no Loan figures are available for Lancashire and Yorkshire, the corresponding yields per thousand acres in the subsidies of 1524–25 were:

Yorkshire (East Riding)	£1.4
Yorkshire (West Riding)	£1.0
Yorkshire (North Riding)	£0.5
Lancashire	£0.5

the counties, the picture we get is decidedly different from that presented by the absolute total yields of money so desirable to the Crown. Again, we are concerned with the yield from the laity only, since these are the only detailed figures we possess.

The wealth of Kent is striking and owed nothing to the proximity of London, as did Middlesex. In the 1330s Kent had stood fourteenth among English counties in comparative wealth.[25] Within two hundred years she stood first. Lay wealth had more than quadrupled in this time. The average growth rate between 1334 and 1515 for England as a whole was rather more than threefold. Some counties had greatly exceeded this growth rate: for example, Devon (8.5 times), Middlesex (8.2), Cornwall (6.6), Essex (5.5), and Somerset and Surrey (5.4). The City of London's wealth had multiplied nearly fifteenfold (14.68) during the same period.

London's contribution to the Loan (probably still below a realistic level) was nearly equal to that of Norfolk and Suffolk put together. It represented just about one-eighth of the lay wealth of the whole country. Yet we must not exaggerate the place of London in the national economy. Its total population was probably 60,000–70,000.[26] Even if we include the borough of Southwark just across the river as an integral part of the metropolis, we can hardly put the population of London at over 80,000: this represents only about 3 per cent of the total population of England and Wales. Ninety-seven people in every hundred lived and worked in the provinces. 'English history is at the bottom a provincial history,' Bishop Creighton remarked ninety years ago, 'but the vigorous undercurrent of a strong provincial life in different parts of England is seldom seriously considered by historians.'[27] If this could be said as late as the 1880s, how much truer it was of the sixteenth century. We must always keep this in mind when we consider such matters as the growth of the London food market and hence of specialized farming beyond the level of mere local subsistence, and even in considering London's place in England's industry and trade, where

[25] Schofield, loc. cit., p. 504, for the figures used in this paragraph. It should be emphasized that Schofield's figures are the *assessments* and not the actual tax yield, so that his figures per thousand acres and mine are not directly comparable. However, this makes no difference in discussing the ranking of the counties in order of wealth.

[26] A Venetian report in 1531 put the population at 70,000. Though statistics about the provinces are often wildly wrong (e.g. it was estimated there were 38,000 churches in the whole kingdom) the other London figures about wards and parishes are pretty accurate.

[27] *Archaeological Journal*, XLII, 1885, 41–2.

the statistics are superficially even more suggestive of its overwhelming paramountcy. In other words we must continually cut London down to size in the Tudor economy as a whole.

The economic upsurge of Kent is abundantly seen in the visual evidence. The 'wealden house' is a well-recognized type, a timber-framed hall-house of some size and considerable comfort, which survives in great numbers to this day. There are said to be between 1,000 and 2,000 of these handsome houses still lived in, built between the late fourteenth century and the early sixteenth by the minor gentry and the larger yeomen. Though it predominates in the Weald, the type could be found all over the county and spread slowly into the adjoining counties of Surrey and Sussex. Mostly it is probably a late-fifteenth to early-sixteenth-century type as we see it today.

The upsurge of Middlesex between 1334 and the 1520s is easily explained by the overflowing wealth of London, though naturally little visual evidence remains for the same reason. But in Devon, and to a lesser extent in Cornwall, the architectural evidence of abounding wealth in the fifteenth century and the early sixteenth is to be found in nearly every parish. There is scarcely a church that was not completely rebuilt or greatly enlarged in these generations. In Devon, too, there are many hundreds of late medieval hall-houses still standing, probably as many as in Kent, but generally heavily disguised by later materials and additions. These, too, were originally built by the same social classes who built in south-eastern England, predominantly the younger sons of old gentry families or yeomen who had climbed solidly throughout the fifteenth century. The Cornish evidence is neither so abundant nor generally of such quality, for Cornwall is and always was the poorer county, but it is still there in every town and country parish.

Somerset, too, was a rich county and had always been so since Romano–British times. The evidence of the buildings at this period, particularly of the parish churches, is overwhelming. Some of it was the work of great monastic builders, like the last two abbots of Glastonbury, but there were plenty of laymen building also. It has been rightly said of Somerset that 'all this evidence indicates a great increase in the tempo of church building on the eve of the Reformation'[28] and this applies also to the money spent lavishly on handsome stained glass and richly carved pulpits, benches and screens. Indeed the historian of Somerset churches concludes that 'never before or since has so much

[28] Wickham, *Churches of Somerset*, p. 34.

26

money been spent on the parish churches of England as in the half-century before the last bad years of Henry VIII'.

Like Somerset, the neighbouring county of Wiltshire owed its great wealth to the cloth industry, to rich and diversified farming, and above all to local wool. The Loan put Wiltshire a close second to Kent in terms of the yield of money per thousand acres: Kent £13.2, Wiltshire £12.7. Third came Essex (£11.4) and then, surprisingly, the inner Midland county of Northamptonshire (£10.9). There was a solid con-centration of high wealth (£9 and over per thousand acres) stretching from the Wash down to the Weald of Kent and the Channel coast; the East Midlands as represented by Northamptonshire and Huntingdon-shire; and a third belt stretching from Middlesex, through Berkshire, up to the Wiltshire edge of the Cotswolds.

The West and North Midlands generally come out as poor, sometimes unexpectedly so as in Herefordshire and Shropshire. The poverty of Staffordshire, Derbyshire, and Nottinghamshire does not surprise us. Their soils were generally poor, their great mineral wealth had scarcely been scratched by this date. Seven counties yielded an average of £10 or more per thousand acres; probably seven others yielded less than £3 a thousand acres, and this excludes the four most northerly counties, for which we have no financial record. The richest parts of England were ten times as wealthy as the poorest.

Yet even the geographical county is an arbitrary unit in assessing the economy of Henry VIII's England. There were wide variations of wealth from one farming region to another within the same county, particularly perhaps in the Highland Zone where the soils ranged from cold pastoral uplands to deep warm arable in the valleys.

The map (Fig. 2) showing the wealth of the various counties in 1524—25 shows the wide variations of wealth that existed within each county, arising mainly from differences in soil-fertility, perhaps proximity to urban markets, but also from the existence of well-developed indus-trial areas and towns.[29] These were almost entirely based on wool and cloth. Mineral wealth scarcely affected the picture at all at this early date, except perhaps the tin of Cornwall and west Devon. Moreover, such wealth as arose from minerals often filled the coffers of rich

---

[29] This map (Fig. 2) is based on the lay subsidy assessments for 1524—25 as worked out by Dr John Sheaill, 'The distribution of taxable population and wealth . . .', loc. cit. I am grateful to him for permission to use his map (rather than my own based on the 1522 Loan) as his figures are more detailed than mine. They reveal a remarkable pattern for the student of agrarian history at this period.

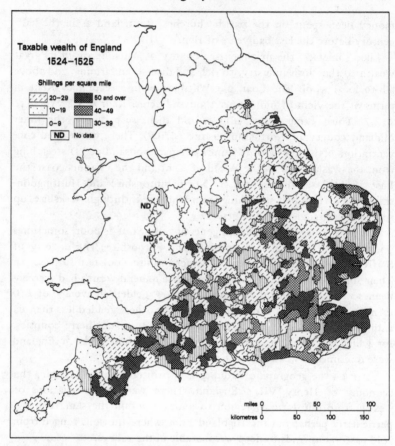

Fig. 2 Taxable wealth of England in 1524–25 (after John Sheaill)

absentee landlords, such as the prince-bishop of Durham in the north-east or the Earl of Devon in the south-west, and was not widely spread in the local economy.

Such, then, was the appearance of England in the early years of Henry's reign: underpopulated, underdeveloped in almost every respect, inward-looking still, based mainly on a pastoral economy of cattle and sheep, vast areas still waste in one form or another, and mostly (with important local exceptions) a subsistence economy based on the land, the household, and family labour.

CHAPTER TWO

The Shearers and the Shorn

THE OWNERSHIP OF LAND

'SOCIETY,' said Talleyrand, 'is divisible into two classes: shearers and
shorn.' This had long been true of Britain, and indeed of all European
countries. By the time of Henry VIII we already see a country in which
the greater part of the land was in the possession of a small minority of
the population; and the same was true of personal estate. The great
mass of people owned little or no land, and possessed but a tiny
fraction of the goods of the kingdom. Whether land was more unequally distributed than goods is impossible to determine, or whether
this gross inequality in the distribution of wealth was more marked by
the end of the sixteenth century than at the beginning. One thing, however, is certain: the century was a golden age for the Shearers, not to be
paralleled until the late eighteenth and early nineteenth centuries when
a combination of the new industrial capitalism with an age-old smooth
and perfected system of political plunder left the shorn with just
enough on their backs to keep alive, and not always that.

If the monumental valuation of 1522 had survived complete, it
would have been possible to depict the overall pattern of landownership. As it is, we must make use of what survives. In Rutland[1] the King
was named as the 'chief lord' in nineteen places out of fifty-two and it
has been calculated that he owned nearly one-quarter of the land. The
Church owned nearly one-third (including benefices, glebe, tithes, etc.),
mostly through absentee landlords like Westminster Abbey and the see
of Lincoln. Only a small part (less than 10 per cent) belonged to
monastic houses. Local laymen owned about a quarter, the majority

[1] Cornwall, 'The people of Rutland in 1522' in *T. Leics. A.H.S.*, XXXVII, 1963,
7–28.

being squires and gentry. The rest was mostly owned by men of high rank living outside the county — three peers and a score or so of knights and gentlemen. In most parishes there were few small freeholders (yeomen or husbandmen) though occasionally we find a sizeable number of peasant owners. Altogether there were 302 landowners listed in the county but of this seemingly large total nearly half owned an average value of only £1 per annum, that is they were mostly owners of but a house or a cottage, and occasionally of a farm. In fact, 4 per cent of the listed population, including the King, owned 43 per cent of the land.

To take a totally different example, let us move southwards to Surrey. Surrey included Southwark,[2] on the south bank of the Thames facing the city of London, a borough in its own right which paid more tax in the 1520s than such wealthy provincial towns as Ipswich, Colchester or Lynn, and considerably more than the city of York. The lands, tenements, benefices, etc., of this crowded borough were valued at £1,977 19s 6d per annum. Of this the Church owned no less than 48 per cent, the laity 52 per cent. Of the ecclesiastical landowners practically 80 per cent were large (£20 p.a. and over).

Unfortunately, the Surrey return as a whole is merely an abstract, giving no names, so that the Crown, if it held land in Southwark or the county, is not separately named. The lay lands of the borough, valued at £1,025 (nearest pound) per annum, were distributed as follows:

	£	s	d	Percentage of total
£20 and over	453	18	4	44.5
£10 to under £20	145	14	1	14
£ 5 to under £10	236	8	0	23
Under £5	188	14	11	18.5
Total	£1,024	15	4	100.0

Of the ecclesiastical lands, etc., the distribution was as follows:

	£	s	d	Percentage of total
£20 and over	748	10	4	79
£10 to under £20	39	18	6	4
£ 5 to under £10	133	7	8	14
Under £5	31	7	8	3
Total	953	4	2	100

(Note 2 on p. 31.)

Thus ecclesiastical landownership was vastly more unequally distributed than lay. The rich ecclesiastics, like the Bishop of Winchester who had a great house on the Bank, neighboured by the Prison (the Clink) and the state brothel (the Bordello), were the most lordly landowners in the borough.[3]

Turning now to rural Surrey, the total valuation of real estate amounted to £14,831 per annum, of which the Church owned 35 per cent and the laity the remaining 65 per cent. Again we have no individual names but the distribution of landed estate (including ecclesiastical property of all kinds) was as follows:

	All assessments		Church assessments	Lay assessments
		(%)	(%)	(%)
£20 and over	£6,841	46	59	40
£10 to under £20	£2,506	17	20	15
£5 to under £10	£2,220	15	16.5	14
Under £5	£3,264	22	4.5	30
	£14,831	100	100.0	99

Here again, in the rural areas, inequality of wealth was much greater in the Church than among the laity. What we may call the Top People were even more separated from the general run of human beings in the ecclesiastical world than in the world at large. If anything can excuse the long-meditated plunder of the Church under Henry VIII — the bishops as well as the monasteries — it was the solemn fact that the Church had departed further from the precepts of its founder than the worldly layman. The richest magnate in England was the Duke of Buckingham, attainted and beheaded in 1521, whose vast estates at the time of his death were bringing in some £6,045 a year; but the Archbishop of Canterbury ran him close, with his various offices, at £5,443 a year net. Next to Buckingham he was the richest lord in the Upper House, and after 1521 the richest.

Let us take yet another region of England for which good information survives — the hundred of Babergh in south Suffolk, which was one of the most highly 'industrialized' parts of the whole country, with its

[2] For Surrey and Southwark, see 'Abstract of the original returns of the Commissioners for Musters and the Loan in Surrey' in *Surrey Archaeological Collections*, XXX, 1917, 13–30. The return for Godley hundred alone is missing.
[3] A detailed topographical description of Southwark is given by Stow in his *Survey of London* (Kingsford's edn, 1908), pp. 52–69.

rich little textile and marketing towns like Lavenham, Sudbury and Long Melford. Of the thirty-two parishes in the hundred, twenty-four had lay lords owning land to the value of £820 a year and eight had ecclesiastical lords, owning land to the value of £411 per annum. The Church was chief lord in a quarter of the places but took altogether 40 per cent of all the revenues, including benefices and tithes. The total valuation of the hundred in lands was £2,339 a year. Altogether, thirty-three chief lords accounted for over half the value of the land. Put in another way, 1.5 per cent of the population owned more than 50 per cent of the land.

Out of 2,277 people named in the hundred, 1,375 had no land or houses at all: just about 60 per cent were propertyless and must have rented what shelter they had. And of the 902 who were assessed on 'lands', no fewer than 620 had land to the value of only £1 per annum or less, probably nothing but cottagers and small householders. Once again the ownership of land in the strictest sense of the word was heavily concentrated in comparatively few hands. Among the larger land-owners, other than the chief lords, the Church numbered 40 out of 161.

For the adjacent county of Norfolk we have a pretty complete picture of land-ownership in 1535, thanks to the work of Dr Swales.[4] Out of a total of 1,527 manors, nearly two-thirds were owned by the gentry, and rather less than 10 per cent by the peerage, among whom the Duke of Norfolk was paramount, with no fewer than 42½ manors. The Church as a whole (including hospitals, gilds, and colleges) owned well over one-fifth of the land. The monastic houses alone held 263 manors, just about one-sixth of all in the county, with a total value of well over £6,000 a year. The Crown held 41½ manors (about 3 per cent of the total) though this holding was greatly increased in the following year by the expropriation of the Bishop of Norwich's lands, which added another fourteen manors in Norfolk, not to mention the town of Lynn.[5]

We all know the hazards of counting manors, which might be large or small; but apart from the Church we have no means of ascertaining the monetary value of the lands of the various social groups. Nor did the lordship of a manor necessarily mean the ownership of all the land within it. In some parts of England (as, for example, the south-west)

---

[4] Swales, 'The redistribution of the monastic lands in Norfolk at the Dissolution', *Norfolk Archaeology*, XXXIV, pt 1, 1966, 14—44.
[5] See Chapter Six, 'The Plunder of the Church', for details of this barefaced transaction.

this was far from true; but such information as we have for Norfolk suggests that very little property lay in other hands — merely houses, cottages, and an occasional farm or two.

To take the manor of Blofield, for example, the Bishop of Norwich was the chief lord in 1522. His lands were valued at £33 6s 8d a year. Of the forty-two names listed, no fewer than twenty-four possessed some land, to the total value of £31 5s 8d. Here the ownership of land was divided roughly evenly between the lord and the freeholders. But in the manor of Calthorpe, where William Calthorpe was the resident squire (his lands are unfortunately not valued), only thirteen out of thirty men other than the squire were assessed on any lands and tenements and it is clear that most of these owned merely a house, or a cottage, and a croft. Once again the majority of the village population rented their houses from the squire. In the tiny manor of Wytton, the squire owned all the land and two-thirds of the total personal estate as well.

Sir Thomas Boleyn, living in Kent, was the Lord of Postwyke in the hundred of Blofield, worth £22 per annum. The other 'land' assessments totalled only £3, one a small farm, and three others cottages. In the two manors of Cantley and Strumpshaw, Lord Matravers owned just under three-quarters of the land. Though there were eleven 'freeholders' out of thirty-two names (roughly one-third) they owned altogether a little over a quarter of the land, mostly in small farms.

Let us take one more hundred in Norfolk, this time the coastal hundred of Happing. Seven out of the seventeen parishes had monastic houses as their chief lords (including King's College, Cambridge), five others belonged to the Calthorpes, and the remainder belonged to various gentry. Out of a total of 737 names in the 1522 valuation, no fewer than 254 had some real property, or rather more than 34 per cent. The number of free tenants varied widely from manor to manor: on the Calthorpe manor of Ingham there were no freeholders in a total of forty-eight households, on the monastic manor of Hickling only fourteen out of ninety-one, but on another monastic manor (Potter Heigham) 63 per cent of the households owned some land and/or a house. Yet the great majority of the 'free tenants' were assessed at levels (3s 4d, 5s, 6s 8d) that suggest they merely owned a cottage — a valuable enough asset in a century of inflation — and few owned their own farms.

It is detailed analyses like these that help to reconcile the apparent contradiction between what is being argued here — that the ownership of land in Henrician England was concentrated into the hands of a relatively small number of families – and the statistics compiled by Tawney from thirty-nine manorial surveys relating to Norfolk and Suffolk.[6] Out of a total of 1,364 manorial tenants, he found 492 described as freeholders (36 per cent), which is not far removed from some of the proportions given in the 1522 valuation. But Tawney gives no *values* for the freeholders' lands, and the Henrician valuation reveals that the freeholders owned far less than 36 per cent of the land in those counties. He goes on to note that in these two counties the proportion of freeholders is about double that for the country as a whole; but they were in fact composed to a considerable degree of smallish peasant proprietors, whereas the 13 per cent or so he counts in western England (certainly in Devon) were mostly larger owners and a different social class, for reasons deeply rooted in English history.

So in the Norfolk coastal parish of Happisburgh, with a total land valuation of £74 7s, Wymondham Abbey owned some 72 per cent; and though 43 per cent of the householders owned some real property they held only 28 per cent of the land between them. Most of the freeholders are clearly only house or cottage-owners. Indeed, of what we may call 'peasant land', three owners alone accounted for nearly two-thirds of the total. If there was a great gulf between the 'chief lords' and the rest in the matter of landownership in England, there could also be a massive inequality in the peasant world itself. This will become even more evident when we turn to consider the distribution of personal estate, what the Tudor taxmen called briefly 'goods'.

We know something, too, of the distribution of land in the West Riding of Yorkshire.[7] It differs in some respects from that of Norfolk at the same period, possibly because the Yorkshire figures are valuations of income and not a mere counting of manors. The Church owned 27.3 per cent of the temporal freehold income, the peerage 8.6 per cent, the Crown 9 per cent, and the gentry 55 per cent. We have no direct information about freeholders other than the gentry, except at a slightly later date and from a somewhat dubious source – the lay subsidy assessments of 1546. Already the subsidy assessments were ceasing to reflect true wealth and income, but those for the West Riding

[6] Tawney, *The Agrarian Problem in the Sixteenth Century*, pp. 24–6. The majority of Tawney's surveys range over the entire sixteenth century, with a few from earlier and later dates.
[7] Smith, *Land and Politics in the England of Henry VIII*, with particular reference to the West Riding between 1530 and 1546; see esp. pp. 73 and 97.

are nevertheless remarkable. Out of 1,763 taxed on lands rather than goods, no fewer than 1,358 (77 per cent) fell into the £1 to £4 class.[8] Unfortunately, Tawney offers no Yorkshire figures at all from manorial surveys, so we are left pretty much in the dark as to how much land the freeholders really held independently.

Turning to the south-west, Devonshire manorial surveys for the sixteenth century show generally very few free tenants. But though few, they are nearly always names of gentry whose holdings were large freehold farms (large by south-western standards, say 100 to 400 acres) and they often own manors and freehold estates in other places. They are essentially gentry; and the strong impression one gets from all the available records is that the Devonshire gentry were as numerous and ubiquitous as those of, say, Norfolk or Kent. They certainly owned the bulk of the land, with the Church probably second in the scale, and the peerage and Crown of no great consequence territorially.

Always we must remember the regional differences in England, and more than that the historical differences from one parish or manor to the next. We see, for example, another kind of pattern of land-ownership in the huge parish of Constantine (8,020 acres), on the edge of the Helford River in Cornwall. The total valuation in 1522 amounted to £93 5s 8d, including the rectory, vicarage and tithes. Of this the Church in the broadest sense of the word accounted for £35 6s 8d, or £30 6s 8d if we exclude the chaplain's stipend: that is, the Church owned in one way and another one-third of the entire parish. Of secular landowners, no fewer than sixty-one are listed out of a probable total of some 208 names.[9] Many of the landowners were absentees (gentry living in other parishes) and none was large. The highest assessment was only £7. More than half the land assessments were under 10s — that is to say, a mere cottage and croft — and only a quarter were over £1. Thus even here, in the far south-west where settlement is scattered among isolated farms and hamlets, the pattern of ownership is not so totally different as might appear at first sight. We still find that seven men owned just over half the parish, excluding the Church. The great majority of parishioners, probably three out of four, rented their houses and cottages from bigger men.

[8] This could well be because the wealthier groups were already learning to evade their real obligations.
[9] The Constantine valuation has been printed in *Subsidy Rolls . . . of the Parish of Constantine* pp. 3—9. The 1522 list is not the complete valuation but the material for the Loan. It omits wage-earners, of whom there were fifty-four assessed in the 1524 subsidy.

An isolated record (1522) from Long Compton, a village in the Cotswolds, shows the total valuation of the manor as £78 5s 4d in lands. Three owners — the Earl of Derby, Sir William Compton, and 'the heirs of Kebull' owned exactly 90 per cent between them. Lady Stodley owned most of the remainder. There were only two small freeholders. The manor was virtually owned by the peerage and the gentry.[10]

So far we have looked at a picture which, for all its regional and even parochial variations, is broadly one in which the ownership of land in the early sixteenth century was highly unequally divided. A very small percentage of English families owned by far the greater part of the kingdom. Yet there could be villages where the free peasants owned a greater share of the land and had done so from perhaps pre-Conquest times. Thus in the Leicestershire village of Wigston Magna at the beginning of the sixteenth century the peasant proprietors owned about 1,100 acres between them out of a total of 2,944 acres. About twenty peasant families out of a possible total of between seventy and eighty, owned about 37 per cent of the land;[11] the rest belonged almost entirely to two great absentee families; the Turviles, who were neighbouring squires, and the Earls of Oxford. They owned just about 60 per cent of the land. The Church owned the rest (the glebe), and Wigston was rare in having not an acre of monastic land within its boundaries. There must have been a great number of such 'peasant villages' in the East Midlands, where land-ownership was much more widely spread than in general: and this fact, combined with absentee lords of manors, produced an entirely different kind of village from the general run under the eye of an omnipotent squire. They were true peasant societies, running their own affairs, generating their own deeply rooted culture.[12]

THE DISTRIBUTION OF PERSONAL ESTATE

Urban wealth and poverty

London was ten times as wealthy in the 1520s as the leading

[10] *L.P.*, III, pt 2, no. 3685.
[11] Hoskins, *The Midland Peasant*, esp. pp. 110–11. The two manors were dismembered and sold off in 1586 and 1606, mainly to the local peasantry, so greatly increasing the number of peasant proprietors. It is important therefore not to mix manorial surveys over too wide a period, as Tawney sometimes appears to have done.
[12] See, for examples of other villages with much freehold land, Thirsk, *English*

provincial city, paying £16,675 to the series of lay subsidies levied between 1523 and 1527 as against £1,704 from Norwich, or £1,072 from Bristol.[13] Foreign observers noticed the riches of London: the Venetian who wrote in the last years of the fifteenth century said it abounded with every luxury as well as necessity. In Cheapside alone there were fifty-two goldsmiths' shops, so full of treasures that all the shops of Rome, Milan, Florence and Venice could not together rival such magnificence. But of the teeming, squalid streets and lanes and alleys of the poor we hear nothing. Just as the Crown gave up the task of fixing an exact sum as a loan from the City of London, putting it down at an arbitrary £20,000, so it is doubtful whether the minute valuation that was inflicted on every other town and parish in the kingdom was ever attempted in the metropolis. All that survives is the so-called Loan Book, which gives no assessments under £5. Below this figure no one was asked to contribute.

An analysis of this record[14] shows the distribution of wealth in the City, adjusted for the missing mass of £0—4 assessments which constituted the bulk of the population. How many people, and how much wealth, fell into this bottom group? Looking at Coventry, a wealthy city for which we have the complete figures, the under £5 group formed almost exactly 80 per cent of the total number of assessments (including nil assessments) and owned between them 6 per cent of the personal estate. In Southwark, just across the river from London, the under £5 group owned 9 per cent of the total personal wealth. We do not know the size of this group, but in any event it is probably safer to assume that London was more strictly comparable with the rich merchant-city of Coventry than the suburban mass of Southwark. If we make this assumption, the complete London survey would have contained about 10,735 names; and the total wealth given in the surviving London assessment should be adjusted by 6 per cent, so raising it to just about £249,000: let us say in round numbers £250,000, as there is clearly a margin of error.

With this adjustment we get the following table of the distribution of

---

[13] Hoskins, *Provincial England*, p. 70, lists the tax yields from London and the twenty-five leading provincial towns (excluding Newcastle, which was not taxed).
[14] P.R.O.(E. 179. 251/15B.) I am indebted to Mr Julian Cornwall for permission to use his calculations from this record. The figures for the £0—4 group are my own estimate.

Peasant Farming esp. pp. 43—4. In the Holland division of Lincolnshire especially the custom of partible inheritance increased the number of peasant landowners, though not of course their total acreage.

wealth in the richest city in the kingdom, and one of the richest in
Europe shown in Table 2.1:

Table 2.1 The wealth of London in 1522

Group	Number of persons	Total personal wealth of group (£)	Percentage of total wealth
£0—4	8,588 (est.)	18,209 (est.)	7.2
£5—9	728	4,016	1.6
£10—19	328	2,655	1.1
£20—39	242	5,666	2.3
£40—99	314	17,008	6.8
£100—499	448	98,147	39.2
£500—999	42	26,347	10.5
£1,000 and over	45	77,952	31.2
Totals	10,735	250,000	99.9

The Top People, to use a loose but convenient expression (those
assessed at £100 and over) constituted just 5 per cent of the population
and owned 80.9 per cent of the personal wealth. Even this is a conservative reckoning, for there is still reason to believe that the richest men
successfully concealed a good deal of their true wealth. This was not
necessarily simple tax evasion. Even today the rich find it difficult to
assess their total wealth at any given time, and in the sixteenth century
the incidence of 'desperate debts', of money that there was little hope
of seeing back, was often very high.[15]

The two highest assessments in London in 1522 were those of Sir
Stephen Jenyns, merchant tailor, and Sir Thomas Seymour, mercer,
rated at £3,500 each. Both had been lord mayors of London. Jenyns
was a native of Wolverhampton, where he later founded the grammar
school, as well as building a great part of his parish church in London of
St Andrew's Undershaft. Yet when he died in 1524 his benefactions
alone totalled £2,693 and presumably he made substantial provision for
his family.[16] We need his probate inventory to obtain a clearer idea of
his true wealth. Thus John Rudstone, alderman of the City, a draper of
Yorkshire origin, was assessed at 2,000 marks in 1522, but his
inventory only nine years later shows a clear total of well over £7,000
in personal estate.

[15] See p. 189 below.
[16] See Stow, *Survey of London*, esp. II, 180; and Jordan, *The Charities of
London*, pp. 222—3, 376—7.

Unfortunately one of the wealthiest Londoners was not assessed in 1522 as he was then resident in Spain. He was a merchant tailor, son of a rich Bristol merchant who had been interested together with Sebastian Cabot in the Newfoundland trade. Robert Thorne the younger died in 1532 and his inventory survives among the *Letters and Papers of Henry VIII*. It shows a personal estate totalling £16,935, plus estate in Spain valued at another £2,623, including 'a house and slaves in Sevyle £94' and doubtful debts in Spain of no less than £1,113 14s. So his total estate was worth round about £20,000. Together with his younger brother Nicholas, who remained in Bristol and made a more modest fortune, he founded Bristol Grammar School.[17]

Altogether no fewer than forty-five London merchants were assessed at £1,000 and over. The richest of all were mercers, merchant tailors, and goldsmiths. In the whole of the provinces only seven men reached this level — three in Salisbury, two in Coventry, one in Norwich; the seventh (richest of all) was Thomas Spring of Lavenham in Suffolk, who died in 1523, assessed at £3,200 in goods — by far the richest merchant in England outside London. He may have been worth more, as the debts owing to him were put at £2,200, of which the 'sperat debts' were put at £1,400, the 'desperate' at £800. Executors sometimes managed to recover some of the desperate debts; but what is more to the point is that he left a very large real estate also. His father (Thomas Spring II) had left in 1486 lands in eight parishes, worth £16 10s a year; but the son died leaving twenty-seven manors, and lands in 130 different places, worth in all some £370 to £380 a year, even at the conventional values of the inquisitions *post mortem*.[18] The next generation saw the inevitable knighthood (Sir John Spring).

In discussing London, it was impossible to say anything of what may be called the Bottom People as the detailed information is lacking. But we can construct a complete picture of the distribution of wealth at Coventry, the fourth richest provincial city after Norwich, Bristol, and Newcastle.[19]

At Coventry the top eleven people owned nearly 44 per cent of the

[17] For a fuller account of the Thornes of Bristol, especially of Robert Thorne, see Moore Smith, *The Family of Withypoll*.
[18] There are two sets of inquisitions on Spring's lands in the Chancery series and the Exchequer series at the P.R.O.
[19] Hoskins, *Provincial England*. Although Newcastle was not taxed in 1523–27, there is good evidence to place her well above Coventry in wealth and population at this date. The analysis for Coventry is based on a valuation preserved among the city records.

Table 2.2 The wealth of Coventry in 1522

Group	No. of persons	Total personal wealth of group (£)	Percentage of total wealth
Nil	699	Nil	Nil
Under £2	176	151	1.3
£2—4	222	564	4.8
£5—9	96	576	4.9
£10—19	59	672	5.8
£20—39	61	1,349	11.5
£40—99	44	2,311	19.9
£100—499	17	3,090	26.4
£500—999	1	667	5.7
£1,000 and over	2	2,333	19.9
Totals	1,377	11,713	100.2

personal wealth. The top 5 per cent of the population owned just about three-quarters of the personal wealth — a figure approaching the London concentration. Conversely, one-half of the people of Coventry possessed absolutely nothing: nothing but the rags they stood up in, a few sticks and boards for 'furniture', and the tools of their trade if any. The bottom three-quarters of the population together owned about 4 per cent of the total wealth of the city.

For Norwich, the richest city in the provinces, we have only rather imperfect information. The 1524 valuation for the subsidy, which generally represented a substantial scaling-down of the great valuation of two years earlier, suggests a total round about £16,080. There were 1,422 taxpayers in 1524; we know that the ninety-nine Top People (those who paid the Anticipation in 1523) paid 73 per cent of the total subsidy. The top 7 per cent of the population paid nearly three-quarters of the tax for the city; but if we assume that half the population (as at Coventry) are not listed at all, then some 35 per cent of Norwich families owned nearly three-quarters of the wealth. At Exeter, again, we have only the tax figures for 1524, but here too 3 per cent of the taxed population owned half the personal wealth of the city.

As a contrast to these wealthy cities let us take the crowded fishing-town of Great Yarmouth.[20] Its total valuation was only £3,508, less than a third of Coventry's. There were 483 assessments, of which exactly one-third were returned as worth nothing.

[20] P.R.O. E.179. 36/25.

40

Table 2.3 The wealth of Great Yarmouth in 1522

Group	No. of persons	Total personal wealth of group (£)	Percentage of total wealth
Nil	161	Nil	Nil
Under £2	75	72	2.0
£2–4	120	316	9.0
£5–9	45	284	8.0
£10–19	33	404	11.5
£20–39	26	639	18.3
£40–99	18	960	27.4
£100 and over	5	833	23.8
Totals	483	3,508	100.0

Compared with Norwich and Lynn, Yarmouth was a poor town at this date. The richest men were assessed at only £200 each; only twenty-three men were worth £40 or more. But these twenty-three owned half the wealth of the town, and the three richest men were all Byschops, who between them dominated the town as shipowners and merchants. The Byschop clan owned one-sixth of the town's wealth. Many towns, if not most, possessed at least one such dominant family, financially if not politically. At Leicester, the two Wyggestons paid nearly one-third of the total 1524 subsidy for the town; and at Bradford-on-Avon in Wiltshire Thomas Horton paid 70 per cent of the tax for the town and was ten times as rich as the next man. But apart from the Byschops, Great Yarmouth's wealth was somewhat more evenly spread. The poor were still a large class, but the middling groups were more conspicuous. There was a great number of small but comfortable assessments, almost like a peasant community.

One curious feature of the Yarmouth economy must be commented on. Although a third of the population had been written off as worth *nil* in 1522, the subsidy of 1524 actually roped most, if not all, of them into the net.[21] True, it was at the minimum rate of fourpence a head, but the crafty Byschops had succeeded in getting their three assessments down from £600 to £500, so the tax screw was turned on to the poorest class. It took a lot of fourpences from poor fishermen to ease the financial plight of their shipowner-employers: an old and familiar story in English history down to the present day.

As a general rule it seems that the richer a town as a whole, the

[21] P.R.O. E.179. 150/210, dated 28 April 1524. This lists 490 names in all, of whom 212 were assessed on wages.

greater the degree of inequality in the distribution of worldly goods — not perhaps a very surprising conclusion. As a town grows richer, the gulf between the Shearers and the Shorn widens. The fruit of economic progress for the wage-earning class is a greater relative poverty, unless offset by a policy of high taxation discriminating against the rich: and this was not the policy in Henry VIII's England, though they paid pretty heavily in the 1520s. But this was less true after Henry's death, when the taxation system became a farce which particularly profited the already-rich.

Rural wealth and poverty

Economic inequality was also deeply marked in rural society. Even in the East Midlands, the home of many free peasants over many centuries, this was so, If we take Leicestershire as an example:[22]

> Only one village in every six or seven had a resident squire at this time, representatives of families settled there in many instances since the time of Henry II or Henry III; the new type of squire — lawyer, merchant, or successful yeoman — had not yet appeared except in one or two places. But in the village where there was no squire we usually find the subsidy list headed by one or two wealthy yeomen who are often themselves the descendants of ancient families who have owned a small freehold in the place for centuries.

The Hortons at Mowsley were assessed in 1524 on three-quarters of the personal estate of the entire village; and at Frisby-by-Galby two old peasant families between them paid more than three-quarters of the tax demanded of the hamlet. Many such villages and hamlets could be found, not only in Leicestershire but in the neighbouring counties also.

There were indeed many villages where the smaller free peasantry had succeeded in maintaining their numbers. At Wigston Magna (Leics.), for example, we find no one dominating yeoman but a number of families, both freeholders and copyholders, of middling wealth. Yet even here, three peasant families between them owned nearly a quarter of the wealth of the village, and a fifth of the taxpayers owned a half. Below this topmost layer, however, wealth was fairly evenly distributed in the village, though it is true that we have no record of the property-less at the bottom of the social structure.[23] Taking Leicestershire as a whole, 'closed villages' as well as 'open villages', and omitting the squirearchy (who were not a numerous class, and many were worth less

[22] Hoskins, *Essays in Leicestershire History*, p. 127.
[23] Hoskins, *The Midland Peasant*, pp. 143–7.

than a rich yeoman) 4 per cent of the rural population owned a quarter of the wealth, and about one-sixth owned a half of it.[24] These are conservative figures — they do not reflect the full degree of economic inequality — as a considerable proportion of the rural population escaped the subsidy on grounds of poverty.

The wapentake of Staincross in the West Riding shows a somewhat different picture, possibly because it is a fuller record (1522) and includes the poor. Much of the wapentake consisted of mountainous upland bordering on Cheshire and much of the rest lay on the Coal Measures, as yet scarcely exploited for coal and giving generally only poor soils. Nearly 58 per cent of the population were assessed at under £1, and would normally have escaped the subsidy of 1524—25. Together they owned only 15 per cent of the total wealth of the region. Indeed, nine out of ten of the households were assessed at under £2, and together owned about 43 per cent of the wealth. The social pyramid here rested upon a very broad base, and reached no great height. Only six people were worth £40 or more, out of a total of 1,635. It was a dismally poor part of England, yet even here the top 2 per cent of the population owned well over 40 per cent of the wealth. Most of the population must have been mere crofters, scratching a living off a smallholding and perhaps combining it with some local small-scale coal-working.[25] The average assessment for the whole wapentake was only £1.4 per head. Such an average is not entirely meaningless, for if we turn to the coastal hundred of Happing, in north-east Norfolk, by no means a richly endowed region, the average wealth per person was £3.63; and in the industrialized hundred of Babergh in south Suffolk it was just about £10.[26]

Happing hundred comprised seventeen parishes, of which half a

---

[24] *Essays in Leics. History*, p. 130. At Preston, in Rutland, an average-sized village for the county, exactly half the people owned practically everything, even in a 'simple, unpretentious peasant community'. See Julian Cornwall, 'The people of Rutland in 1522', *T. Leics. A.H.S.*, XXXVII, 1963. But Cornwall points out that some labourers and servants bore the same names as husbandmen and were very likely serving their apprenticeship in husbandry. In Rutland, the bottom half of the population together owned only 5 per cent of the goods.

[25] Such a dual economy of farmer-craftsman has been studied for a large parish bordering upon Staincross by D. G. Hey, 'A dual economy in south Yorkshire', *A.H.R.*, XVII, 1969, pt ii, 108—19. The evidence however is mainly from the late seventeenth century and the eighteenth.

[26] Another indication of comparative wealth between the different regions is that Staincross was valued at less than £10 per thousand acres; Happing at £99 per thousand acres; and Babergh at £302. Both Surrey (excluding Southwark) and Rutland were valued at £97 per thousand acres, and Buckinghamshire at £76.

Table 2.4 Distribution of personal wealth in Happing hundred in 1522

Group	No. in group	Total wealth of group (£)	Percentage of total wealth
Nil	195	Nil	Nil
Under £2	146	169	6.3
£2–4	243	657	24.8
£5–9	83	523	19.7
£10–19	50	582	21.9
£20–39	14	330	12.4
£40–99	5	257	9.7
£100 and over	1*	140	5.3
Totals	737	2,658	100.0

* The prior of Hickling.

dozen bordered the North Sea. It was a farming and fishing economy, a countryside of small men. Out of 736 names (that is, excluding the resident prior of Hickling) only three were classed as gentry. As in Leicestershire, the resident squire — one of the most persistent myths of English rural history — was an anomaly: about five villages in six had none.

More than a quarter of the population had no goods at all worth noticing. The middle group (£2 to £9) were the most important: 45 per cent of the names listed owning 44.5 per cent of the total wealth. Apart from the prior of Hickling again, only five men out of a total of 736 were worth £40 or more. It was an almost untouched peasant economy. About one household in three owned some real property also, mostly houses, cottages and small farms. Monastic houses and gentry owned nearly all the land, as we have seen: but this does not invalidate the picture of a peasant/fisherman economy. It was a hard life, summer and winter (fishing was a winter occupation off this coast), but there was a rough measure of equality in worldly goods — certainly far more so than in most parts of England.

Turning now to a completely different economy, but still in eastern England, we find the picture of distribution of worldly goods in four textile towns and villages in Babergh hundred shown in Table 2.5.[27]

As to the distribution of wealth in these rich little places, we can state the basic facts simply as follows: at Lavenham, the bottom half of the population owned 1 per cent of the personal wealth, at Long

[27] A transcript of the 1522 valuation for Babergh is in the Ipswich public library.

Table 2.5 Distribution of personal wealth in Babergh hundred in 1522 (selected places)

Wealth group	Lavenham			Long Melford			Sudbury			Nayland		
	No. in group	Total group wealth (£)	Total wealth (%)	No. in group	Total group wealth (£)	Total wealth (%)	No. in group	Total group wealth (£)	Total wealth (%)	No. in group	Total group wealth (£)	Total wealth (%)
Nil	23	nil	0	28	nil	0	43	nil	0	28	nil	0
Under £2	33	35	0.5	25	27	1.3	38	38	1.5	26	28	1.7
£2–4	32	80	1.1	26	66	3.2	64	166	6.6	35	87	5.4
£5–9	11	65	0.9	13	84	4.1	25	169	6.6	12	77	4.9
£10–19	17	196	2.7	14	173	8.4	29	349	13.7	7	79	5.0
£20–39	11	270	3.7	7	147	7.1	12	270	10.7	4	90	5.7
£40–99	18	1,044	14.3	4	217	10.6	11	544	21.4	5	297	18.7
£100–499	10	1,934	26.4	4	733	35.7	8	1,000	39.4	4	933	58.7
£500–999	1	500	6.8	1	600	29.3	0	0	0	0	0	0
£1,000 and over	1	3,200	43.7	0	0	0	0	0	0	0	0	0
Totals	157	7,324	100.1	122	2,047	99.7	230	2,536	99.9	121	1,590	100.1

Melford 2 per cent, at Nayland 2.5 per cent, and at Sudbury 4 per cent. Looking at the Top People, at Lavenham 5 per cent of the population owned 71 per cent of the wealth; at Long Melford 70 per cent; at Nayland 66 per cent; and at Sudbury 50 per cent. The presence of the Springs at Lavenham distorted the picture slightly, but not as much as one would imagine overall.

In Surrey, excluding Southwark, the total valuation of all goods and chattels amounted to £40,162 2s 6½d.[28] Of this total the £20 and over group owned rather more than half this wealth. Taking lands and goods together, the Top People, as defined in this way, owned 63 per cent of the wealth of the county, but we do not know the size of the group.[29]

The final official return of the yield of the Loan for thirty-three counties shows that the £20 and over class paid just two-thirds of the total, and the £5 to £19 class the remainder. Those with less than £5 were not included on this occasion. The figures show a wide variation from county to county in the pattern of wealth distribution as revealed in this rather elementary way. And the pattern is an odd one: sometimes it reveals what we might have expected, elsewhere it does not. Thus the counties where the Top People paid over 70 per cent of the Loan included Wiltshire, Suffolk, Essex, Kent, Berkshire and Warwickshire (the last undoubtedly inflated by Coventry's contribution); but we also find Derbyshire (76 per cent) and Shropshire (79 per cent), regions that come low in the total wealth of the country. The counties where the Top People paid least (as percentages) were Cornwall and Staffordshire, which we might expect (42 and 47 per cent respectively), but also Leicestershire (44 per cent). To put it in another way, the middling-group paid more in these counties than in any other (53 to 58 per cent). Perhaps we can detect here regions of England where the middling peasant and merchant predominated: certainly they reflect a somewhat more widely spread distribution of wealth; but taking England as a whole the gulf between rich and poor was already enormous by the third decade of the sixteenth century.

The social structure rested on a vast base of people who owned little or nothing more than what they stood up in, who rented their houses

---

[28] *Surrey Arch. Coll.*, loc. cit., The hundred of Godley is missing from the record.
[29] 'Lands' were reckoned at so much per annum (i.e. income) while goods and chattels were valued as capital. Strictly speaking, therefore, the two categories should not be added together, but the final official return of the yield of the Loan as given in *L.P.*, IV, pt i, no. 214, does this for each county, being interested only in the total yield. See Appendix IV for details.

and cottages from others, who had no reserves to fall back on in a bad year, and who therefore formed a potentially explosive foundation of which any Tudor government was continually aware. They stood, as Tawney said, up to their necks in water; the slightest ripple could have drowned them, and often did.

The social background

The statistical picture we get, so far as the bottom half of the population is concerned, might seem one of almost unrelieved gloom and misery. It clearly cannot be the entire story. How did men and women tolerate such a life, beset by poverty, liable every few years to devastating epidemics in which half a family or the whole could perish in a few days, and liable to acute periods of hunger when the grain harvest failed as it did on an average about twice in every decade? Not only that, but one bad harvest generated another, so that there were often two, three, or four in a row. Poverty, plague and hunger: the three ancient enemies of the human race. Yet the fact remains that suicide was rarely employed as a final escape from such a life. It is difficult to arrive at any estimate of the suicide rate in the sixteenth century. All one can say is that those who have combed local and other records over the years in minute detail rarely come across instances of self-destruction. It was a felony, and the suicide's goods and chattels were forfeit to the Crown. Thus one might argue that a family would tend to conceal such a death for purely economic reasons and no doubt sometimes did; but there was also the inducement for someone to probe where the rights of the Crown were involved. As far as we can tell, then, suicide was rare in the Tudor period.[30]

Many explanations could be advanced for this fact. Before the Reformation, certainly, suicide was a mortal crime in the eyes of the Church, with its own penalties; but it was rare too even in Protestant England. One might also say that life for the majority was so short in any event (probably an expectation of under forty years at birth) that self-destruction may have seemed an act of supererogation, especially in so far as few people attained an old age with its own special problems of degenerative diseases and loneliness. But these are rather negative

[30] Gough's *History of Myddle* (in Shropshire), written in 1700–01, contains hundreds of potted biographies and anecdotes about seventeenth-century inhabitants of the parish, but the number of suicides recorded is exceedingly small — possibly two or three at the most over several generations.

explanations: and when we postulate more positive reasons involving discussion of the quality of life, which is not susceptible to statistics, we run the risk of being accused of creating unprovable myths, of talking about a vanished golden age. The statistical picture painted so far, which there is no gainsaying, forms a sufficient answer to any such accusation. What, then, did men and women live by, especially when their religious faith seemed thin or hollow, as it must have done at times of hunger and meaningless pestilence?

Above all other positive facts was the sense of *belonging* to a place and to a community of people one had grown up with, a place that was, even in most sixteenth-century towns, even perhaps in London itself, a community still, whether one was rich, or merely comfortable, or poor. 'Men are attached to places', says Lewis Mumford, 'as they are attached to families and friends. When these loyalties come together, one has the most tenacious cement possible for human society.' There was, to quote Mumford again, an essential relationship between the human spirit and its physical background, a relationship that has almost been forgotten in the modern industrial world. The twentieth century is a century of displaced persons, not only as the result of political tyrannies and devastating wars but in a much wider sense as a result of the industrial changes of the past two centuries. We have either forgotten this profound relationship with our ancestral background, or we underestimate and even deride it. But historians at least should not underestimate its power, for it explains much that is otherwise inexplicable.

Even in London, such small communities within the Great Wen existed within living memory. How much more so in the sixteenth century, and even more in the smaller towns like Norwich and Bristol, York and Exeter, Newcastle and Coventry? Men and women, however poor, lived in a small and personal community, whether it was a town or a hamlet in the backwoods of northern or western England, a community in which the odds were they had been born and grown up. The Family was all-important, not only as the dominant economic group in a pre-industrial society but also as a social group which looked after the old or those unable to work. It was frequently an 'extended' family of three generations, and sometimes of four. The old had a special place in it, respected as those who had done their life's work, and honoured at times as the repositories of folk memory and tradition, to be called on to testify in some local crisis. Oral tradition was vitally important in a society where few could read or write.

Not only were men and women living in a place where they belonged, to which they were deeply attached in a multitude of ways, and in a family which was a present help in time of trouble, so that the terrible loneliness of a modern industrial society was not known, but their work, however ill-paid, brought them into daily contact with old friends and acquaintances. And they worked at their own leisurely pace, ungeared to any machine except in rare cases like the watermill or the windmill.

Then, too, they lived in what was for the most part a natural economy. For most people, especially in country areas, the barter of goods and services — especially in the first half of the sixteenth century at any rate, before the widespread Elizabethan revival of markets and fairs — was far more pervasive than the exchange of money. Money played only a marginal part in the lives of perhaps four people out of five, possibly even more. A money economy is impersonal to a greater or lesser degree; a natural economy is highly personal and the barter of services and of goods to some extent was widespread in the century we are now talking about. This, too, is essential to a proper understanding of the century, for it was — from the 1540s onwards — an age of inflation when the cost of living trebled in two generations, and money wages far from kept pace. On statistics alone, the poor should have sunk without trace in these decades. The answer is, once more, that they did not live in such a money economy, but only on the fringe of it.

Even in economic life, then, living was more personal than it became in, say, the nineteenth century, when suicide began to reach epidemic proportions in most 'civilized' countries. Loneliness amid crowds became a fact of life and a theme of nineteenth-century poetry, as in the threnodies of Matthew Arnold. The old set forms of life had either dissolved altogether or were no longer believed in.

There were yet other compensations in sixteenth-century life, even — perhaps especially — among the very poor. Like their descendants in Edwardian England they had what is to us an astonishing faculty for enjoying life on next to nothing. 'Some men', wrote Thomas Hardy in his *Notebooks*, 'would manage to whistle in Hell.' And he goes on to speak of what he calls 'the determination to enjoy'. 'It is achieved of a sort under superhuman difficulties. Like pent-up water it will find a chink of possibility somewhere. Even the most oppressed men and animals find it, so that out of a thousand there is not one who has not a sun of some sort for his soul.' Unless we understand this side of human nature, too, we cannot understand the social history of the sixteenth century, why there was so little suicide, why there was no massive uprising of the poor against the rich, but only pathetic rebellions for some local and passing provocation.

Death, too, was a commonplace event, most of all among the poorer classes. They faced it with a stoical fortitude. Montaigne writes about their attitude towards plague (the severe plague of 1586—87 in this instance) in words that must reflect precisely how the English peasantry would also have behaved:

> Now, what example of resoluteness did we not see then in the simplicity of this whole people? Each man universally gave up caring for his life. The grapes remained hanging on the vines . . . as all prepared themselves indifferently, and awaited death that evening or the next day with face and voice so little frightened that it seemed that they had made their peace with this necessity. . . . I saw some who feared to remain behind, as in a horrible solitude. . . .
> Here a man, healthy, was already digging his grave; others lay down in them while still alive. . . . In short, a whole nation was suddenly, by habit alone, placed on a level that concedes nothing in firmness to any studied and premeditated fortitude.

Men and women lived their lives according to a regular cycle throughout the year, a rhythm based in Catholic England on a series of 'holy days' but also on certain secular events, perhaps of pagan origin such as May Day. Charles Phythian-Adams has shown how elaborate this cycle could be even in an urbanized society such as Coventry in the first half of the sixteenth century, and how important it was to the mass of the population. In rural communities the cycle was equally highly organized throughout the year, regular events which involved the entire population, such as the blessing of the crops at Rogationtide, or Plough Monday: a series of communal occasions in addition to those that were purely local such as the annual procession to commemorate the day of some local saint. It is significant that, early in the seventeenth century, the parson of Cole Orton in west Leicestershire had to report that the Rogationtide procession was no longer well attended as so many of the men now worked underground as colliers. The industrial system was beginning to impinge on the ancient order of things and was ultimately to wreck it. This raises the question whether suicide was commoner in large towns than in the countryside, but this is unlikely except perhaps in London. We have no evidence one way or the other at this date; but even towns like Norwich and Coventry or Exeter were not far from green fields and the ancestral taste of country life. It was still a very long way to the inescapable grimness and rootlessness of the towns of the Industrial Revolution.

Life was hard as hell for at least half the population, and death a commonplace, but there were these fundamental compensations and suicide was rarely thought of. There was, indeed, an easy alternative, a temporary oblivion, and that was cheap drink. Whether the English drank more than the natives of wine-growing lands can never be proved, or whether they drank as much and continually as censorious bishops and Puritans continually said they did. It seems probable that they did, judging by what little independent evidence we possess. The British climate is on the whole chilly and wet, and in those towns and country districts where wood was scarce or too dear, drinking was the best way of keeping warm. Stow, writing at the end of the century, remarks that excessive drinking had always been a feature of life in London and he thought it had 'mightily encreased, though greatlie qualified among the poorer sort, not of any holy abstinencie, but of meere necessitie, Ale and Beere being small, and Wines in price above their reach'. At Coventry in 1544 the governing body grappled with the problem of the excessive number of ale-houses. Many people had forsaken better occupations to become brewers and tipplers, whereby the common-wealth of the city had decayed and vice and idleness had increased. This may well have been so, but it is one of the oldest complaints in the history of the world that the poor no longer work as they used to. The regulation of ale-houses continued to be a civic problem at Coventry: in 1547 the leet ordered that no labourer, journeyman, or apprentice should enter any inn, tavern, or ale-house on a workday, the penalty for the offence being fixed at imprisonment for a day and a night. A few years later (in 1553) there were further regulations concerning drinking and card-playing by the labouring class in ale-houses and inns.[31]

The history of the Shropshire parish of Myddle, already quoted for the rarity of evidence for suicide, is full of anecdotes about hardened and excessive drinkers in the local ale-houses, and of many a small estate being guzzled away over the years, sometimes by women also. It is abundantly clear from this parochial survey, aptly subtitled 'Human Nature displayed in the History of Myddle' that what we should now call alcoholism was common. Yet the drinkers were often men who were moderately well-off and not in despairing poverty. Harrison, writing in an earlier generation (1577–87), has a kinder verdict. After

[31] Harris, ed., *The Coventry Leet Book*, III, pp. 771, 786, 808.

51

saying that no man of position would overeat or get drunk, he goes on to observe that the poorer sort were given to 'verie muche babbling' and got drunk now and then. Even so, he is charitable enough to say that this was largely because at home they had 'a hard and pinching diet' so that drink affected them quickly; and they felt afterwards that in being 'cupshotten' they had disgraced themselves. On the whole the verdict must be that the English (and what of the Scots with their potent whisky?) were copious drinkers and spent an excessive amount of time in taverns and ale-houses. Only in this way could they soften the hardness of their working lives. Drink was plentiful and cheap, and was indeed the only consumer good readily available in early Tudor England. It was an economy with practically no consumer goods as we would term them, with no frills to buy except perhaps a few at the annual fair, and hence an economy of low wages and low productivity, despite the extremely long hours of work ordained by various statutes.[32]

---

[32] For hours of work and wage rates at this period see Chapter Five.

CHAPTER THREE

Rural Society and Agrarian Change

THE SOCIAL STRUCTURE

THE ownership of land was the source of all political and social and military power. The King was the largest single landowner. At the beginning of his reign Henry VII possessed about £10,000 a year in lands, a figure which rose to about £35,000 a year after a deliberate attack on the richer magnates, the relics for the most part of the old medieval baronage, the great warlords who had dominated their regions like local kings. The fall of Sir William Stanley alone was said to have added £1,000 a year to the royal revenues from land. In addition to the crown lands proper, the annual surplus from the Duchy of Lancaster, which was separately administered, grew to some £6,500, so that Henry's total income from land was well over £40,000 towards the end of his reign.[1] Out of this he accumulated the largest fortune ever known in England, which he left to his profligate and disastrous son.

When Henry VIII came to the throne many of the great medieval families had been liquidated. The number of temporal peers in the Upper House had never exceeded fifty-five in the Middle Ages: by 1500 they numbered perhaps forty, mostly living in a healthy fear of the new monarch. A dangerous chasm had been created between the Crown and the rest of the nation. Not until the 1530s did the ageing Henry begin seriously to fill this gap. Of the sixty-one peerages existing in 1559, twenty-six — the New Men — had been created within the preceding thirty years.[2]

As to the incomes of the peerage, they varied relatively as widely as

[1] Elton, *England under the Tudors*, pp. 48–9.
[2] MacCaffrey, 'The Crown and the new aristocracy', *Past and Present*, no. 30, 1965.

those of other social classes. The Duke of Buckingham, attainted in 1521, possessed lands in England and Wales to the value of some £6,045 a year. Next to him in wealth came the Archbishop of Canterbury with a clear income of £5,443 at the taking of the *Valor*. A few other magnates, like the Percies in the north and the Courtenays in the south-west, had about £3,000 a year. There is no point in pursuing exact figures as the income from a large estate, scattered over many counties and taking varied forms, varied from year to year. According to the subsidy assessment of 1523, only a third of the peerage possessed incomes of £1,000 a year or more but these were certainly considerably underestimated.[3] The average assessment for a peer was about £800 a year. Allowing for underassessment and variations, the average – for what this figure is worth – might have been £1,000 a year.

Beneath the peerage in the social hierarchy were the knights, whose territorial interests were more localized. Thomas Wilson (*c.* 1600) put the number of knights at about 500, and esquires at some 16,000. It is difficult to give similar estimates for the early sixteenth century, but a detailed scrutiny of the lay subsidies of the 1520s for East Anglia alone suggests that Norfolk had nineteen knights with an average landed income of £180 to £200 per annum. There were the usual magnates such as Sir Roger Townsend, assessed at £600 a year in lands, and Sir William Paston at £300. Like many leading families of Norfolk, Sir Roger was heavily engaged in sheep-farming with some 3,000 to 4,000 sheep. Sir William Fermour of East Barsham was keeping sheep in 1520–21 on twenty-five different grounds and probably had some 20,000 sheep in all.[4] The incomes of the greater landlords came not only directly from rents and fines but to a considerable degree from their large-scale farming activities. They constituted a major grievance in Ket's Rebellion of 1549, where half the twenty-seven complaints related to the agrarian situation and two were specifically aimed at limiting the number of sheep owned by large landlords.

The Suffolk subsidy names some twenty knights, again with a wide variation of income. Sir William Waldegrave of Bures had lands to the annual value of 400 marks (about £270 p.a.) but Sir William Clopton of

[3] Miller, 'Subsidy assessments of the peerage in the sixteenth century', *Bull. Inst. Hist. Research*, XXVIII, 1955. J. M. W. Bean, in *The Estates of the Percy Family 1416–1537*, O.U.P., 1958, found that while the Fifth Earl of Northumberland was assessed at £2,920 per annum in 1523, his clear income was about £1,000 a year more. But not all discrepancies were as large as this.
[4] Simpson, *The Wealth of the Gentry 1540–1660*, pp. 182–3. Dr Allison gives the Fermour total as 15,568 from twenty out of twenty-five flocks.

Long Melford's estate was put at half that value. He may, however, have possessed lands in other counties.

Knights were comparatively rare on the ground, and even esquires were not common. The traditional picture of the English village ruled over by a resident squire is one of the most persistent of historical myths. Suffolk, for example, had about forty-eight resident squires in the 1520s, in some 500 parishes — about one parish in ten. Bures had one resident knight and two esquires in the village, but in this was quite exceptional. Other counties, such as Buckinghamshire and Rutland, show the same low proportion.[5] But if Thomas Wilson's figure of 16,000 esquires at the end of the century is anywhere near the truth, then the Elizabethan village must have shown an entirely different picture. The Henrician figure suggests a total of about 1,000 esquires. Three generations later there were sixteen times as many: 'the rise of the gentry' indeed. Over England as a whole the esquires had an average income of some £80 a year, but there must have been considerable differences between the Kentish squire and his counterpart in the wilder parts of the south-west or in west Yorkshire.

In a way it is unrealistic to distinguish closely between esquires and gentry in Henrician England, though contemporaries often make the distinction in various legal records. The gentry were more numerous than the true esquires. Perhaps the best distinction is that an esquire tended to own at least one manor, and often several, while the gentleman merely owned lands and enjoyed a lower average income. Whereas the 'squire' enjoyed an average landed income of some £80 a year, for what such a statement is worth, the gentleman enjoyed some £10 to £20 a year; but again there are poor gentry with much smaller incomes. Most of the gentry were in fact the younger sons of esquires, and many would rise in the social scale before their lives ended. Many of the so-called gentry, too, in the 1520s were rich merchants — a London origin being the most common — and others were up-and-coming lawyers and officials with local power, such as David Cecil of Stamford, the founder of the Cecil fortunes and the original begetter of two famous peerages. But even gentle status did not automatically give entry to local power (e.g. as a justice of the peace): indeed only a minority of the gentry in the widest use of the term reached this status.[6] Quite possibly a considerable proportion of backwoods gentry did not trouble their heads

[5] Julian Cornwall, 'The early Tudor gentry', *Econ. H.R.*, sec. ser., XVII, no. 3, 1965.
[6] Ibid., p. 469.

about such local power but were content to devote their time and energies to their lands, where they were often active and practical farmers.

Esquires and gentry, as often lumped together in some records as they were separated in others, together made up between 2 and 3 per cent of the total population, but again there were considerable variations in different parts of the country. What is more generally true is that the resident squire or gentleman was comparatively rare in English villages. In Rutland and Suffolk, for example, four villages out of five had no resident squire or any other sort of gentleman living in them. In Leicestershire only one village in every six or seven had a resident squire in the 1520s. The village with a resident squire is largely a Victorian creation.

Occasionally a careful record distinguishes between esquires and gentry: thus in a list compiled in 1539 Cumberland had seven knights, twenty-two esquires, and eighty-four gentry, but Westmorland at the same date with twenty-two esquires had only thirty-seven gentry. Rutland had eight esquires, and twenty-seven gentry. Probably in the West Country, and perhaps in Kent also, there were more gentry, but they tended to be smaller fry altogether. A count through the feodary surveys at this date, which classify men more scrupulously, shows that out of forty-two gentry more than a half had landed incomes of £10 to £20 a year, and none had as much as £30 in lands. But again local power and recognition as a J.P. mattered more in the social structure of the countryside. Many of the squires and gentry were of ancient origin, often bearing the name of the parish from which they originated some time back in the twelfth or thirteenth century, such as Clopton of Clopton in Cambridgeshire, Shirley of Shirley in Derbyshire, Cruwys of Cruwys Morchard in deepest Devon, and hundreds of others.

Beneath the gentry in the countryside were the yeomen, again a term not capable of precise definition (often men were called yeoman or husbandman in different records) but it is safe to say that the common people made a clear distinction in their own minds though they could not have defined how and why. Even in the early twentieth century, village people made a subtle distinction among the farmers of the parish between Mr White and Farmer Brown: perhaps if they could be pinned down it was that Mr White owned his own land and Farmer Brown (as the very word 'farmer' indicates) did not. This may have been the biggest distinguishing mark, yet we must always recall Latimer's well-known words in a sermon preached before Edward VI, that his father was a yeoman though he had no lands of his own. It seems to have been by the early sixteenth century a matter of a man's personal wealth and the scale of his farming and living.[7]

> Generally speaking, the Leicestershire yeoman occupied a farm — perhaps two or three — running into a hundred or two hundred acres and rented pastures in addition; his activities extended into two, three, or four parishes, whereas the husbandman's horizon was bounded by the fields of his own village; his live-stock were ten times as numerous as the husbandman's; and altogether he lived on a wider and more comfortable scale.

This summary description of one Midland county is probably true of most parts of England at this time.

Among the yeomen, too, we know from tax assessments that there were wide variations in personal wealth as well as in their lands. Indeed in many villages, especially where there was no resident squire monopolizing most of the land, two or three big yeoman families dominated the place nearly as effectively.[8] Even so, this is not the whole of the story. The squire, where he existed, was on the whole a being apart, whereas while economic inequality might be very con-spicuous among the peasantry, there was still a considerable measure of social equality. The big yeomen did not get away with much against the regiment of smaller peasant farmers, not least because most village com-munities (above all where there was no resident lord) were governed in all their farming arrangements by village by-laws which had to receive the consent of the majority and be obeyed by all. This was probably true of all open-field villages; but in the pastoral regions of isolated farms and hamlets no rules were required except those that governed the use of the common pastures.

The social structure of English villages varied from place to place, and region to region. It seems almost impossible to generalize at all use-fully. Some peasant families had accumulated lands in a steady persistent way during much of the fifteenth century and became the big yeomen of Henrician England; others went to the wall and entered the new century as husbandmen or even less, perhaps labourers or at best craftsmen. The determining factors were the amount of freehold land that was available: that is, whether a village was 'closed' or 'open' in the matter of ownership: whether there was a local land market at the peasant level, or whether a resident or distant squire controlled most of the land so that little ever came on to the market. And beyond that

[7] Hoskins, *Essays in Leicestershire History*, p. 151.
[8] Ibid., pp. 127–8.

again there was the equally important factor of the local customs of inheritance. If land passed by primogeniture (with perhaps some token provision for the younger children) then a village might develop into a tightly closed one. But where partible inheritance was the custom and a man's lands were more or less equally divided after death among all his sons, it produced an entirely different social structure and way of life, and a different kind of farming. There would tend to be more land available for buying and selling in small parcels: on the other hand a tenement might be so fragmented that it could not produce a decent living at all. Here much depended on the quality of the soil. The rich fenlands and marshlands of eastern England could support a dense population off quite small holdings, whereas in the wilder dales of Northumberland, leading up into the Cheviots, the generally poorer lands (not all) produced a lawless element among the younger men who throve on cattle-stealing because their smallholdings could never satisfy them; yet they did not wish to migrate and leave their ancestral countryside.

Thus, for historic reasons, the social structure and indeed the very field system of country parishes might differ considerably within a few miles of each other, yet the peasant culture, for such indeed it was, had many features in common wherever one found oneself in Tudor England. It is not easy to describe its fundamental characteristics shortly, but I have done so at length in *The Midland Peasant* (1957). It formed a powerful social cement that held the village and the parish together when disruptive forces from outside might have been expected to dissolve it. In most Midland parishes, and over an even wider field, it was not until the parliamentary enclosures of the period 1750 to 1850 that this distinctive culture was finally killed; and even so remnants of it could still be detected early in this century. It was perhaps at its strongest in the Tudor period, and even then there were forces making for its dissolution as well as its strengthening. Yet the balance remained in favour of a well-knit community of people and common interests despite such obvious weaknesses as a very unequal distribution of wealth. Powerful social forces mitigated these economic differences, not least the Catholic Church to which all 'belonged'.

In Henrician England the husbandman, whether he farmed under an open-field system and communal rules or in an anciently enclosed countryside in an isolated farmstead set among closes of pasture, farmed about 10 to 30 acres of land, rarely owning any, but holding it on leases that varied in the protection they offered. Thus in the west of England the lease for three lives or ninety-nine years had established itself by this time, and under a good landlord, content to renew with fresh lives at an agreed rent, such leases tended to be thought of as tantamount to freehold. They went on from generation to generation. Elsewhere, where such long leases were almost unheard of, the protection might be only that afforded by a seven- or ten-year term, with the very real possibility of the rent being raised at each renewal.

At death the husbandman rarely left more than £20 in personal estate. The average in Leicestershire was £14 to £15, and in Somerset about £12. Often such a small farmer carried on a craft as a sideline — the dual economy referred to elsewhere — and sometimes it is hard to see which side of his living he regarded as paramount. Most if not all village craftsmen had some land on which family labour helped out.

Cottagers, below the husbandman in economic status at least, have sometimes been described as an 'agricultural proletariat', a view formed probably from looking too exclusively at manorial surveys and at the small amounts of land (if any) a cottager might till or graze. But this is far from the truth. There were bad times, of course, a harvest failure being the worst of catastrophes, and these were the class (and the purely wage-earning class in so far as they can be separated) whose heads went under in an economic storm. But most years were not like this, and they lived in what may truly be called a 'cottage economy', a term which Cobbett tried to revive in the early nineteenth century. The essence of this economy was *thrift*, and the barter of goods and services rather than a money economy, which played but a small part in their lives; the careful use of all the natural resources of their parish, even the humblest; an unyielding meanness at its worst which is so characteristic not only of the French peasant but of parts of rural England to this day. So in north Devon it is a common saying that it takes two Jews to get the better of a Devon farmer. Such a mental attitude, a bulwark in Tudor England, became too often in the nineteenth century an all-enveloping and inhuman meanness that made farmers in the peripheral parts of England repellent in their attitude towards their labourers. It produced widespread unrest and emigration to the New World to escape from the horrors of the England's green and pleasant land. On the other hand, there is good reason to believe that in sixteenth-century England this was not so, without pretending that it was in any way a golden age for the cottager and the labourer.[9]

[9] I develop this theme in greater detail in *The Midland Peasant*, pp. 190–4.

THE MANORIAL POPULATION

Every manor, however loosely held together in practice, consisted of free tenants (freeholders), customary tenants (who were mostly but not all copyholders), and possibly some leaseholders or conventionary tenants. Our information comes chiefly from manorial surveys, which become increasingly common as the sixteenth century goes on, probably because of the renewed pressure on land as population rose steadily. Because of this it has been suggested that the peasantry paid greater attention to family rights, litigation became more common even at that level, and the drawing-up of manorial custumals by lords and tenants increased in number in order to settle growing disputes or to prevent disputes in the future.[10]

It is again virtually impossible to say what proportions of the manorial tenantry were freeholders and/or customary tenants. The leaseholders are usually easier to identify. Tawney's figures in *The Agrarian Problem in the Sixteenth Century* are vitiated to a considerable degree by the fact that he drew on manorial surveys covering the whole of the century, and there may have been important changes between the early part of the century and the later; and also by the fact that many of the tenantry overlapped more than one category. A free tenant might hold customary land, and vice versa; without counting individual names one cannot be sure of the extent of this overlapping. Further, as has been shown elsewhere (see pp. 33—5) the percentage of free tenants as calculated by Tawney can itself be misleading. Tawney found that in Norfolk and Suffolk free tenants amounted to 36 per cent of the total manorial population, and in Devon the proportion was only 23 per cent. But this takes no account of the size of the free tenement: it has been suggested earlier that many of the East Anglian freeholders held merely a house and a small piece of land, perhaps merely a cottage and a croft; while in the south-west a considerable proportion of the free tenants as listed in the surveys were esquires and gentry whose holdings were usually farms of 100 to perhaps 400 acres. All we can safely say is that on the majority of manors the free tenants were an important element in the manorial structure, enjoying absolute security. They paid a token rent (variously called a quit rent or a chief rent) to the lord of the manor: but this rent, fixed in medieval times,

[10] Rosemary Faith, 'Peasant families and inheritance customs in medieval England', *A.H.R.*, XIV, pt ii, 1966, 77—95, makes this suggestion that the sixteenth century was really following the precedent of the thirteenth century when there had been a similar pressure on land.

remained unchanged over the centuries. Thus the Aclands, who are recorded at Acland Barton as early as the mid-twelfth century, were free tenants of the episcopal manor of Bishop's Tawton in Devon, holding in free socage at a chief rent of ten shillings a year, a rent which remained unchanged into modern times. Hundreds of other Devon gentry held land of other lords on similar terms and ranked under the heading of 'free tenants' in manorial surveys.

The customary tenants were by the far the most numerous class in the manorial population. If we accept Tawney's figures in default of more exact calculations made since, on average, three out of five tenants were customary tenants. Unsatisfactory as such a statement is, it is nevertheless clear that they were by far the most numerous class, and also the class most open to exploitation in various ways by the lord. The sixteenth-century copyholder evolved from the medieval villein who had held at the lord's will, and who obeyed the customs of the manor under the penalty of forfeiting his holding. During the fifteenth century the central courts of law stepped in to protect the copyholder from the grosser dangers and abuses, greatly strengthening his position. We must always remember, however, that seeking the aid of the central courts in London, whatever the law said in theory, might prove too unrealistic for an oppressed copyholder in the backwoods. In bad cases, however, perhaps involving the rights of all the customary tenants, they might well band together against the lord and bring him to court.

Again, not all customary tenants had the protection of an entry on the manor court roll. They could be *custumaria sine copia*, a not uncommon tenure even in the reign of Henry VIII. Glastonbury Abbey had no fewer than 215 families of bondmen on its estates in 1533, and as late as 1549 the most oft-quoted request in Ket's Rebellion was 'that all bond men may be made free for god made all free with his precious blood shedding'. The position of customary tenants without copies improved during the sixteenth century as the courts tended to treat all customary tenants alike, with the very important qualification (which the courts themselves could not upset against the proven facts) that not all copyholders were of equal strength. Strongest of all were copyholders by inheritance, holding by a fixed entry fine and a fixed small annual rent. But there were masses of copyholders who did not necessarily inherit automatically: they depended on the goodwill of the lord whether they followed on at all. If the custom of the manor was such that entry fines were not fixed by ancient practice, but variable at the will of the lord, then the hopeful tenant might find himself competing in terms of money, through the entry fine or the annual rent or both, for his dead father's tenement. The fine, calculated at so many years' rental value, was the dangerous loophole in such a struggle, above all when the demand for land grew in the later decades of the century and inflation more or less forced landlords to revise fines, rents, and other terms of tenure.

A copyholder for the term of his life, on a tenement burdened with an uncertain fine (one that would probably rise at his death) was in the weakest position in any tussle with the lord over the succession. But there are two important qualifications to the bare economic facts. That there were thousands of disputes and lawsuits between landlords and tenants during the sixteenth century cannot be denied. Tawney's book *The Agrarian Problem in the Sixteenth Century* still stands, despite inevitable criticism after some sixty years, as the classic statement of the subject. But our evidence is very largely based on legal records that survive in the national archives, and by their nature they are pathological in origin. They represent situations where the normal machinery of the manor or the village had broken down, and they may be no more representative of everyday life than the divorce rate in modern England represents the state of marriage as a whole. The evidence, then, of legal struggles between landlords and tenants in sixteenth-century England is heavily biased towards the abnormal

There have always been good and bad landlords, but the good landlords rarely record the smooth working of the manorial system though it could be painfully calculated from thousands of entries on the manor court rolls. Even the upheavals that accompanied the dissolution of the monasteries and the rapid disposal of their lands did not necessarily alter fundamentally the picture of a fairly stable rural society. So we find in Bedfordshire that Sir John Gostwick, a Tudor official with access to monastic spoils and who benefited thereby, nevertheless counselling his heirs *c.* 1540: 'take not above one year's rent for a fine. . . . Heighten no rent unless your farmers have heightened theirs to subtenants.' Gostwick was one of the New Men, so often criticized by economic historians; but he could well have been typical of a great number as he makes it clear that his heirs should get the goodwill and favour of all their neighbours, not only in their manor of Willington but in the whole shire. The desire to stand well in local esteem and to conform to the decent usages of rural society may well have been acute in men rising from one social class to another.[11]

(Note 11 on p. 63.)

From medieval times onwards the leasing of the demesne land was always an important element in the manorial economy. By the early sixteenth century the leaseholder or conventionary tenant was probably more important than mere numbers would indicate. Tawney gives one tenant in every eight over all England as a leaseholder, generally holding land for a term of years at a rack-rent. But in all probability the lease-holder leased the whole, or part, of the demesne and was therefore a bigger man than the average copyholder in the manor, taking a lease of the demesne land to add to his existing farming enterprises. There was therefore a considerable overlapping of tenures, which makes it difficult if not impossible to differentiate them. In East Anglia, for example, Spratt found that of nearly 13,000 acres of land, nearly 60 per cent was held by tenants who were both freeholders and copyholders. Again, the statistics do not show how much land was held in terms of acres, especially in the case of the free tenants. They probably held more land than their bare numbers would suggest. The same applies to lease-holders who were perhaps more important than their numbers would suggest as a dissolvent of the peasant economy through the tempted eyes of the landlord with visions of rack-rents.

As to the landless, we know even less about these and have little idea about their numbers. They supplied the labour for the manorial economy and often had a little land, above all in an open-field economy where the land was greatly subdivided physically in the form of strips. It is therefore a great mistake to dismiss these cottagers and labourers with perhaps one, two or three acres listed in the manorial surveys, as an 'agricultural proletariat'. An acre of land could make all the differ-ence in this class between poverty in the face of rising prices and com-parative economic security: not to mention the possibilities of rising in the economic scale through the old-fashioned, and now derided, virtue of thrift by adding strip to strip, as the opportunity arose. Such a labourer, with even an acre of land, had his foot on a ladder in the open-field economy, which was not possible in a countryside of enclosed fields which were necessarily larger and harder to acquire.

Tawney has immortalized the phrase 'the agrarian problem' in the sixteenth century. It was a problem that had two major elements. First there was the renewed pressure of population on the supply of land, which was greatly aggravated by the engrossing of farms into fewer and larger hands; and secondly there was the increased pressure of prices on

[11] A. G. Dickens, 'Estate and household management in Bedfordshire *c*. 1540,' in *Bedfordshire Hist. Rec. Soc.*, XXXVI, 1956.

incomes, especially of landlords, though this was far more important after the middle of the sixteenth century. Not that this was merely a onesided pressure. Rising prices could just as well increase a landlord's income through the sale of surplus produce from the demesne and of tithes in kind in a period of rising prices.

After the great fall of population since the middle fourteenth century, followed by the 'land plenty' of the fifteenth century, there was a change in the agrarian economy. Population was probably rising fairly steadily by the early sixteenth century, though the greatest rise came in the last quarter of the century. It is possible that the population of England in 1600 was no greater than that of the 1340s. Why then a 'problem'? Why did not the rising population of the early sixteenth century, and beyond, merely take up the slack of the late fourteenth and fifteenth centuries?

The answer is probably to be found in the engrossing of farms which had been going on for generations, especially among freeholders, partly by the natural processes of death and marriage, and partly by the deliberate act of acquisition of the smaller freeholds by the larger man with greater reserves to withstand a temporary agricultural depression. The pace of engrossing increased greatly in the Tudor period. Thus there were fewer farms available for the rising population and, further, there were no great areas of 'waste' land left to reclaim and be colonized, except limited areas as in, say, the Forest of Rossendale. The entire district of Rossendale was developed as farming land enclosed from royal forests after the disafforestation of Rossendale by Henry VII. Here we find a growth of small copyholders who outnumbered all others by the early seventeenth century. But not much land was available in England by, say, 1550, except the commons and wastes which were vital to the agrarian economy of peasant husbandry itself. So even a 'peasant village' with no dominant or grasping landlord imposed its own limits on taking in more common land for arable farming: the use of the village common was as strictly regulated as the arable. It is not true to say that England consisted of islands of cultivation in a sea of waste, but rather the reverse: precious islands of commons in a sea of cultivation, certainly in the lowland commons.

The real price revolution did not become apparent until the late 1540s, but there was probably pressure on landlords' incomes because of their heavy expenditure on rebuilding their old houses. This applies not only to those who were building grand country houses for display, but also to a considerable number of the smaller gentry, as is evident from the extraordinary number of houses of the period 1480 to 1540 which survive all the way from Devon up to Kent, and probably northwards into the Midlands.

With the rising expenditure on building, and possibly rising household expenses, the tenant was an inviting target. If we say that roughly three tenants out of five were customary tenants to some extent or other, many of whom paid but modest fines and rents, then they presented a clear temptation to the early Tudor landlord. As the prices of farm produce rose the 'unearned increment' drained at first only into the customary tenants' pockets, with their fixed costs. To that extent they were a legitimate target even for an easy-going landlord.

The agrarian problem had various aspects, the more obvious of which was the legal aspect. Here the struggle was fought out in the law courts, either to oust copyholders with a weak tenure, and convert their farms to leasehold at a rack-rent, or to raise the entry fines of copyholders who could not be ousted because of the strength of their title. A great number of local disputes turned on whether the entry fines were certain or arbitrary, at the will of the lord. The importance of entry fines which were not certain for one reason or another, is made clear in the Pilgrimage of Grace of 1536 which made an economic demand that the gressom (*ingressum*) be limited to two years' rent. Henry VIII himself defined the duties of the Council of the North in 1537 as, among other things, to make diligent inquisition 'who hath taken and enclosed commons, called intakes; who were extreme in taking of gressoms and raising of rents'. The prayer of the Reformers under Edward VI has often been quoted: 'O Lord, we pray thee that the landlords may not rack and stretch out the rents.'

We therefore get from the early sixteenth century onwards a great increase in the number of custumals of manors, that is to say, written records of the customs of particular manors which differed from one manor to the next. This setting down and writing of the customs of the manor was of benefit to both landlords and tenants, and even if the custom of the manor was that entry fines were not fixed but remained at the will of the lord, it does not follow that this led to eviction of copyholders unwilling to pay, or to the raising of the fines. We must always remember that legal records, however numerous, represent the pathology of society. There was no uniformity in this matter, even of the manors in the same region belonging to the same lord. In East Anglia, in the first half of the seventeenth century, Spratt found that while forty-six of eighty manors in Norfolk and Suffolk had uncertain fines, there was no evidence of entry fines being raised to exorbitant rates. Similarly in Devon the general picture is one of stability. This was probably even more true of the less commercialized time of Henry VIII. We are in danger of seriously underestimating the monumental stability of rural society, which was bound together by stronger ties than the purely financial to which we, in our besotted modern way, attach so much importance.

Long before 1500 demesne lands had been leased out for years at a time, and to some extent, in Henry VIII's time, the leasing of land at competitive rents or competitive fines continued. But what is equally striking is that in south-west England at least, we find the development of leases, not for a term of years, but for the lifetime of the lessee plus two other living persons nominated by him. Well before the sixteenth century ended, therefore, we find the standard form of lease in the south-west becoming a lease for three lives or ninety-nine years, a long term which had great merits both for the landlord and the tenant and, in later centuries, great demerits.

The agrarian problem can be exaggerated because of the pathological nature of our sources. We obviously rarely hear of amicable settlements between landlords and tenants over the entry fines or their rents. There was another aspect, however, to this problem which arose from a conflict of views about the nature of land. From time immemorial land had been regarded basically as a source of military service, according to the number of tenants 'able to do service'. It is significant that the first statute against depopulation (1489) applied to the Isle of Wight alone, the most vulnerable part of Britain from the military point of view. This was the old, the feudal, point of view, and it naturally persisted longest among the magnates of the north with their virtually private armies against the Scots or anyone else who dared to cross their path. But as the sixteenth century advanced we find land being regarded more as an economic investment. In other words, it must yield a monetary return and the number of tenants became of little or no consequence. Generally, the feudal view was supported by the government, sometimes for obvious reasons and sometimes for somewhat odd rationalizations. For example, when vast areas of open-field arable were being converted to sheep and cattle pastures in the later 1400s and early 1500s the argument was used, when one shepherd could take over the work of perhaps a hundred arable labourers, that shepherds made bad archers. It is difficult to fathom why this should be so unless shepherding was regarded as a contemplative occupation, of gazing into space where a precise target did not matter. There was also the more serious argument about the social importance of a solid base of peasant husbandry as the best possible basis for conservative government. Husbandmen made the best infantry, fishermen made the best seamen.

This argument was not held by the new landed proprietors and was strongest in the southern part of England especially within a radius of say, eighty to ninety miles from London, the kind of radius which London merchants considered the maximum in finding new farms and in building grand new houses, safely embedded in the Midlands and far from the strife of the Scottish border.

The agrarian problem had, of course, a number of other economic aspects. The engrossing of a number of small peasant farms into a larger unit had its reaction on the methods of subsistence farming, especially with the growing importance of the great food market of London. This was reflected most obviously in enclosures for sheep and cattle pastures; but apart from that it is probably true to say that this aspect of farming was not of much importance until the second half of the sixteenth century. Apart from specialist crops, and even these on a small scale, specialist regions of English farming remained basically subsistence farming down to the middle of the century, producing for the smaller and nearer local markets, in so far as there were surpluses, rather than for a larger market like London. But London was not the only growing food market: the major provincial towns like York, Exeter, Newcastle and Bristol must also have had an increasing influence on the nature of farming in their own regions. Another economic aspect of the agrarian problem was the development of competitive rents for land, but even this must not be overstressed before the middle of the century. England was still slow-moving underneath the apparently visual revolution in the countryside.

There were other factors at work which were having their effect on the new economy, though here again the main pressure came after the middle of the century. There was the building up of large estates by the new aristocracy; and their fashionable demand for deer parks which took land out of cultivation and aggravated the local pressure on the remainder. Such extensions of parks or creation of new parks were a not infrequent cause of bitter legal disputes, and so far as the supply of land was concerned there was the increasing engrossing of farms by rising yeomen. The importance of engrossing of farms by bigger men was possibly a greater social problem than the much more noisy controversy over enclosures, if only because it was more general. The enclosure problem was largely confined to the Midlands, though this is an oversimplified statement; but the engrossing of farms was going on all the time all over the country. The controversy over enclosures which usually involved almost immediate conversion to pasture was primarily a Midland problem. The greater part of the south-west of England, south-east and the north had already been enclosed in some form or another; yet even in these regions there were serious local changes. The price of labour had risen and pasture-farming reduced labour costs greatly for landlords. Probably the reduction of labour costs was more important than the actual rise in wool prices and this in spite of the growth of native cloth manufacture and the constant demand for English wool at home. The development of food markets has already been touched on and was possibly not very important during Henry VIII's reign except, perhaps, for an increased consumption of meat.

The enclosure controversy appeared to have reached its height in the early decades of the sixteenth century but it is clear from the now well-recorded history of deserted medieval villages that the bulk of the damage caused by enclosure and conversion to pasture had been done before 1485. It seems likely that the spread of printed books had a great deal to do with the increased noise of the controversy after 1500. Moreover, there was a growing knowledge of land use and of the different kinds of soil, which not only gave progressive landlords a rational defence for their actions, but also legitimately increased agricultural production.

The earliest printed book on agriculture comes, as one might expect, from Augsburg in 1471: Peter Crescent's *Liber Ruralium Comodorum*. Some fifty years later came the first book of the kind in English, FitzHerbert's *Husbandry*, followed by his *Surveying*, both published in 1523. FitzHerbert's *Husbandry* went through eight editions by the end of the sixteenth century. Not until 1557, thirty years after FitzHerbert, did a second book appear, Thomas Tusser's *A Hundred Good Points of Husbandry*, later enlarged in 1573 to *Five Hundred Good Points*. So FitzHerbert held the field as a printed guide to the practice of farming all through Henry VIII's reign. It shows, as Dr Fussell says,[12] a thorough knowledge of farming, dealing purely with the best principles of arable farming of his time, the tools, the capital required, the value of manuring, the practice of draining and, above all, perhaps, his belief in

---

[12] Fussell, *The Old English Farming Books*, pp. 4 *et seq.*, on which this paragraph is largely based.

the value of enclosure for the improvement of farming standards. What we do not know, of course, is how far the best standards were widely practised, or on what regions FitzHerbert's experience was based; and, above all, whether the average farmer possessed any or all of the tools and implements needed for the best farming. Thus he speaks of rollers being used to roll barley ground after a shower of rain to make the ground even to mow; but a study of Leicestershire farm inventories shows that rollers were almost unknown throughout the county before the seventeenth century. FitzHerbert did not doubt that enclosure enhanced the value of land considerably and, in the growing knowledge of the different types of land, their possibilities, if only among the gentry and the larger yeomen. When certain east Leicestershire squires were summoned at different times for enclosing their land and turning it to pasture they defended themselves in some instances by saying that the heavy lias clays in their part of England were better suited to pasture, as indeed they were. But this does not mean, as was once argued, that the open-field arable land had been exhausted by centuries of cropping.

We may take Leicestershire as a good example of the general picture in the enclosure controversy. It was in the heart of open-field England; it was highly cultivated, with very little real 'waste' left except in Charnwood Forest. Possibly 95 per cent of the land was under cultivation: mostly good land, though heavy clays predominate and here too most of the damage, if damage it was, had been done before the date set for investigation by the first of the three commissions on the subject. It is almost impossible to give figures about the total acreage involved in this conversion from arable to pasture. A detailed investigation by Dr Parker showed that possibly one-tenth of the open-field arable at the very most was converted in this way; even allowing for the fact that the jurors under Wolsey's commission of 1517—18 understated the amount of land so converted. Local juries could be packed by local squires: and, even if not packed, the tenant would show a healthy regard for his landlord's goodwill. So, for example, the jury declared that William Ashby in east Leicestershire had enclosed 120 acres of arable for pasture, back in 1487, but other records show that he had enclosed and depopulated the whole manor, amounting to some 1,000 acres. As to the dating of enclosure in Leicestershire, most had happened before 1485, but taking the period 1485 to 1530, 43 per cent of the recorded total, affecting 45 different places, occurred between 1485 and 1530. After that, there was a great falling off and, for 50 years, from 1531 to 1580 only 9 per cent of the total acreage (involving twenty-seven places) was affected.

There are thus peak periods at the beginning and end of the sixteenth century and in so far as there was a climax it was reached about 1510.

Acreages alone, however, do not give the full picture. The number of places affected is more important. Thus, between 1485 and 1607 enclosures in Leicestershire affected about 140 places out of some 370 villages and hamlets − in other words, more than one community in three suffered complete or partial enclosure and conversion to grass. About forty places of the 140 were completely enclosed. Former writers[13] have described the controversy about enclosure and conversion to pasture as 'hysterical exaggeration' and this may be so if we look merely at the acreages involved; but when we look at the number of places affected we can understand the feeling of the time. This is especially so in the early sixteenth century when enclosure was much more a matter of the squire and perhaps one or two of the big freeholders working their will on the whole community; whereas later enclosure, in the second half of the sixteenth century, tended to be done by agreement among a larger number of tenants and spread over a number of years. Then, too, so far as 'hysterical exaggeration' is concerned, even the partial enclosure of land from arable cultivation at a time when the demand for farms was rising created serious local problems, of little or no national importance statistically but shattering for the community concerned.

The enclosure of the open arable fields was generally followed by conversion to grass, though some arable was generally kept for essential purposes. But basically there was wholesale conversion, arable tenants were evicted, and, as the record (the so-called *Domesday of Inclosures*) not infrequently said 'departed in tears'. Some must have been fortunate to find another farm in an 'open' village not too far away, but most probably went to swell the ranks of the urban poor. In many instances, certainly in the Midlands, such wholesale enclosure and conversion to pasture farming was often forced on a landlord because of sheer lack of labour to maintain the old farming economy with its predominance of arable husbandry. The successive waves of plague

[13] I. S. Leadam had published his edition of *The Domesday of Inclosures 1517−18* in 1897, with a minute discussion of the statistical evidence. In 1900, E. F. Gay published articles in *T.R.H.S.* which were largely critical of Leadam's work. It was Gay who used the phrase 'hysterical exaggeration' about sixteenth-century writers and others.

during the fifteenth century had reduced many a once populous village to half a dozen small farmers and a few labourers. So when Sir Robert Brudenell evicted thirty people (probably half a dozen households) at Holyoak on the Leicestershire—Rutland border in the autumn of 1496 — and the record says 'they have departed thence and are either idle or have perished' — these were but the remnants of a much larger village that had been decaying over a long period. Recent archaeological investigations have revealed a much larger village, extending over many acres. Sir Robert Brudenell merely gave the *coup de grâce* to a place which had long been suffering from a dwindling population and was perhaps no longer a viable community of the common-field type. The tax quotas of the fifteenth century for the Midland counties reveal serious economic decay generations before the early Tudor landlords roused such fury in print and in sermons for their enclosing activities. Depopulation was therefore both a cause and a consequence of enclosure and conversion to pasture.

The social status of the enclosers has been discussed inconclusively by Leadam in his pioneer work.[14] The evidence is not always complete; but a detailed investigation by Parker in Leicestershire produced results which give a fuller picture.[15] Here, in the period 1485 to 1550, the Crown was responsible for 2.1 per cent of the total enclosure of the period (a new hunting park for Henry VIII just outside Leicester and therefore not typical); the monasteries for 17.6 per cent; the nobility for 12.1 per cent; and the squirearchy for no less than 67.5 per cent. Peasantry and merchants do not figure at all in this early period. No doubt the proportions differed from county to county. Leadam found that in Northamptonshire, which bordered Leicestershire, monastic enclosure accounted for 29 per cent, thanks largely to the activities of the rich abbey of Peterborough, but the record is incomplete and too much must not be made of this difference. In Leicestershire, and probably in other Midland counties, enclosure was the work of old-established, indigenous families, not of newcomers seeking a quick profit. Altogether two-thirds of the enclosure in this county was the work of twenty-one squires, nearly all of them native to the county. It is much what we would expect, and it is a similar picture to that presented by the disposal of monastic lands (see Chapter Six).

In the early period (1485—1550) enclosure was almost entirely for

---

[14] See note 13.
[15] L. A. Parker, 'The enclosure movement in Leicestershire, 1485—1607', unpublished thesis, University of Leicester.

pasture, but having said this we must add that both sheep and cattle were involved. Most of the controversy of these years, as witness Sir Thomas More's oft-quoted words about sheep eating up men, centred round sheep, but there is considerable evidence that in the Midlands the growing leather industry, not to mention the meat market in the towns, also called for far more cattle than hitherto.

Although Wolsey's commission allowed for prosecution where enclosure and conversion could be proved to have damaged the community, and hence the commonwealth, it was almost impossible to secure any worthwhile results. In Leicestershire only twenty-two cases were brought to court, and only one conviction secured out of fifteen known results. Packed juries made conviction difficult, and many landlords got away with the plea that the enclosed land had been reconverted to tillage. There is little likelihood that this was true; after all, some of the biggest offenders were justices of the peace, unlikely to convict themselves or their friends. They were a closely packed caucus, both by marriage and by financial interest.

Even so, there was no general uprising against enclosure. There were, it is true, small disturbances in 1549 and 1553, but no general movement in the Midlands until the famous rising of 1607. The reason may well be that in the early Tudor period the communities involved were already small and decaying. No mass revolt could arise in such lonely countrysides, which remain so even to this day.

ENGLISH FARMING UNDER HENRY VIII

The regnal dates of monarchs have no significance for agrarian history: in this field cabbages are more important than kings. Comparatively little is known about the detail of English farming during the first half of the sixteenth century, certainly before 1540 where 'Tawney's Century' has attracted so many scholars, to the unwitting neglect of earlier generations. There is perhaps a good reason for this concentration on the period after 1540. It is that the records and printed sources are scarce until the great flow begins after the Dissolution, for obvious reasons. Moreover, probate inventories, on which we now rely so heavily for detailed pictures of farming all over England, scarcely get going (with a few exceptions) until the second half of the century, and often not then. Estate maps, manorial surveys, and terriers are also scarce until the last quarter of the sixteenth century.

Our knowledge of farming in Henry VIII's England is therefore patchy and will remain so until we have far more local studies. It used to be thought that so far as farming was concerned in England and Wales the country could be divided roughly into a drier arable half in the east, and a wetter pastoral half in the west: a Lowland Zone and a so-called Highland Zone divided approximately by the Exe–Tees line on the map. These zones had different field systems, different types of farming, different social and physical structures, as well as the more obvious differences in climates, soils, and geology. But as long ago as Elizabethan times, William Harrison in his *Description of England* had made a more fundamental distinction in dividing the countryside into champion and woodland which did not necessarily coincide with the rough and ready modern distinction between highland and lowland. 'It is so that,' he writes, 'our soil being divided into champaign ground and woodland, the houses of the first lie uniformly builded in every town [i.e. village] together, with streets and lanes; whereas in the woodland countries (except here and there in great market towns) they stand scattered abroad, each one dwelling in the midst of his own occupying.' The champion or champaign country was distinguished mainly by open-field arable farming; and the woodland by mainly pastoral husbandry.

Dr Thirsk's brilliant opening chapter to the fourth volume of *The Agrarian History of England and Wales* broke down this wide distinction into a much more complex pattern and gave us the better name of 'wood-pasture' for Harrison's simple woodland, emphasizing more clearly its pastoral nature. Thus by the sixteenth century, and probably long before that, the pattern of English farming was extremely complicated even within the two broad zones of highland and lowland. In the pastoral west, thought to be the home of single farmsteads and hamlets rather than true villages, with small fields enclosed from the still abundant woodland and moorland, one could yet find considerable pockets of flatter and more fertile land with larger communities of the lowland type, growing more corn in what were still common fields. Such fields, much diminished in size within recent times, may still be seen at Braunton in north Devon and more remarkably on the Isle of Portland in south Dorset and on the Isle of Axholme in Lincolnshire. On the other hand, in the arable east there were large areas of wood pasture where the picture was more like the highland model, where pastoral husbandry was paramount and settlement dispersed into single farmsteads, often surrounded by a medieval moat. Thus the county of Essex has no fewer than 760 moated sites, and more are being found every year. Suffolk is almost equally rich in such sites. Most occur in the wood pasture areas of eastern England, particularly but not always on the heavier clays which had originally favoured dense woodland. And the extensive marshlands that bordered most of the east coast and some of the south constituted a farming world and a social world of their own.

The farming world in Henry VIII's time was not a static world, though changes were usually slow and the fruit of much meditation and discussion in the village or the parish. In open-field country there could, at the most dramatic, be wholesale enclosure of hundreds or even thousands of acres of arable land, and conversion to sheep and/or cattle pastures. And even where the open fields remained there were many places where more complicated arrangements than the classic two- or three-field system of farming were introduced to give a greater flexibility in cropping and hence greater productivity. Wigston Magna, in mid-Leicestershire, whose history has been studied at length in *The Midland Peasant*, kept its three open fields from time immemorial down to the parliamentary enclosure of 1766, and so did many other villages up and down the country. These may have been a minority; a great number of villages and parishes possessed a much more complicated pattern of common fields before the middle of the sixteenth century.

H. L. Gray, in his classic work of sixty years ago on *English Field Systems* (1915), was the first to notice that, at a fairly early date, many parts of England had what he called 'irregular fields'. His map showed the approximate distribution of the simple two- or three-field system, but there were other types which he called for example 'Celtic runrig', and even then he was left with field patterns that could only be called 'irregular'. In recent years many articles have studied irregular field systems of one sort and another, or traced the evolution of the field system of one manor or small region over a long period, as for example Dr Alan Baker's close study of 'Field systems in the Vale of Holmesdale' in Kent, with particular reference to the complicated agrarian history of the archiepiscopal manor of Wrotham.[16] The manor of Tottenham probably had twenty or so common fields as early as the fourteenth century and the manor of Edmonton had seventeen in 1605, ranging from the Hyde Field with 173¼ acres down to Broomfield with 3 arable acres.[17] The simple question occurs, 'When is a common field

[16] *A.H.R.*, XIV, pt i, 1966, 1–24.
[17] See Avery, *Manorial Systems in the Edmonton Hundred* and *The Irregular Common Fields of Edmonton*.

not a common field?' We may need a new terminology before we finish the study of field systems through a mass of detailed local studies.[18]

The assessment for the Loan of 1522 was by far the most sweeping of all tax assessments since Domesday, and vastly more detailed and searching than that ancient record. Allowing as always for the errors of Tudor arithmetic, probably small in this case, the richest counties as measured by the assessment per thousand acres were Kent (£13.2), Wiltshire (£12.7), Essex (£11.4) and Northamptonshire (£10.9). The poorest counties were Derbyshire with only £1.4 and Shropshire with £1.6. There are no figures for Yorkshire, Lancashire, Cheshire and the four northern counties. The richest parts of England were ten times as wealthy as the poorest, as measured by this test. There was a solid concentration of farming wealth which stretched from the Wash down to the Weald and so down to the Channel coast. Other farming regions of high wealth were in the East Midlands (chiefly Northamptonshire and Huntingdonshire); and a pretty solid belt from Middlesex running through Berkshire to the Wiltshire edge of the Cotswolds. Seven counties yielded £10 or more per thousand acres, and seven yielded less than £3. Among many smaller farming regions the South Hams of Devon were particularly rich.

But the county is not a valid unit for the study of farming wealth at this date or any other. Even in purely farming areas, excluding as far as possible the regions with much industrial wealth (though we must still remember that much of this was generated directly in farmsteads and cottages), there could be a sixfold difference between the good lands and the poor lands within a given county. Suffolk, one of the rich counties, showed a fourfold difference, even excluding the highly industrialized hundred of Babergh which contained most of the clothing towns. The lowest region in Suffolk, as we should expect, was the Breckland, with an average valuation of £2.4 per thousand acres. In this connection it is significant of the general accuracy of the valuations that the Norfolk side of the Breckland (for it stretched over the two counties) was £2.1 in Grimshoe hundred.

Norfolk presents us with at least one inexplicable fact for farming history. The 'Good Sands' region of the north Norfolk coast and its hinterland, as the modern geographer would designate it, was the richest in all Norfolk. The hundred of Brothercross, roughly round the

[18] For a recent discussion of this complex subject see Alan Baker, 'Some terminological problems in studies of English field systems', *A.H.R.*, XVII, pt ii, 1969, 136–40.

Burnhams, was valued at £9.9 per thousand acres, and its neighbour on the Good Sands (North Greenhoe, which included Holkham) at £8.9: these were some of the highest valuations in East Anglia if not in farming England. Generally in Norfolk, as in Suffolk, there was a fourfold difference between the best lands and the worst. But the Good Sands region raises a problem which is at the moment unsolved. As far back as the 1334 assessment the hundred of Brothercross produced the highest yield of tax per thousand acres, with North Greenhoe not far above just the average for the county. In 1522 they were almost on a par as the richest lands in Norfolk. Yet it is precisely here that the legendary Holkham estate of the eighteenth century lay, the estate of which it was said by old Lady Townsend when the great Coke of Holkham came into his own: 'All you will see will be one blade of grass and two rabbits fighting for that.' No doubt this was a bit of country gossip and grossly exaggerated, but it seems pretty clear that the Holkham estate had gone back badly at some point in time. What had happened to this good farmland between 1334 and 1522, and above all between 1522 and Coke's day? The third hundred of the Good Sands region (Smithdon) had in fact decayed relatively even by the early sixteenth century, but why? Even in this one small and homogeneous Goodsands region one part had decayed heavily, whereas the other two parts had increased in taxable value.

And what of the marshland of western Norfolk, lying to the south of the Wash? In the 1330s and long before it had been one of the richest farming regions in all England, as both its tax assessments and its magnificent medieval churches testify; yet by the 1520s it was worth only about the average for Norfolk as a whole and scarcely more than one-half of the richest hundred of Brothercross. The marshland had fallen back relatively, though it was still prosperous. We shall have to rewrite the economic history of England county by county, region by region, before we understand it fully.

Essex was the richest of the three eastern counties and the best lands were generally worth twice as much as the poorest. Could this be, in contrast to Norfolk and Suffolk, that the general level of farming in Essex was higher, that there was not such a gap between the good and the bad lands? Perhaps a greater commercialization of farming on the doorstep of London?

Oxfordshire and Northamptonshire also reveal that the richest regions were just about two and a half times as valuable as the poorest. Northamptonshire just included the hundred of Nassaburgh in the extreme north-east (alias the liberty of Peterborough), one of the few parts of England that yielded more than £10 per thousand acres in the 1520s.

To take a final example, from a county which overlapped the pastoral and wet Highland Zone and the drier more arable Lowland Zone: the county of Devon. The soils of Devon vary as much as any in England, from the deep red sandstone, most valuable of all to this day, to the yellow clays of the west, beaten by heavy rain and high winds for the greater part of the year. Here we take the actual tax yield in 1524—25 rather than the Loan figures for 1522, which were generally higher. The scaling-down for the subsidy does not affect the conclusions noticeably. In Ottery St Mary hundred the tax yield was as high as £14.4 per thousand acres; and in the warm South Hams, also a fertile region, the yield was £12.2. Contrast these high figures with Sherwill hundred (only £1.2) on the Exmoor foothills (heavy rain and poor soil) or with Lifton hundred (£1.5) on the even rainier western slopes below Dartmoor. This part of Devon, and indeed all the yellow clays that stretch over most of west Devon, has broken the hearts of many thousands of farmers over the centuries, above all the poor optimists who returned from two wars in our own time and lost everything within a few years. For Devon as a whole, then, there was a tenfold difference between the good lands and the bad. If the highest figures are inflated by the wealth of busy little cloth-making towns (though they are, as had been said, part of the whole farming scene) and we carefully choose regions not affected by domestic industry on any appreciable scale, we still find a sixfold difference between the good and the bad lands. Cornwall was poorer altogether. The highest tax yield was only £4.8, the lowest as little as £1.5: a threefold difference. So the disparity in the Essex regions may not be so easily attributable after all to the proximity of London.

This discussion is perhaps the nearest we can get to assessing the manifold differences in farming in Henrician England: it is the best possible approach and as such it serves to keep in mind the figures we derive from such sources as the probate inventories, thinly spread as these are before 1540 at any rate. Another approach is the detailed study of one county's farming such as Joan Thirsk's *English Peasant Farming* (really Lincolnshire) and my own study of one Midland parish (*The Midland Peasant*). The unexpected (at times) results thrown up by examining the valuations and tax assessments of the 1520s should provoke yet more specialized local studies of agrarian history, to clothe

the dry bones of taxation statistics with some flesh of local detail.

As to what was actually grown, two counties have been studied in detail from probate inventories: Leicestershire (Hoskins) and Lincolnshire (Thirsk).

In Leicestershire the spring corn (peas and beans, and barley) took up just over 80 per cent of the average peasant farmer's land, the winter corn (wheat and rye) just under 20 per cent. Thus the common field could not have been the unit of cultivation; and indeed we now accept that the furlong was much more likely to have been the unit round which the crops rotated. In using the probate inventories, however, we must remember that at this early period they are those of peasant farmers, a small sample ranging from 8 to 49 sown acres. Peas, beans and barley were not only the largest crops sown, but also the least variable from farm to farm. The average area under peas and beans was about 43 per cent, the variation ranging from 25 to 57: a large range one might think, but more than half the sample had between 40 and 50 per cent under peas and beans. Possibly the variations depended on differences of soil types, even in a small county like Leicestershire, but the sample is far too small for us to break it down further. Barley was also a staple and general crop. Two-thirds of the sample of fifteen farms had 30 to 40 per cent of their sown area under this crop. Wheat occupied about a seventh of the sown area, and every farmer grew some. Rye was grown by most farmers on a small scale, but oats were almost unknown in Leicestershire in Henry VIII's time. The great predominance of peas, beans and barley was of long standing in Leicestershire farming. Peas and beans almost invariably occupied the whole of one field. Barley was sown in the same field as wheat and rye, so that the furlong system of rotation apparently applied only to one field.

Dr Thirsk in *English Peasant Farming* was working over a longer period and with a far larger sample of inventories, hence she is able to divide the large county of Lincolnshire into four distinct regions: Fenland, Marshland, the Chalk and Limestone Uplands, and the Claylands and miscellaneous soils. On the other hand, most of her information comes from later in the sixteenth century and from the seventeenth. Some conclusions are, however, possible: in the Fenland in the 1530s the average sown area was only 11 acres as against 24 acres in Leicestershire in the same period. Barley was the most important crop in Lincolnshire, as much as 61 per cent in the 1530s. Peas and beans came next, as in Leicestershire. In the Lincolnshire marshland, so far as the arable was concerned, there were usually only two open fields, one of which lay fallow every year. This was not wasteful, as Dr Thirsk points out, in a region in which cattle and sheep were far more important: fallowing half the arable could well have been as great an asset as corn. The claylands had a mixed husbandry, with a bias towards cattle-rearing and dairying, but unlike the fenlands and marshlands where pasture stretched to the horizon, the clayland farms carried more arable than pasture. However, the detailed statistics here are drawn from early seventeenth-century surveys and must not be used as a guide to a hundred years earlier.

The chalk and limestone uplands were largely arable, and barley, beans, and peas took up just three-quarters of the total sown area, with barley pre-eminent. But again the details of crops sown are not good enough for the reign of Henry VIII. We need more inventories, not only of other regions far away from the Midlands, but also from the larger peasantry, not to mention the lesser gentry. One of the rare larger inventories, in Leicestershire, that of Thomas Bradgate of Peatling Parva, the richest yeoman in the county in 1524, shows that when he died in 1539 he owned small farms in five places, besides holding a ninety-nine-year lease of a grange farm from Merevale Abbey. He also rented large enclosed pastures miles away from his home farm. Of his total farm goods, grain crops of all kinds in the barns amounted to 15 per cent by value; livestock to 82 per cent, and implements to some 3 per cent. Though he had a considerable number of cattle of all kinds, including horses, worth half the total of all his livestock, his 400 sheep were the biggest single item. Nevertheless, as a big man, representative of a rising type in the East Midlands, his farming showed a much heavier bias towards cattle and sheep than did that of the much more typical peasant farmer. The fact that much of the Leicestershire clay-lands, above all the liassic clays of the eastern half of the county, were better suited to pasture than arable was well understood by the larger landowners, such as the monastic houses, well back in the fifteenth century; but it was the gentry in Henry VIII's time who first exploited this knowledge extensively, and here and there a rich yeoman like Thomas Bradgate.

It is now time to turn to the pastoral side of farming under Henry VIII. Here in some respects we are better informed. We no longer depend on probate inventories: we have something much better — the sheep accounts kept by large-scale graziers, chiefly in East Anglia. Thus Sir William Fermour, who built the still lovely Hall at East Barsham in

Norfolk, had sheep pasturing in twenty-five different 'grounds' or fold-courses (to use the special East Anglian term) totalling probably some 17,000 sheep. Dr Allison's valuable article in the *Economic History Review* for 1958 on flock management in the sixteenth and seventeenth centuries shows that those other great Norfolk landowners, the Townsends, had 8,000 or 9,000 and more sheep in the 1480s, though fewer than 4,000 by 1546. Sir Robert Southwell, an officer of the Court of Augmentations and a considerable landowner, had more than 13,000 sheep on fourteen different fold-courses. Several Norfolk families had 10,000 to 20,000 sheep each. A statute of 1533 referred to some sheep farms with up to 24,000 sheep. It was people like these to whom we turn when we ask the fundamental question: how far was English farming geared to commercial markets, and how far was it — in the first half of the century at least — merely the subsistence farming of hundreds of thousands of peasants?

Already in the 1470s and 1480s much of the Townsend wool was sent direct to Lynn merchants, most probably for export; but a great number of Norfolk sheep-farmers more often dealt with middlemen (wool-broggers) who in turn sold to clothiers in Norfolk, Suffolk, and Essex. The whole of the Norwich Cathedral Priory clip in 1535—36 went to the Springs of Lavenham, the richest clothiers in England at that time, and most of Sir Richard Southwell's wool — over 15,000 sheep in fourteen flocks — went to the clothiers of Dedham. And twice Bedingfield sold the whole of his clip from some 5,000 sheep to the men of the Suffolk clothing town of Stoke-by-Nayland. Wool and store lambs were the primary products of these huge East Anglian flocks. Some mutton was sold to the prosperous city of Norwich through local butchers; but it was not until the mid-century that Norwich and the growing maw of London encouraged mutton production which went mostly through the big East Anglian fairs like those of Newmarket in Suffolk and Reach in Cambridgeshire and eventually found its way to the metropolis.

Where the great clothiers of the Cotswold country and Wiltshire, Somerset and Devon, bought their wool we have little idea. There must have been large-scale sheep-farmers in the West Country to supply such men as Horton, Lane, Greenway, and Jack of Newbury, but their accounts have not survived. We cannot imagine them buying hither and thither in local fairs and markets. In Elizabethan times Devon was one of the biggest sheep counties in England, but as a contemporary writer observes the sheep were all hidden inside the high-banked enclosures and not visible to the casual eye as on the Norfolk fold-courses or the Wiltshire and Berkshire downs.

Most of the peasant farmers of whom we know anything from their probate inventories carried on mixed farming, with the emphasis one way or the other. In Leicestershire in the early sixteenth century the typical farmer carried thirty-four sheep; in Lincolnshire rather fewer but probably more cattle at least in the richer fenland and marshland. Yet in total the number of livestock in an ordinary open-field village could be large — running into perhaps a couple of thousand sheep or more. Even cottagers contributed a not inconsiderable total: a survey at Nassington in Northamptonshire made in 1550 showed that fifty-two cottagers had some 1,200 animals in all. In the early seventeenth century — if one may dare to venture so far — a landless labourer of Brigstock, a forest village in Northamptonshire, had 100 sheep. Possibly he was a shepherd who was allowed to pasture his flock on his master's land, as was often done.

There were far more sheep than human beings in early sixteenth-century England. Though the huge flocks of the Norfolk gentry made a more spectacular sight and a mightier account book, we must not over-look the millions of sheep owned by the peasantry who kept no such accounts and who sold their wool and lambs in local markets and fairs rather than in great masses to capitalist clothiers. There can be no doubt that the range of sales, and the amount of ready money, increased greatly during the second half of the sixteenth century.

So much is known about sheep-farming in early sixteenth-century England, not least from the violent controversies, literary as well as on the ground, over wholesale enclosures of common-field arable and con-version to pasture, for which the all-devouring sheep and their wool were almost universally blamed. On the other hand we know remark-ably little about large-scale cattle-farming at this period.

Dr Clarkson has drawn our attention to the growing importance of the leather trades in Henry VIII's time, and to the multifarious uses to which leather was put; not to mention the meat that went in increasing quantities to the Midland towns. There can be no doubt that cattle-farming was an important branch of English farming when one thinks of the high level of employment in the leather trades at places like Leicester, Northampton, Birmingham, and, higher than all, probably London itself. The skinners and leather-sellers of London were listed among the more important livery companies by Stow, quoting a list of 23 Henry VIII.

Hundreds of miles of the English coastland, chiefly on the eastern side from south Yorkshire around to Romney Marsh in Kent, were already rich fattening pastures by Henry VIII's time. Cattle were driven scores of miles, even hundreds of miles at times, in order to reach these marshland pastures. Thus the grain shortage of 1528 was attributed locally to the great numbers of Welsh cattle that were fattening on the Romney marshes to the detriment of arable cultivation[19] and we find Midland graziers competing for pastures on Sheppey in Kent in the 1520s. In an inventory made in 1522 of the personal estate of Thomas Fuller, a Kentish gentleman, we find that he had no fewer than 1,389 sheep of various kinds (including 555 lambs) feeding on Sheppey where he lived. He had a small number of cattle and a mere 24 acres of corn in the ground. He also had wheat, barley, oats, tares and peas all in the barns, and a stack of hay to the value of £3 6s 8d. The total value of all his crops, in the ground and in the barn, was however worth only some £21, or just about one-tenth of his personal estate, as against livestock worth some 50 per cent of the total personal estate.

More than that, he had leases valued at £45 6s 8d, which became the subject of dispute four years after his death. Thomas Hynman, grazier, 'now farmer of Grafton in Northants', declared that five or six years ago he had offered to Thomas Fuller, then citizen and mercer of London, to take a twelve years' lease of land in the Isle of Sheppey on terms which he would willingly accept now. Shortly after this offer Fuller had leased to Thomas Hynman of Lubthorpe in Lincolnshire, grazier, his lands in Sheppey for the large sum of £130 a year for a term of twenty years. Thomas Fuller was on his part to keep the mansion, barns and seawall in repair. Here we have the complete cycle of English farming on a rather large scale, beginning with the newly rich citizen and mercer of London buying lands in Sheppey with a high potential value as grazing land, then termed gentleman when he lived in style on the island, and finally the large lease to a Lincolnshire grazier some two hundred miles distant. Clearly, cattle were moved over considerable distances by the beginning of the sixteenth century.

It is often difficult to see which way the cattle were moving at this date. The Welsh Road was the most famous route by which cattle had moved from Wales into England since at least the thirteenth century, winding its way south-eastwards for the most part, across the centre of England to some unknown destination; but at the same time thousands

---

[19] *L.P.*, IV, pt ii, no. 4414.

of English cattle were being driven over the Welsh border from Hereford, Shropshire, and Staffordshire for fattening on the almost unlimited upland pastures of Montgomeryshire and adjacent counties.[20] They left on the first of May and returned home in mid-September, 'full fed'. The payment for this grazing was fourpence or sixpence a beast. Even then it was said that not a tenth of the upland pastures were eaten away. The numbers engaged in this migration must have increased greatly during the rest of the century, as by the third quarter of the century there were various complaints about the overstocking of the Welsh commons, particularly by the cattle of strangers.

Again, as early as the 1520s the bigger English landlords were keeping large numbers of cattle, above all in the Midlands. When John Spencer of Wormleighton, the founder of the great Spencer fortunes, was ordered by the enclosure commissioners to destroy his hedges and put the newly enclosed land under tillage once more, he petitioned against the order on various grounds, one being that he would have to destroy all his cattle for lack of sustenance. As it was the dead of winter he could only sell at a loss 'for he hathe no maner of fatt cattell now left him at this tyme but his brede'.[21]

Enormous numbers of sheep depended on the common pastures, whether upland pastures mostly in the north and west, or the lowland commons that were to be found almost anywhere in England, even in and immediately around London. A proposal made in 1548 to abolish the royal right of purveyance supposed that there might be some 4.5 million sheep all told, of which 1.5 million were kept on the commons, presumably throughout the year. The common pastures were an integral and vital part of the farming economy, above all in the lowland areas where they were often under different forms of attack. It might be the squire wishing to enlarge his old park by taking in a large part of the village common, like Sir John Rodney, knight, at Draycott and Stoke Gifford in Somerset who had taken in hundreds of acres that had been used time out of mind for villagers' cattle and sheep. They had a number of other grievances also, and banded together to bring him before the Star Chamber, with what result we do not know.[22] Or it might be, certainly later in the century, a pressure of population and

[20] *A.H.E.W.*, p. 139.
[21] *T.E.D.*, I, 16–17.
[22] *T.E.D.*, I, 29 *et seq.* Not dated but some time in Henry VIII's reign. For a prolonged struggle between landlords and tenants over valuable lowland commons near London in the fifteenth and sixteenth centuries, see Pam, *The Fight for Common Rights.*

hence a need for more food, which led village meetings to discuss the ploughing-up of part of the ancient commons in order to expand the arable; but this was usually done by general agreement and the problem was still to keep a nice balance between additional arable and enough common pasture for the livestock. Again, there could be bitter disputes between adjacent communities, especially on the windswept uplands where there were few boundary marks, as to the respective shares each village had. A high proportion of the village by-laws which survive are concerned with disputes over commons and common rights within a community, whereas disputes involving the lord of the manor usually went to one of the courts in London. At any rate, open-field husbandry could not have survived without a considerable proportion of land left in its natural state as common grazing, though constant grazing must have improved the sward as opposed to the true 'waste'. The commons were so important, too, that they were in constant danger of being overgrazed, so that the device of 'stinting' (that is, fixing the precise share of animals allowed on the village commons for each tenement) appeared at an early date, in the thirteenth century in some places. Even this did not avoid the invasion, or alleged invasion, of many commons by animals owned by 'outsiders' whom it might be difficult to discipline. Within the village community itself there might well be one overmighty yeoman who was considered by the rest to be hogging more than his fair share.[23]

The great majority of farmers in Britain, even in the richer parts of England, were small peasant farmers living in a subsistence economy, producing small surpluses in good years which could be sold in the nearest local market town but generally only fortunate enough to be able to hold their own. The indirect evidence for this is that in the early sixteenth century probate inventories (admittedly few in number) money is rarely mentioned, beyond a pound or two or even a few shillings. In the second half of the century, larger sums of money appear in yeoman inventories, consistent with the growth of more specialized farming among the top yeomen at least, and larger sums of money change hands when leases are negotiated. But before the middle of the century, and somewhat later, money was a rare sight. Harrison makes the same point when he says in later years, speaking of the old days:

[23] For a fuller discussion of the importance of commons and their management, see the *Report of the Royal Commission on Common Land, 1955—58*, Appendix II, esp. para. 21 for early stinting.

Such also was their poverty that, if some one odd farmer or husbandman had been at the ale-house, a thing greatly used in those days, amongst six or seven of his neighbours, and there in a bravery, to shew what store he had, did cast down his purse, and therein a noble or six shillings in silver, unto them . . . it was very likely that all the rest could not lay down so much against it.

and he proceeds to contrast this with the much greater show of wealth, in cash and in goods, in his day (the 1570s).

England was a country of subsistence farming; even more so were Wales and Scotland. Here and there, as among the great landed proprietors of Norfolk, there were sheep flocks running into thousands, even into tens of thousands; and there may have been cattle-farmers in the Midlands and the northern fells who farmed in a big way for a specialized market; and the great barley-men of the country to the north of London who were building up the malt trade well before 1500; and here and there, anywhere in England except the wilder parts, were solitary pioneers a century or so ahead of their time in working for a specialized market. But over the country as a whole, nine farmers out of ten in all probability worked as a household to get the where-withal to eat and the small annual surplus to buy household goods and clothes at the nearest fair. This was undoubtedly so before the 1550s: the great advance comes, in farming as in so much else, during the reign of Elizabeth I. Henrician England was a country of very slow economic growth, if any.

HARVEST FLUCTUATIONS

A little has already been said about the importance of fluctuations in the annual harvest: the annual harvest was the greatest single fact of life in every generation.[24] Every harvest was a gamble, largely dependent on the capricious British weather, or on the seed-corn left over from the previous harvest, which itself was a product of the weather. Harvests ran in a series of good or bad, perhaps a run of three or four good harvests full of 'belly-cheer', and then a run of bad harvests when the smaller men struggled to survive and the urban poor depended on prompt municipal or government action, usually the former as being more immediate. There were all kinds of complicating factors which

[24] This was still profoundly true of rural England well into the nineteenth century. Thus Parson Hawker of Morwenstow in north Cornwall wrote in July 1862, of the harvest, 'our worry is now unutterable.' In the following year he was writing, 'To me it is life or death in the harvest field and to how many more of my poor parishioners' (Brendon, *Hawker of Morwenstow*, pp. 76–7).

make sweeping generalizations open to criticism: the weather in the west might be ruinous, but in the east reasonably favourable to the harvest. Local differences were important; unfortunately we do not possess anything like enough regional price series to speak confidently. And it is possible that a season bad for corn might be tolerable, or even favourable, for grass-farming. Yet occasionally a season or two could be disastrous for both arable and pastoral farmers. So the below-average harvest of 1543 was followed by a very wet spring (1544) which brought about a great mortality among cattle. For some reason, too, the price of fish — a vital food in Henrician England — rose to great heights at the same time, possibly due to continued stormy weather or, equally likely, to the scarcity of corn and meat which naturally forced up other prices. In the famine years of 1527–28, when corn prices were almost universally high, heavy rains all through the winter of the same years destroyed not only cornfields and pastures, but drowned many sheep and cattle. So the rough balance between the pastoral west and the arable east, which some historians consider to have been a saving grace in that the weather that ruined one suited the other, was easily upset; and again a dearth of grain drove up all other prices, so that nature was frustrated.

In detail, the 1490s were a bountiful decade, followed by bad years in 1500–03; and bad years again in 1519–21, three years in a row. The critical factor was the seed-corn. Enough had to be saved from each harvest to sow for the next; but with two bad years in succession, perhaps disastrous years, there was an overwhelming temptation among the mass of peasantry with no reserves to eat next year's seed corn; and so the dreadful cycle was repeated until a fine season restored the balance that had been destroyed by man.

Apart from the problem of the seed-corn, there was little rhyme or reason in the harvest fluctuations. The three bad years of 1519–21 (at Exeter corn prices reached the highest level for over two hundred years) were followed by five good harvests in a row: 1522–26. These were the years of the most ferocious taxation and so-called loans under Henry VIII and Wolsey, and must have helped to prevent popular disorder. As it was there were sufficiently serious disturbances in Kent and Suffolk.

The next three years were bad years, worse in some parts than others. At Norwich the mayor viewed the situation in 1527 as one bordering on revolution, and in the following year many young men were hanged at Norwich and Great Yarmouth for attempting to hinder the export of corn to other parts when it was scarce at home. In other

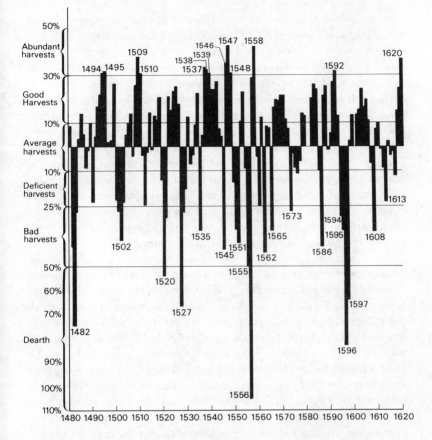

The percentage figures in the left-hand margin represent the deviation of the annual average price from the thirty-one-year moving average for that year.

Fig. 3 The quality of English harvests 1480 to 1620

words, the true capitalist spirit was beginning to manifest itself: more money at any cost. Greed before human life. Then in 1529 there was trouble at Yaxley, a river-port up in the Fens, when Lynn merchants attempted to load their ships with grain for export to Scotland, at a time of local shortage. Excessive rain was the major cause of this shortage also, combined also with the recurring problem of saving the seed-corn.

Taken as a whole the 1530s were a good decade: only one bad

harvest out of ten, four of average quality, and no fewer than five abundant, again with three successive very good harvests (1537–39). And so into the 1540s with yet three more good harvests, making a series of six good harvests in all. Two average years followed, then the bad harvest of 1545; but Henry's reign closed with two abundant harvests. It had opened with an abundant harvest, and ended with one. Roughly speaking one harvest in six in Henrician England was bad, but the effect of good and bad harvests varied among the farming community. A dearth could bring the big farmer a modest fortune, as nothing could stop him selling in the dearest market; the middling peasant struggled through; but the poorer men, always living from hand to mouth, faced the temptation of eating the precious seed-corn and so ensuring yet another poor harvest. Perhaps we exaggerate the intensity of this problem. Tightening the belt and eating cheaper substitute foods for the time being may have been the most common answer.

There was yet another line of defence in many parts of England, inadequate though it may have been by itself, and that was the dual economy in which so many peasant households lived. There were farmer-nailers in the future Black Country, farmer-miners at intervals from Cornwall up to Derbyshire and beyond, farmer-fishermen off the east and south coasts, farmer-potters especially in the West Midlands. Nothing could overcome a basic shortage of food, it is true, but such a combination provided a little ready money for some cheap substitutes. The dual economy was not simply to eke out a poor living, but presented a way of dividing the year and its labour in the most economic way, and in a human way by providing a change of scene and occupation. We may rediscover this same way of living in time to defeat the dreadful consequences of our modern economy, based as it is for the most part on large-scale and monotonous work and on the grand illusion of economic growth from which our Tudor ancestors unwittingly spared themselves.

CHAPTER FOUR

Urban Life and Structure

TOWNS IN THE LANDSCAPE

WHAT constitutes a town defies anything but a tortuous and arid socio-logical definition with little reference to the realities of human life. Leland, whose description of England and Wales in the late 1530s is the fullest we possess, had little doubt that he knew a town when he saw one, and it was certainly not a matter of mere size. The Holy Roman Empire at this date contained some 3,000 cities and towns, of which five out of six counted their inhabitants only in hundreds.[1] Cologne was the largest city in the Empire, with some 30,000 people, and there were five others (Nuremberg, Strassburg, Hamburg, Ulm, and Lübeck) with about 20,000 inhabitants in the early sixteenth century. Frankfurt had only 10,000 people, Leipzig about 6,000. The Italian cities were much larger, Florence and Milan with 80,000 or so, and Naples with a larger population even than Paris (230,000 and 200,000).

English towns and cities were more comparable in size with those of Germany. London, with some 60,000 people, was twice as big as Cologne, but no other city approached the size of the major German towns. Norwich, with between 12,500 and 13,000 people, was the largest town in the provinces; Bristol and Newcastle had about 10,000 each; Salisbury, York, and Exeter about 8,000; Coventry and Worcester about 6,000 to 7,000 each. Below this level there were something like thirty towns, clearly recognizable as such, with 2,000 to 4,000 people.[2] Reckoning all the towns together we get a total at the most of about

---

[1] Strauss, *Nuremberg in the Sixteenth Century*, pp. 5, 35–6.
[2] Hoskins, *Provincial England*, pp. 72–3. Dyer in 'The economy of Tudor Worcester', *Univ. of Birmingham Historical Journal*, X, no. 2, 1966, is inclined to put Worcester's population at under 4,000 at this date.

300,000 people. There were many places that were either market towns or incorporated boroughs which also regarded themselves as towns (Banbury had only about six or seven hundred inhabitants, for example), but here we reach a level where urban character is really dominated by country trades and interests. Many of the larger towns, too, had considerable roots in the surrounding countryside. This is what makes any precise definition of a 'town' at this period a futile exercise in words. The best we can say is that about one person in eight, at the most, lived in a recognizably urban environment, possibly as few as one in ten. Ninety per cent of English and Welsh people lived on and by the land in Henry VIII's reign, and all were dependent on it in the last resort as the major source of food, drink, and the major raw materials of industry.

Many of the English towns were still strongly walled, towns like London, Exeter, York, Chester, Lynn, Coventry and Leicester. Leland makes special reference to the strength and magnificence of the walls of Newcastle, surpassing all others in England and most in Europe, as well they might so near the eternally troublesome Scottish frontier. Other towns which had once been walled around had let their defences fall down. At Nottingham most of the walls were down, and at Barnstaple in north Devon all were down. Such towns felt safe. They were small and remote from possible attack; but the walls of Exeter were kept in good repair, remote though the city was, as the key to the west of England. Indeed, they had to withstand long and serious sieges in 1497 and in 1549.

Some towns had great gates of stone or brick but no walls, relying on ramparts and ditches for the rest. Such a town was Beverley in east Yorkshire; and at Portsmouth there was only a mud wall crowned with a timber palisade. It was a naval dockyard but Leland observes that 'the town ... is bare and little occupied in time of peace'. Much of the ground inside the walls was vacant ground; but this was true of many other towns, such as Leicester, where the decay of medieval times had not been made good.

Even within the walled towns and cities there were considerable areas not built up, not merely because of late medieval decay but because important buildings such as castles, cathedrals and monasteries occupied much ground. The earliest reliable town plans show large open spaces still devoted to orchards and gardens well into the seventeenth century. On the other hand, such towns usually had at least one extensive suburb outside the walls, often two or three, mostly occupied by the wage-earning class. Leland speaks of two such suburbs at Northampton, one outside the south gate and a smaller one outside the west gate. Exeter had large suburbs outside the east and west gates, both dating from early medieval times. Leicester had considerable suburbs outside the north, east, and south gates from early times, so that by the 1520s as many as 45 per cent of the tax-paying population lived outside the walled area. Leland's pages are full of references to suburbs, and tax records generally reveal that these were, as we might expect, working-class districts. So usual was it to find suburbs by this date that he particularly mentions that the important east-coast town of Hull had none; and it is likely that Great Yarmouth similarly had little or nothing outside its walls. These towns were the most exposed to enemy attack from the sea. Inland cities like Canterbury and Lincoln seem to have developed suburbs as far back as pre-Conquest times.

It is naturally more difficult to distinguish suburbs where a town was not walled — as, say, at Sherborne in Dorset — but even here one can detect from the records expansion beyond the truly urban area around church and market-place into ribbon development along the outgoing roads, mainly for housing the working class. Not that even in the walled towns were wage-earners all pushed beyond the walls: we often find that the central parishes were occupied by the well-to-do, that some parishes beyond these were mixed in social composition, and that the parishes that abutted on to the walls were occupied mostly by the working class. The suburbs were simply the result of an overflow from a tightly constricted area where much land was 'sterilized' by the Church or the Castle. But in human terms, it meant that the walled towns, and the unwalled towns, were not as heavily congested as might be supposed. As many as half the total population might be living beyond the strictly urban area in relatively open spaces where fresh air could blow and sanitary problems were not as formidable as they became with the urban infilling of the eighteenth and early nineteenth centuries.

URBAN OCCUPATIONS

What of the occupations of the urban population, divorced as it largely was from the land except for a fair-sized garden outside the walls? Here Leland, detailed though he is at times, fails us. He was not much interested in the niceties of economic and social structure, but noticed the obvious things like specialized market towns and towns that 'stood much by clothing'. Markets and fairs appealed to him; but we catch occasional glimpses of industrial beginnings in places like Birmingham and Walsall. Coal is mentioned only rarely. We must turn to other sources to discover the hard facts about how towns really got their living, how important the different trades were locally, what were the basic trades in every town, and how many openings there were for young men apart from the clothing trades we hear so much of, and probably overestimate in the national scene.

To discover the occupational structure of towns we must use free-men's lists and such occasional taxation records as specify trades and callings. Even this is not as straightforward as it sounds, for the majority of towns were not sophisticated enough, or had not the powers, to create a special privileged class of freemen. Or if they had the powers, they were sometimes so selective in creating the distinction that the freemen's list is no guide to the trading community as a whole. Thus the list for Kings Lynn[3] is, certainly for the sixteenth century, too brief as compared with, say, the much smaller town of Leicester to inspire any confidence in its scope. Even the best lists will have their defects (omissions and occasional ambiguities of terminology). Yet for all this there are certain towns where one can reconstruct the occupational structure pretty accurately; and what is more the results as between different towns agree in certain fundamental respects. The largest single omission in any town is, of course, the labouring class who were rarely important enough to become freemen; yet most of these must have fitted into various of the listed trades and occupations at the bottom level.

Northampton and Leicester, with about 3,000 people each in the 1520s, specify sixty-three and sixty different trades respectively. Coventry, twice as large, had ninety separate trades. York could show ninety to a hundred different trades. Bristol had over a hundred trades in the Elizabethan period. At Norwich, 103 separate occupations are specified in the period 1500–58.[4] These are, on the whole, the larger towns. Nothing can be said on this score for the smaller places like Sherborne, of which Leland says it stood partly by cloth-making but

[3] See *A Calendar of the Freemen of Lynn, 1291–1836*, Norwich, 1913. The list is far from valueless for the economic historian, but is clearly covering only a minute proportion of the population in any given decade.

[4] For most of these figures, see Hoskins, *Provincial England*, p. 79. For York, see Palliser, 'Some aspects of the . . . history of York', unpublished Oxford thesis, 1968, p. 273; and for Norwich, see J. F. Pound, 'The social and trade structure of Norwich, 1525–1575', *Past and Present*, no. 34, 1966, p. 65. I am indebted to Mr Pound personally for much further information about the Norwich freemen throughout the sixteenth century.

'most of all manner of crafts'; or of Swaffham in Norfolk 'one of the quickest markets of all Norfolk ... it standeth much by handy craft [men] and buyers of grain'. We shall never know more than this, but it would not be surprising to find that bustling little towns like these had fifty or so different trades.

Altogether there were some 760 market towns in Tudor England and fifty in Wales. Though the population of the country in Henrician England was about one-twentieth of what it is today, there were far more market towns, most of them serving a radius of only a few miles. As Professor Everitt says, 'the intense localism of society and the absence of mechanical transport demanded their proliferation'.[5] Even so, there were far fewer markets than in medieval times. The Black Death and the subsequent continued fall in population had killed off many of the smaller markets for good, and others struggled to keep alive during the sixteenth century. But on the whole new markets were being created, some as early as the 1520s but most later in the century and in the early seventeenth. So the 800 or so 'market towns' (many of them mere villages) were probably not quite so numerous in the early part of the century, but were still thick on the ground. Many were already highly specialized, as is clear from Leland's pages. Bishop Auckland in Durham was 'a pretty market of corn', Luton and Ware were pre-eminent for barley, Warminster (in Wiltshire) for corn in general. There must have been scores of markets that were noted for wool and cloth and leather goods; and it is possible that specialization among markets increased during the Elizabethan period and under the early Stuarts. The larger market towns were also important social centres, with public buildings (notably a market hall) and an increasing number of inns; and they drew on a much wider area of the surrounding countryside than the great majority of such places.

Two other important features of the urban economy emerge from such an occupational analysis. First of all, three basic groups of trades — clothing, food and drink, and building — were essential to every community that called itself a town and furthermore gave employment by and large to a third of the occupied population. Secondly, most towns had a more or less strong leaning towards some specialization. This was usually textiles, as we might expect from all we know of the general economic history of the period, but by no means always so. Then, too, we can detect in those towns which had borough status and a governing

[5] Everitt, 'The marketing of agricultural produce', *A.H.E.W.*, IV, 467. The following paragraph is based on this notable essay.

body, those occupations which ranked highest in the local wealth scale, simply by studying the occupations of those who were chosen for governing the town, and above all the aldermen and mayors. These positions went almost without exception to men with money, for various reasons we shall examine later. Merely to examine the occupations of the mayoral group alone over the century tells us much about the economy of a town we would otherwise never know.

Table 4.1 Occupational structure of English towns in the early sixteenth century (classified as percentages of all occupations)

Trades	Coventry	Northampton	Leicester*	Norwich†	York
Clothing	14	15	15	8	17
Food and drink	15½	15	21	13	19½
Building	4½	7½	4	9½	10
Leather (and allied)	11	23	19	11½	5
Textiles	33	13½	8½	30½	8½
Metal	8	3	3	not known	not known
Distributive	14	23	29½	18	17
Others				4½	23
	100	100	100	100	100

* The Leicester figures cover the period 1510–40.
† Pound's figures for Norwich have been translated from decimals and rounded up and down slightly, with no difference to the conclusions.

Despite minor differences of classification, these figures show that the three basic groups of trades employed 30 to 40 per cent of the occupied population at this date. Only York is out of line with 46.5 per cent so employed. These trades were the solid basis of the urban economy almost everywhere, but less so in a small town that had developed a highly specialized economy. Coventry and Norwich specialized heavily in textiles – about a third of the occupied population in each were so engaged – but they still remained widely diversified in other respects. On the other hand, the cloth-making districts of Suffolk, particularly along the Stour valley and nearby, showed marked signs of a lopsided (perhaps top-heavy is a better term) economy. It is here that one finds the most highly capitalistic industry in early Tudor England, dominated by rich clothiers and to an increasing extent by the demands of the foreign market; and not surprisingly it was the most sensitive spot in Britain during the tax troubles of the 1520s.

Even Sudbury, an old and well-established Suffolk market town, had some 32 per cent of its occupied population employed in textiles; but overgrown villages like Nayland and Stoke-by-Nayland had 70 to 90 per cent so employed. The rich little town of Lavenham, still one of the best surviving late medieval towns in England, had some 60 per cent directly engaged in the cloth industry, even excluding labourers as a class (some fifty-two of them), most of whom probably depended on the textile trades for their work. In all probability between 70 and 80 per cent of the population of Lavenham depended on the cloth industry, and the other trades, so universal in bigger towns, were correspondingly less important.

Certain Midland towns specialized in the leather trades, notably Northampton and Leicester, and to a lesser degree others like Birmingham where some of the wealthiest men were tanners. The Midlands were perhaps as important for cattle and leather as they were for wool. But by the early seventeenth century the greatest centre for the leather trades was London, centred in Bermondsey and Southwark; and there is little reason to doubt that it had been the most important centre a hundred years earlier. Unfortunately, we know almost nothing about the occupational structure of London, or indeed of the distribution of wealth within it. No records survive to give us anything like an overall picture: possibly the complexity of the urban economy in London and its large suburb of Southwark defeated all administrative efforts, just as it had done when it had been a question of assessing the city for the Loan of 1522. The great mass of Londoners in their alleys and tenements were scarcely worth the infinite trouble of tracking them down, for any purpose.

Birmingham is a good example of how misleading Leland can be as a source for the economic historian. He notes that it is a good market town, and that 'there be many smiths in the town that use to make knives and all manner of cutting tools, and many lorimers that make bits, and a great many nailers. So that a great part of the town is maintained by smiths.' As Birmingham was an unincorporated town, with no urban governing body, we do not possess the usual administrative records to help us, but it is clear from other sources that tanners (and hence butchers) were the most important class of traders, followed by cloth-workers. The metal trades were an important part of the local economy, but the other trades made the most money. And again, we are safe in assuming in a lively market town that the food and drink, clothing and building trades formed the usual large element in the economy.[6]

95

In all probability the distributive trades formed a fairly consistent fourth group of trades in any town of local consequence. If we may judge by Norwich and York, the only towns for which we have the necessary information, they employed 17 to 18 per cent of the occupied population, though as these towns were regional capitals it is likely that this proportion is unduly high for smaller towns.

Apart from these general reflections on the occupational structure of various towns, we can learn something of their individual flavour also from listing the dozen leading trades in selected towns in the early sixteenth century, see Table 4.2.

THE URBAN PYRAMID

Urban society was a plutocracy. In shape it was a pyramid with a very broad base, rising to a fine and high point. The richer the town the higher this point, though this was not invariably so. Some cities were dominated by one or two very rich families.[7] At Coventry, Richard Marler, grocer, was one of the three or four richest merchants in England. Julian Nethermill, draper, and Henry Pysford, merchant of the Staple, were the next wealthiest, all richer than anyone at Bristol where the Canynges dynasty had died out fifty years earlier and no one family had taken their place. At Norwich, Robert Jannys, also a grocer, was even richer than Marler, but in a larger city he was not the same dominant figure. At Coventry, Richard Marler paid nearly one-ninth of the entire subsidy for the city in 1524; at Exeter, the Crugge family paid a tenth of the whole yield. Neither Bristol nor Ipswich contained one overmighty family. Yet smaller towns might have such a plutocratic family, like the Wigstons at Leicester, merchants of the Staple, who paid (two cousins together) just under a third of the entire subsidy for the town. The cloth town of Bradford-on-Avon in Wiltshire was completely overshadowed by Thomas Horton, who paid ten times as much tax as the next wealthiest clothier, and had also considerable interests in Trowbridge where he built 'divers fair houses of stone'. In a small town the disappearance of such a great business might well be disastrous for

[6] For early Tudor Birmingham, see Court, *The Rise of the Midland Industries*, pp. 34–6. The various leather trades, from tanning to shoe-making, were also prominent in Worcester, where the tanners ranked next to the clothiers in prosperity. See Dyer, 'The economy of Tudor Worcester'.
[7] This section is based largely on my essay 'English provincial towns in the early sixteenth century', reprinted in *Provincial England*, pp. 68–85.

Table 4.2 Leading trades in five selected towns

	Coventry (1522)		Northampton (1524)		Leicester (1510–40)		York (1500–25)		Norwich (1500–29)	
1	Cappers	83*	Shoe-makers	50	Butchers	27	Merchants	118	Worsted Weavers	160
2	Weavers	41	Bakers	21	Shoe-makers	24	Tailors	87	Mercers	71
3	Shearmen	38	Tailors	20	Tailors	18	Cordwainers	61	Tailors	71
4	Butchers	36	Weavers	20	Mercers	16	Fishers	47	Shoe-makers†	42
5	Shoe-makers	28	Tanners	15	Weavers	16	Butchers	43	Grocers	37
6	Drapers	28	Mercers	15	Bakers	15	Bakers	41	Shearmen	31
7	Dyers	28	Butchers	14	Tanners	11	Tanners	41	Carpenters	30
8	Bakers	27	Glovers	13	Glovers	10	Weavers	39	Masons	23
9	Mercers	26	Fullers	12	Smiths	7	Haberdashers	37	Rafmen‡	23
10	Tailors	21	Drapers	9	Millers	7	Tapiters	37	Butchers	21
11	Tanners	15	Dyers	9	Barbers	7	Millers	35	Smiths	18
12	Smiths	14	Millers	9	Shearmen	7	Carpenters	32	Barbers	16

* Includes twelve hat-makers.
† Including cordwainers.
‡ Probably 'chandler'.
Note that the above figures are not comparable between the different towns, as some cover a period of time and others a single year.

the whole economy, rather like the abandonment of a medieval castle by some noble household, as at Leicester in the early fifteenth century. Conversely, a small town might grow rapidly in numbers and prosperity because a noble family took up residence there. Leland speaks of how Petworth had grown because the wealthy Earls of Northumberland dwelt there. Leominster had decayed because of the removal of the market, and presumably many of the subsidiary trades it had engendered.

Big businesses might dissolve because the second or third generation bought lands and moved away, or for some quite accidental reason. Small towns might be hard hit, if not ruined; but larger towns and cities, with their widely diversified economy, could usually take the blow in their stride. Other plutocrats took the place of the old, and the oligarchy at the top of the social pyramid remained small, exclusive, and as powerful as ever.

Just as the City of London drew all the time on the younger sons of provincial landed families, for whom under the custom of primogeniture there was little prospect at home, constantly recruiting its merchant class in this way, so the provincial towns and cities drew on the same class in their own regions and often much further afield.[8] Those who made their fortunes generally moved away in a generation or two: few urban businesses lasted as long as three generations. But newcomers flowed into well-established towns without hesitation. There was constant mobility in Tudor England, especially at and round the top. There was also considerable mobility at the bottom, in the labouring and journeyman class, to judge by detailed inquiries into taxation and manorial records, though it is likely that the lower down the social scale the smaller the radius of movement. The merchant class might well be recruited from a hundred miles away; but the labouring population probably drifted round within a ten-mile radius. The people we know least about, as regards mobility, are perhaps the middling group — the skilled craftsmen, the shopkeepers, and the lesser merchants; they may have been more deeply rooted, since it is riches and poverty which mostly lead men to move about.

We can measure the size of the topmost class (wealth being the criterion) precisely by looking at those who paid the so-called Anticipation in 1523. All those who were assessed at £40 and over for the comprehensive subsidy of 1524–27 were called on to pay their tax in

[8] Mayors of Exeter came from Suffolk, Cheshire, Worcestershire, and Wales at this period.

anticipation in the autumn of 1523. In London this class paid 66 per cent of the tax required;[9] at Norwich they paid 73 per cent, and at Bristol 72 per cent. The highest proportion was reached at Lavenham (86 per cent) due largely to the presence of the Springs, and this must be regarded as an exceptional case. As to the numbers in this class, there were ninety-nine in Norwich, twenty-nine in Lynn, and only seventeen in Yarmouth: the three largest towns in Norfolk evidently had a different wealth structure. At Coventry there were forty-nine in this select group, at Exeter sixty-two, but at Plymouth only eleven. At the other end of this scale we may cite Birmingham, where only two men paid the anticipation and owned one-eighth of the wealth between them. But even £40 is too low a limit for identifying the oligarchy who ruled a town: it is merely a convenient way of finding out the proportion of the comfortably-off and the rich.

Turning to the Bottom People, those assessed on 'wages' in 1524, at Exeter they were 47 per cent; at Salisbury 48 per cent; at Lavenham 50 per cent. Even so, we know that many of the labouring class escaped paying even fourpence on their wages, and it is pretty safe to estimate that some two-thirds of the urban population lived on or near the poverty line in the 1520s. Roughly one-third owned nothing at all and escaped the tax; and another third of the population depended wholly or largely on wages. They could exist provided employment was fairly regular and harvests were good or at least not deficient. But they had no reserves against bad times. Even a poor countryman had his garden and possibly a strip or two in the open fields to tide him over in the matter of food; the real poverty was to be found in the towns, not least because the rural poor drifted into towns in the hope of finding jobs in the fifty to hundred trades of a reasonably sized town. But in bad times of slack employment or high grain prices the urban oligarchy was sitting on a dangerous bomb. Members of town councils, and above all mayors, were liable to be called on suddenly in a time of dearth to contribute substantially out of their own pockets towards the purchase of grain or herrings elsewhere, which were then sold below the prevailing market prices for the benefit of the poor. There was no machinery for invoking aid from London, nor the time to do it even if it had been there.

The constitutions of town councils provided for more or less exclusive oligarchies as their governing bodies, and these oligarchies, with the occasional addition of a lawyer to guide them, were drawn

[9] Actually, they owned 88 per cent of the wealth but were more successful in getting their subsidy assessment scaled down.

from the wealthiest section of the urban population. Wealth was not the only criterion, though it was by far the most important. Some trades were socially acceptable at the councillor level but not at the aldermanic; and some occupations were socially unacceptable at the mayoral level.[10] Hence the analysis of the occupations of mayors in early Tudor towns is a sharp guide to the social ethos as well as the relative prosperity of different occupations. Even so, there are two exceptions to this general statement. The first is that occupations that were socially unacceptable at one period became acceptable at a later date, and one can thence trace changes in the economy of a town (for example, the replacement of mercers and merchants at Leicester by butchers and tanners in the mayoral chair, a social and economic change that was beginning to make itself felt in the middle of the sixteenth century). Secondly, trades that were socially unacceptable at certain levels in a large and rich town might well be acceptable in a smaller town with less extreme wealth.

TOWN GOVERNMENT

Oligarchies were nothing new in urban government. They may indeed be as old as urban society itself, for men vary widely in ability, in ruthlessness, in the flair for making money, and not least in the desire for power. The great mass of people — Shakespeare's 'groundlings' — have never had much interest in the way they are governed or in who governs them, provided there are no wanton abuses of power by their rulers. And this occasionally happened, usually over money matters as we might expect.

From the thirteenth century onwards, and possibly earlier if we possessed the records, urban society had been classified as consisting of the *potentiores*, the *mediocres*, and the *inferiores*. The actual terms used varied slightly from place to place and time to time, but this is what they all came down to. At times during the fourteenth and fifteenth centuries the lesser classes quarrelled rancorously with the 'powerful ones', with a view to acquiring a greater say in the govern-

---

[10] Yet even this must be slightly qualified, provided there was the money. Thus a baker became mayor of Exeter in 1517–18, and a scrivener mayor of Norwich in 1553. A brewer was mayor in 1549. But we must remember that even simple descriptions like 'baker' or 'brewer' covered a very wide range of wealth, as did the omnibus word 'merchant'. A close modern parallel is, of course, the word 'farmer', ranging today from abject poverty to millionaires.

ment of the town, but these revolts were shortlived and achieved little or nothing. The *potentiores* were equated with the rich. That seemed natural enough to most people, even down to the nineteenth century (if not the present day) and trouble only broke out over specific grievances, above all if, as happened in various places, the rich evaded their fair share of local taxes and tallages and passed the burden to the rest by manipulating the assessments. But there was no general feeling against the deeprooted inequalities of society; they were taken for granted.

Despite the occasional revolts, then, in past generations most town governments seem to have become increasingly closed and oligarchical by the beginning of the sixteenth century. Thus the new charter of 1499 for Bristol put an end to what little popular control there had been in the past by appointing six aldermen for life. In theory the forty common councillors had been chosen by the mayor and sheriff 'with the assent of the community' and the new charter continued this, but it was a shadowy sort of assent. Probably any dissent got short shrift. From 1499 onwards the mayor was chosen from among the aldermen, and the aldermen from ex-mayors and the common council men. The government of the town 'became wholly oligarchical', especially when later charters allowed the council to fill its own vacancies and the number of aldermen was increased to twelve. The government of Bristol became close in form as well as in fact.

At Exeter democratic risings against the oligarchy in the two preceding centuries had produced no lasting results. The last years of the fifteenth century saw fresh dissensions, probably over the choice of mayor, but Henry VIII's charter of 1509 effectively put an end to any perverted notions of popular participation in government. The choice of mayor was tightly limited; councillors sat for life and were not removable save for serious cause and then only by their own body, which filled all its own vacancies. 'The government of Exeter at the beginning of the sixteenth century could hardly have been more oligarchic.'[11]

Lynn, then under the overlordship of the Bishop of Norwich, and one of the most prosperous ports along the east coast, had had continual trouble during the fifteenth century, again mainly over the way in which the *potentiores* manipulated matters (again financial) to their own advantage. Some slight popular element was thereafter allowed a

---

[11] Tait, *The Medieval English Borough*, p. 333; for Bristol see ibid., p. 331.

say, but even this was swept away by the new charter of 1524 'which made Lynn one of the closest of close boroughs . . . every vestige of popular participation in the town administration disappeared'.[12]

The charter of 1524 set up a mayor, twelve aldermen, and eighteen common councillors. The mayor was chosen by the common council from among the aldermen. The first twelve aldermen were appointed by the Crown and held office for life, and vacancies were afterwards filled by the common council. Members of the latter were chosen by the mayor and aldermen from such burgesses as they pleased. Thereafter the common council had the power to remove any member and fill any vacancies. The closing of the plutocratic ranks is evident at once when one looks only at the names of the mayors for the period 1500 to 1547. From 1500 to 1509 there were ten mayors, drawn from nine different families. But out of forty mayors between 1509 and 1547 there are only twenty-two different names; and, more striking, seven families occupied the mayoral chair no fewer than twenty-six times. These certainly were the *potentiores*. Thomas Miller, merchant, was mayor no fewer than six times between 1520 and 1546 — three times in succession in the early 1520s.

The choice of the first aldermen can be discovered from various records. Nearly all of them stood high in the subsidy assessment for 1524 (assessments of £100 to £200 are common) and nearly all were big merchants, the only exceptions being apparently a brewer, a baker and a chandler. The council members were a somewhat more mixed bag, but merchants, drapers and tailors predominated. They also included a fishmonger, a baker, and an organ-maker.

Most incorporated towns, if not all, had oligarchical structures of government, which tended to become even more tightly drawn as the century went on. There were various reasons for this tightening, ably summarized by Peter Clark.[13] 'The two hundred or so borough charters issued during the Tudor and early Stuart regimes reduced the democratic element in town government. . . . Conciliar membership was now small and intermarriage common', so much so that as time went on the government of the smaller boroughs at least became a family party. The causes of this closely oligarchical trend were both local and national. At the national level the Crown, obsessed with the growing problems of

---

[12] Ibid., p. 321. For fuller details of the Lynn charter see *HMC Report on the Manuscripts of Southampton and Kings Lynn*, 1887, pp. 206–7.
[13] Introduction to *Crisis and Order in English Towns 1500–1700*, pp. 21–2.

social order, needed 'small knots of reliable men in every town'; and locally, too, the fear of public disorder was strong among the rich and successful. Further, the rising administrative pressure on town government demanded more time and discouraged men from serving (an age-old complaint in towns); not to mention the growing financial difficulties of towns as inflation generated its own problems and at the same time made it more difficult to solve them. Office-holders (down to aldermen at least) were expected to subsidize the town finances, especially in times of crisis. At times a man otherwise well qualified would be passed over for the mayoralty because he was not wealthy enough to meet the costs of office; and as time went on more and more men refused to serve in town government, paying the stiff fines rather than do so. On the other hand, membership of the governing body brought what opponents thought were flagrant financial abuses of power, but which might be charitably regarded as the rewards for spending so much time and money on public affairs. English local government, in the boroughs at least, still works on this principle (or lack of principle.)

Yet some Tudor towns were more 'open' than others, or perhaps we should say less exclusive. Both Lynn and Exeter, for example, seem more exclusive than the average, for even when we have narrowed down the select circle who provided mayors we are still taking no account of family relationships by marriage. There is much evidence of this inter-marriage in mayoral biographies as portrayed in Hooker's Commonplace Book in the Exeter records, and in the wills of the mayoral class that survive. The same was true of the aldermanic class, to judge by Dr Palliser's study of 'civic dynasties' at York.

If we take the Elizabethan mayors as our criterion, since they are somewhat easier to trace in most towns than their early Tudor counterparts, the fifty Elizabethan mayors of Exeter (there were two mayors in some years) were drawn from only twenty-six different families, and intermarriages probably reduced the ruling class to about a score of families out of some 2,000 in the city as a whole. At Norwich, a much larger city, the forty-seven mayors in this period came from twenty-nine families. Here one family in a hundred could aspire to the mayor-alty, but this takes no account of interrelationships by marriage, so that the choice at Norwich was possibly more exclusive even than at Exeter. But at York the thirty-nine mayors were drawn from thirty-three different families and at Bristol, the second richest city in the kingdom at this date, no fewer than thirty-eight families were represented in the mayoral list. Winchester and Chester, too, made a somewhat wider choice than Exeter, Norwich, or Lynn.[14]

But Norwich was more 'open' than Exeter in one respect, and that was the wider range of occupations drawn on for the mayoralty. At Exeter only four of the fifty Elizabethan mayors came from outside the merchant class, whereas at Norwich thirteen out of forty-seven mayors came from the non-merchant class. At Bristol there was a shift of emphasis in the last quarter of the century. Between 1558 and 1576, ten out of eighteen mayors were merchants; from 1576 to 1603 twenty-five of the twenty-eight mayors were merchants. Bristol too was becoming more oligarchical. Mr McGrath has shown that in the seventeenth century the key positions of mayor, sheriff, and chamberlain were all held by merchants. Finally, as an example of a small town, though important in its own region, Leicester, like Exeter, drew upon twenty-six different families for its mayors; but since its population was only a third of Exeter's its range of choice was far wider. Thus even if pretty well every corporation was oligarchic, some were much more open than others to penetration by 'outsiders'. We still have much to learn about the social history of urban government in the sixteenth century (or in any century for that matter), and many questions important to the historian and sociologist remain unexplored. This discussion has centred largely on the office of mayor, but we need to examine also the personnel of the other offices, such as sheriff and chamberlain, and of the aldermanic class, and that of the common councils. Not only their relative wealth and occupations are of interest, but also the degree of mobility in different towns from the bottom of the governing class to the top. An enormous field of social history is awaiting exploration. But the fundamental fact of Tudor urban life was that the great majority of the population were completely excluded from all government and gilds and any kind of civic recognition.

[14] Hoskins, 'The Elizabethan merchants of Exeter', p. 165; Palliser, loc. cit., p. 168 for York, Chester and Winchester.

CHAPTER FIVE

The Condition of the People

THE WAGE-EARNING CLASS

THE great mass of the people in Henry VIII's England, perhaps two out of every three, consisted of wage-earners and their dependants. It was a pre-industrial society, based on the family and on a household economy. Apart from the building trades, including shipbuilding, the majority of people worked in or near their homes. This was a saving grace in a hard life. Mills and mines were small and scarcely affected the lives of any but a tiny minority. England was underdeveloped and underpopulated, slow-moving in every way, almost totally unmechanized except for the watermill and the windmill, dependent on hand labour and the power of the ox and the horse.

The existence of this huge substructure of society was rarely noticed except in times of crisis and internal dissension. Foreign observers, notably the Venetian ambassadors whose reports on England are the best we have for this century, have nothing to say about them. The single exception is the author of the so-called *Italian Relation of England*,[1] already quoted, who tells us 'there are three estates in England, the popular, the military, and the ecclesiastical', and then in a casual line adds, 'the people are held in little more esteem than if they were slaves'. Elsewhere he says that 'there is no injury that can be committed against the lower orders of the English that may not be atoned for by money'. The lengthy reports of Barbaro and Soranzo in the *Calendar of State Papers Venetian* for 1551 and 1554 say not a word about the working class, except to note — they all do this — that the English were a lazy people who, if they would make the effort to

---

[1] Edited by C. A. Sneyd, Camden Society, XXXVII, 1847, pp. 26, 34.

develop the natural fertility and resources of their country, could be much better off. But they preferred not to make the effort. The Venetian envoys did not penetrate far into England — much of what they say about us beyond London is hearsay and guesswork — and they mingled only with the rich and the powerful as an ambassador would today. They may or may not have been right about the laziness of the working class.

That the English Establishment (to employ that useful word) similarly regarded the mass of people as little better than slaves, existing only to work for the few, is revealed in an unguarded moment in the year 1547 when Parliament passed 'the most savage Act in the grim history of English vagrancy legislation, imposing slavery as a punishment for refusal to work'.[2] It is true that the Act proved to be unenforceable and was repealed two years later, but the fact that it could be passed at all is significant of the mentality of some at least of the ruling class. It provided for branding (with a V for Vagabond), for a diet of bread and water and meat that no one else would eat, for beating and chaining if necessary. This personal slavery was to last for two years; but a runaway slave could thereafter be enslaved for life and branded on the face with an S. On a second escape he could be put to death. Although this Act was repealed in 1549, the mentality that had first envisaged it remained. When Ket's Rebellion had been put down in that same year, it was the reactionary Earl of Warwick himself who felt obliged to call a halt to the hangings at Norwich by reminding the bloodthirsty and triumphant Norfolk gentry that they had better leave enough men alive to plough and harrow their land for them.[3] The leopard had not really changed his spots. Whether or not they were legally slaves, the working class led a life of slavery. As Tawney says, Sir Thomas More had no illusions about their lot. The Utopians were 'not to be wearied from early in the morning to late in the evening with continual work, like labouring and toiling beasts. For this is worse than the miserable and wretched condition of bondmen. Which nevertheless is almost everywhere the life of workmen and artificers, saving in Utopia.'

Nor was there much escape in the real world through a good educa-

---

[2] This Act is discussed critically by C. S. L. Davies, 'Slavery and Protector Somerset', *Econ. Hist. Rev.*, sec. ser., XIX, no. 3, 1966.
[3] Jordan, *Edward VI: The Young King*, p. 491. The idea that 'idle persons and vagabonds' should be made slaves was revived in 1559. Apparently Cecil was toying with a revival of the old statute (*T.E.D.*, I, 325).

tion. The sons of merchants and yeomen might be fortunate enough to live in a town which had a monastic or other school, and some — a small proportion — might rise high in the social scale. Wolsey was despised by his rich and well-born enemies as the son of a butcher, and Thomas Cromwell as the son of a tanner. But men of such outstanding ability could afford to ignore these charges by a class interested only in its own survival. This attitude persists to this day among the more backward and unintelligent knights of the shires. They dread the spread of education among the lower orders who are quite likely to take the posts in the State, the Church and the finance houses previously reserved for their own progeny.

Many schools perished during the dissolution of the monasteries: few new schools were founded under Henry VIII. Most of the well-known schools of this period are refoundations, as at Canterbury, Worcester and Ely, rather than due to the scholastic zeal of the King. The great age of the English grammar schools begins with the dissolution of the chantries under Edward VI. Under Henry the battle for a wider spread of education had to be fought from the ground up, and the classic case[4] was the discussion about the education of 'poor children' when the school at Canterbury was to be refounded. The odious Lord Rich, evil beyond measure in an evil age, argued (and he had some support from the other members of the Commission) that education should be reserved for the offspring of gentlemen. 'Husbandmen's children, they were more meet . . . for the plough and to be artificers than to occupy the place of the learned sort. So that they wished none else to be put to school, but only gentlemen's children.' Others agreed with him, but Cranmer, also on the Commission, argued the case for the other side. Poor men's children were often endowed with gifts of nature and were frequently more studious than the sons of the gentry whose position in the next generation was assured in any event. Cranmer told his opponents that though they were now gentlemen by birth, their families had sprung from lowlier origins (this was quite true historically), and if a poor man's child was apt for learning he should be admitted in preference to a gentleman's son who was not. Cranmer may have won this particular battle, but the Shearers were determined to preserve an adequate supply of cheap and servile labour for their farms and estates.

[4] See Ridley, *Thomas Cranmer*, p. 197, and Tawney, *The Agrarian Problem*, pp. 134–5. Both Wolsey and Cromwell were born into the well-to-do 'middle class', rich provincial men on a par with successful merchants in the towns. However, their enemies did not scruple to diminish them.

THE WORKING WEEK

Hours of work were regulated by the Statute of 1495, and they remained virtually unchanged until the nineteenth century. After reciting that many artificers and labourers 'waste much part of their day and deserve not their wages, sometimes in late coming to work, early departing therefrom, long sitting at their breakfast, at their dinner, and their noon-meat', the Act proceeds to regulate the working day. Between 15 March and 15 September, the wage-earner shall be at his work before five o'clock in the morning and shall leave between seven and eight in the evening. Out of this time he was allowed half an hour for his breakfast, and an hour and a half for his dinner and afternoon sleep. The afternoon siesta was authorized only between 15 May and 15 August, and was an old custom (it is referred to at York Minster in the mid-fourteenth century). When the afternoon sleep was not allowed, the worker was allowed an hour for his dinner and half an hour for his noon-meat. The final effect was the same: a total of two hours' break out of a fourteen- or fifteen-hour day.

From mid-September to mid-March, every artificer (i.e. craftsman) and labourer was required to work from 'the springing of the day' until nightfall. Failure to observe the statutory working hours at any time involved a proportionate reduction of wages.

Clearly, the hours of work between autumn and spring were very variable according to the month of the year — they could be only eight hours in the depth of winter — but the master-cappers at Coventry sorted this out in the following year (1496) by fixing a twelve-hour day (6 a.m. to 6 p.m.) all the year round. The masters also fixed journeymen's wages at 12d a week. Any master paying more, in order to tempt away other employers' men, was to be fined 6s 8d. Both masters and journeymen were to give eight days' notice of terminating employment.[5]

By 1520 the master-cappers felt strong enough to lengthen the working day substantially. From Michaelmas to Easter journeymen were to work from 6 a.m. to 7 p.m. (13 hours) and from Easter to Michaelmas from 5 a.m. to 7 p.m. (14 hours). Presumably there were the statutory two-hour breaks, though the Coventry leet books do not mention them. The ordinances of 1520 were also tougher in requiring the journeyman to give fourteen days' notice of leaving his job, under a penalty of 6s 8d, but there was no longer any obligation on the master's side to

[5] Harris, ed., *The Coventry Leet Book*, II, 1908, p. 574, and III, 1909, pp. 673, 693.

give any notice. It is possible that these new regulations met with silent opposition as six years later the journeymen cappers were ordered to keep the hours and times laid down under the penalty of a proportionate reduction of wages.

Another set of regulations, for workers in the building trades, was passed by the Common Council of London in 1538.[6] They covered all manner of carpenters, masons, joiners, tilers, plasterers, bricklayers, gardeners and labourers. From 8 September to 25 March they worked from 6 a.m. to 6 p.m. The breaks were fixed at a quarter of an hour for breakfast (9 to 9.15), an hour for dinner (12 to 1), and a quarter-hour 'for his drinking' (4 to 4.15). The net working day was therefore 10½ hours, for which the wage was fixed at 7*d*. During the rest of the year the working day was from 5 a.m. to 7 p.m., again with 1½ hours off for meals. For this longer working day (12½ hours) the wage was fixed at 8*d*. No siesta time is referred to either in London or in Coventry. Already, then, the employers had begun to make the Act of 1495 even more onerous. The problem of reducing the wage-earning class to some sort of industrial discipline — the great problem of the Factory System that still lay far ahead — was taking shape.

The hours of work were long: the London building workers would have done a net 63-hour week for about six months of the year, and a net 75 hours for the rest of the year. The cappers of Coventry in 1520, if we assume that the regulations included the usual breaks (though they do not say so) worked even longer — a net 69 hours for about half the year, and 75 for the remainder.

These hours seem monstrous, but there were mitigating factors. In the first place, the pace of work was slow. Since most work was not geared to a machine, men did not exert themselves overmuch but adapted their pace to the long day ahead. We must remember, too, that most of them were poorly fed for a good bit of the year, and would be incapable in any event of working hard over such a long stretch of time.

Again, there was almost nothing to buy, apart from meeting essential expenses such as food, drink, and rent, by way of consumer goods and services. This is unquestionably why men spent so much time in ale-houses, as the sixteenth-century moralists were so apt to point out; drink was the only consumer good that was widely available, and one that was relatively cheap. Alcoholism was almost certainly widely prevalent in Tudor and Stuart England.

Besides the slow pace of work, with frequent pauses for chats with

[6] *T.E.D.*, I, 115—17.

passing friends (one of the advantages of working in or near their homes), there was a good deal of underemployment. This is characteristic of all primitive economies. Employment was irregular, for craftsmen as well as labourers, partly because the economy was primitive and badly organized, and partly because so many people's work was directly affected by the weather in a variety of ways. Prolonged rain stopped many trades altogether (e.g. building) and prolonged drought could stop others, where water-power was involved.

There was also an extraordinary number of official holidays. In Catholic England before the Reformation there may have been fifty or more holy days in the year, though it is not clear how many of these were actually taken. By the sixteenth century the number of holidays was constantly under attack. Latimer, as early as 1536, was among many who preached against the excessive number of holidays for the working class which led, he thought, to idleness and drunkenness.

> But what doth the people on these holidays? Do they give themselves to godliness or ungodliness? . . . God seeth all the whole holidays to be spent miserably in drunkenness, in glossing, in strife, in envy, in dancing, dicing, idleness and gluttony. . . . Thus men serve the devil, for the devil hath more service done unto him on one holiday than on many working days. . . . The foolish common people think it to be a belly-cheer day, and so they make it a surfeiting day: there is no wickedness, no rebellion, no lechery, but she hath most commonly her beginning upon the holy-day.

The well-fed have always been prone to this sort of speech. The working class were condemned for enjoying themselves in the only way they knew, and for letting themselves go when they had the chance. In 1549 the writer of a treatise on 'Polices to Reduce this Realme of England unto a Prosperus Wealthe and Estate' includes a large reduction in the number of holidays per annum as one of his many proposals for a more vigorous economy. According to his reckoning there were still thirty-five holy days a year besides Sundays, 'whereof 24 or 25 may be well put down'. If the numerous holy days were spent in listening to good sermons or homilies and daily prayers 'the people might . . . be far better disposed than they now are'. But they were not. If, then, twenty of these days were spent in labour, 'this realm should be richer yearly by 5 or 6 hundred thousand pounds and by means thereof much more Bullion to be brought unto the mints'. Our imports, always a sore point, would be cut by producing more nails at home, for example, and our exports of corn, lead, tin, cloth and other merchandise could be

[7] *T.E.D.*, III, 311 *et seq.*

doubled. An Act of 1552 did indeed reduce the number of 'holy days' in the year, but only to twenty-seven. There were three days off at Easter and Whitsun, for example, and four at Christmas, besides numerous odd days. But they were holidays without pay, and as the cost of living rocketed decade after decade more and more wage-earners preferred to go to work for much-needed money.

The full attack on the number of holidays came later in the century, when employers saw the advantages of uninterrupted labour. It is significant of a new attitude that the Protector Somerset built his great house (Somerset House) in the Strand between 1547 and 1552 without the work stopping either on Sundays or on holy days.[8] No doubt the fortunate craftsmen and labourers did not mind this unwonted influx of money wages. At Cole Orton in Leicestershire the parson complained very early in the seventeenth century that the traditional Rogationtide procession round the parish could not be held as all the men were now working in the coal mines. It was a foretaste of the industrial discipline of the nineteenth century.

The irregularity of employment, whether arising from working conditions like the weather, or from numerous holidays, makes it exceedingly difficult to calculate the average weekly wage of a wage-earner and the length of the normal working week. The best information we have comes from the seventeenth century, or from underdeveloped countries in the modern world. Tawney found in the China of the 1930s that for many half-employment was the rule. In general in backward economies today the average seems to be about 150 to 180 working days in the year. In particularly backward areas, such as modern Sicily, labourers average only 100 days' work in a year, or only two days a week. Writing as late as 1705, John Law assumed that in the England of his day about 50 per cent of working days, in farming at least, were lost for one reason and another.[9] Some major activities virtually closed down altogether for months on end, such as farming and fishing, and building must often have stopped for weeks. In the England of Henry VIII, then, it would be rash to assume an average of more than three working days a week, possibly as few as two and a half. In these circumstances the 70 to 75-hour week becomes bearable, but the problem of poverty becomes all the more acute.

---

[8] Gairdner, *The English Church in the Sixteenth Century*, p. 281.
[9] Coleman, 'Labour in the English economy of the seventeenth century', *Econ. H.R.*, sec. ser., VIII, no. 3, 1956, esp. 288–9.

WAGES

What do we know of wage rates in the early sixteenth century? The London building ordinance of 1538 speaks of 7*d* a day during the autumn and winter months, and 8*d* a day during the rest of the year. At Coventry the master cappers in 1496 fixed journeymen's wages at 2*d* a day — 12*d* a week. But here we must be careful to make clear an important distinction. Wages were calculated in two different ways: sometimes 'meat and drink' was provided by the employer, and the money wage reduced accordingly. This must be the understanding at Coventry, whereas the London figures obviously allowed for no meat and drink. Wages also varied slightly from trade to trade, but more commonly as between craftsmen and labourers. In 1519, when the common ditch of the City of London was cleansed and scoured, Stow tells us that the chief ditcher (presumably the foreman) got 7*d* a day, the second ditcher 6*d*, other ditchers 5*d*. Every vagabond ('for so they were termed' says Stow) got a penny a day with meat and drink at the charges of the City of London. Here the skilled men found their own victuals, and the labourers were provided for. The use of the term 'vagabond' as a synonym for 'labourer' is significant; clearly the labouring population, in a town at least, was largely composed of a wandering and homeless crowd of men who would drift from job to job or from place to place. Gradually the word acquired a more pejorative meaning. The word merely meant originally a 'wanderer', from the Latin *vagabundus*, and acquired a derogatory meaning from being coupled in legislation with rogues, so that 'rogues and vagabonds' became indistinguishable in the public mind. In point of fact a wandering or floating population of labourers must have been essential in an underdeveloped economy where so many trades were seasonal, not least in farming where many men and women must have followed the harvest from south to north as was customary in the United States of America within quite recent times.

The building accounts for Hampton Court for 1536—37 show that board wages were reckoned to be worth a shilling a week. In other words, craftsmen and labourers got 2*d* a day less when meat and drink were provided. Ships' carpenters in 1514 got 8*d* a day, with meat and drink reckoned at 2½*d* a day.[10]

The Exeter cathedral accounts (Fabric Rolls) show all master craftsmen getting 6*d* a day in 1425, their assistants 5*d* and labourers 4*d*. In

[10] *L.P.*, I, pp. cxii-cxiii; ibid., no. 5790.

1540 labourers at Exeter were getting 5*d* a day for picking ivy off the city walls, and demolition workers at St Nicholas Priory about the same time were paid 6*d* a day for more skilled and dangerous work. Not until the Statute of Artificers in 1563 do we get fuller information about wage rates in the different trades, and for different levels of worker, and by that date wages had risen appreciably over the levels that had prevailed a generation or two earlier. Most of the information about wage rates in Henry VIII's England is still awaiting excavation from such building accounts as survive, either of new country houses or of public works of national or local character.

Broadly speaking, wage rates had not moved for over a hundred years. Both Salzman and Thorold Rogers agree that they remained virtually unchanged from 1400 down to the 1530s, with master craftsmen getting 6*d* a day, their assistants 5*d*, and labourers 4*d*. There were variations from time to time — the time of the year, the nature of the job — but these were the basic facts of life.[11]

Assuming that on average labourers worked only half the possible number of days (master craftsmen might have fared slightly better), the average income of the lowest class of wage-earner over the whole year could not have exceeded a shilling a week, perhaps a little more in summer and less in winter. In other words, we have to reckon a man's income at about 50*s* a year, excluding what his wife and children might be able to earn in certain favoured parts of England, above all the textile districts. In farming, too, the seasonal employment of women and children would have made a vital difference to the household budget.

THE WORKING-CLASS BUDGET

Is it possible to say anything about how this meagre income was expended, to construct a 'working-class budget'? Such a question is as fundamental as that of irregularity of employment, for we cannot talk about the vicissitudes of the working class throughout the sixteenth century unless we know something about the way they spent their money.

The major items were food and drink, far and away the most important; then rent, fuel and light, and clothing. Even in the twentieth century a veracious weekly or monthly budget is often a rather

---

[11] Salzmann, *Building in England*, esp. p. 77. The statute of 1514 gives fuller details of the wage rates for various specialist jobs.

hypothetical affair, and the lower we go down the social scale the more we are left guessing about imponderables. In 1688 Gregory King calculated that, for nearly half the total population, annual expenditure exceeded the family income.

The vast majority of the wage-earning class lived in rented cottages and houses in the sixteenth century and earlier. At Coventry in 1522 a detailed survey of wealth, occupations, and property, shows that some labourers paid 2s to 3s a year in rent but the typical rent was about 5s, probably paid half-yearly or perhaps quarterly. Here rent came to 1d or 2d a week. As a comparison, we find the city of Augsburg in south Germany building 400 houses for poor people 'in a convenient air' with three rooms, a chimney, a privy, and a little yard, for 4s a year rent. This was palatial accommodation as compared with most English towns, as we shall see.

At Exeter, rentals of city property show that cottage rents were 4s to 5s a year in the 1580s. This is a bit late in date for our purpose but it is doubtful whether in fact urban rents for poorer property in the provincial towns had risen during the century. A Winchester rental for the 1580s also shows that out of 115 tenements and cottages, eighty-three were small houses. Of these, forty were generally described as 'cottages' and paid rents ranging from 4s to 6s 8d a year. Ten properties described as 'small houses' paid only 1s to 3s a year. It is noteworthy that 'cottages' were regarded as by no means the lowest kind of accommodation.

In the city of York the chantries held much small property with very variable rents. The cheapest were yielding as little as 4d or 8d a year, but these lay in narrow lanes and were certainly in a bad state. Other 'decayed' cottages yielded 2s a year. A reasonably sound cottage brought in 3s or 4s a year, and upwards. At Ripon cottage rents tended to be slightly lower, at 2s, 2s 8d, and 3s 4d, but it is difficult to generalize freely about urban rents anywhere. Much depended on which part of the town the property lay in, and more than that upon its physical state. A 'decayed' house could be found for less than a shilling a year. There was a wide range of cottage and other small property in any town, and the poor could rise to the better or sink to the worst within their own class. As prices rose they substituted lower-quality food, drink and housing; hence the worst effects of Tudor inflation were hidden and will never be susceptible to definitive statistical statements.

Cottage rents in the country were pretty much the same as in the town. The chantry certificates of 1545 for Leicestershire give many details of the rents of chantry property. Cottage rents in most villages ranged from 3s 4d to 5s, with 4s as the commonest figure. Some cottages were rented at as little as 1s 6d and 2s 8d, but at Noseley in the uplands of south-east Leicestershire a cottage with an acre and a half of land was rented for 3s 8d, and another with two acres for 6s 8d.[12] Such cottagers were exceptionally well off. Even the labouring class had its own wide inequalities.

About the money spent on clothing we are completely in the dark. It would have been a world of cast-offs and rags just as it was in the England of Edward VII. New clothing, apart from shoes and caps or hats, must have been almost unheard of. The number of shoe-makers in both town and country suggests that even the working class had to spend some money in this direction, but we are still in the dark about how often and how much. In the Statute of 1514 we find that 'a bailiff in husbandry' was allowed 26s 8d a year plus 5s for his clothing, with meat and drink. In other words he lived in with all found. He was the highest paid of the farm workers, being what we would call a farm fore-man. A 'common servant of husbandry' (the labourer) got 16s 8d a year with 4s allowed for clothing. A woman servant got 10s and 4s for clothing, and children up to fourteen years of age got 6s 8d in wages plus 4s for clothing. All these rates are for workers living in, who formed a considerable proportion of the rural labouring class. This point is important in considering the impact of the price revolution on the working class, for this large group — how large again we do not know — paid no rent, bought no clothes or fuel, and were fed. They were effectively cushioned against inflation, unlike their fellows in most urban occupations and those country workers who lived out.

Four shillings a year per person seems to be the agreed figure for working-class clothing, but that the wage-earning household fending for itself ever rose to this level is most unlikely. How could such a family, with even two or three children, have faced an expenditure at this level? Moreover, we have to remember that farm servants living in were probably far better clothed than those fending for themselves, if only as a matter of pride for the farmer's wife.

[12] For Coventry, see the so-called military survey of 1522 in the city archives; for Exeter, see a rental of 1584 in the city archives; for Winchester, see Atkinson, *Elizabethan Winchester*, p. 128; for York and Ripon, see *Yorkshire Chantry Surveys*, Surtees Soc., XCI and XCII, 1892—93; for Leicestershire, see *Reports and Papers of Associated Architectural and Archaeological Societies for 1910*.

Most clothing was made at home. So Eden records in the closing years of the eighteenth century, and there is no reason to believe it was any different in the time of Henry VIII. The two chief exceptions to this were shoes and hats. A pair of shoes 'for poor people' cost a shilling in the 1550s — that is, three days' wages.[13] The price of hats and caps had been fixed by law in 1511–12, in the face of foreign competition. The best caps were priced as high as 3s 4d but these were of no interest to the working class. The fourth quality of Leominster wool cap cost a shilling, but there may have been even cheaper headgear as lesser qualities of Cotswold wool caps were left to 'such price as buyer and seller may reasonably agree'. Whatever the prices, we are still left with the unanswerable problem of how often a wage-earning family bought shoes or hats or caps.

Fuel and light present another problem. Neither could have cost much. Rushlights made at home cost nothing. As for fuel, it was there for the picking up in wooded country, above all where there existed the common right of estover (collecting wood for burning). But where woodland was scarce, as in the East Midlands, even as early as Henry VIII's time, the poor were reduced to burning the dried haulms of peas and beans, the largest crop, and even dried cow-dung. Few country dwellers could have spent anything on fuel, but the town-dweller was worse off. Towns were small, the countryside within a few minutes' walk, and many must have collected firewood in this way. Cobbett remarked in the early nineteenth century on the vast difference in comfort between those parts of England where the poor had access to good supplies of fuel, and those which had not.

Lastly, we have food and drink. If we put the expenditure on rent at 6 to 8 per cent of the total income, possibly as little as 5 per cent when the whole family's earnings were pooled, and clothing at another 5 per cent, it is clear that some 90 per cent of a working-class income was absorbed by food and drink. Not only that, but most of the food came from the harvest, as did all the drink (ale made from barley). Bread was the great standby, eaten with cheese or fat bacon on a good day, various messes of pottage made from peas and beans, especially in the Midlands where these were the biggest crop, and ale the universal drink.

On and near the coast, sea fish formed an important part of the ordinary diet, above all the invaluable herring — one of God's greatest gifts to mankind and especially to those nations that bordered the

[13] Beveridge, *Prices and Wages in England*, p. 457. These were Maundy shoes. By the end of the decade the price had doubled (*T.E.D.*, I, 329).

North Sea. England was rich in freshwater fish also: various foreign observers note this in contrast to their own countries. But even sea fish could be carried as far inland as Coventry, a hundred miles from the east coast, by the early sixteenth century. Regulations of the court leet make it clear that sea fish was coming by road from 'the se-syde' and it was forbidden for any trader to 'lye by the wey' and to forestall supplies en route. Herrings, oysters, and mussels are particularly mentioned. All such fish had to be viewed by the mayor before sale in the market, presumably to ascertain its fitness for human consumption.[14]

Meat was probably rare in the working-class diet, except where workers lived in, but a whole sheep's head could be bought for a halfpenny at Coventry in 1513, a price fixed by the city fathers. This was within the reach of a labouring family when the father was in work. But for all the meat, the fish, and the occasionally poached rabbits, the greater part of the diet of most people in England depended directly and precariously upon the size of the annual harvest.

SOCIAL SEGREGATION

The wage-earning class was largely segregated in its own particular areas, in the larger towns at least, and had been so long before Tudor times. In some streets the well-to-do and the poor lived side by side (some urban parishes were still mixed in this way) but on the whole the social classes were segregated physically. A clear example is that of Totnes in south Devon, a wealthy little town dependent largely on the cloth industry. Fifteenth-century tax assessments show that the richer sort lived within the walls, along the High Street and Fore Street, while the suburb outside the West Gate at the top of the town consisted mostly of the poorer sort who contributed comparatively little to the taxable capacity of the town. This segregation persisted into later centuries, as witness the remarkable number of fine Elizabethan and Stuart houses which survive within the walls to this day.

Exeter, a much larger city, shows the same segregation of rich and poor areas, with a middle group of parishes that were evidently mixed in social composition. Again the richer sort, the *potentiores*, lived along the four main streets in the centre of the walled city; the poor were massed in the lanes and alleys of parishes either near the city walls or outside them altogether. The subsidy assessments for the 1540s vary slightly in their ranking of the parishes by wealth (measured here by the

[14] Harris, ed., *The Coventry Leet Book*, III, pp. 646–7.

average assessment per taxable person) for one rich merchant moving from one parish to another could alter the picture in detail, but the basic fact remains that the same five central parishes head the lists in taxable wealth, and the same five occupy the bottom place. Just outside the walls, and not at that time within the tax jurisdiction of the city, lay two parishes (St Edmund and St Sidwell) which had been largely populated by the poorest of the working class since early medieval times. All that can be said in favour of this segregation of the wage-earning class beyond the old walls or adjoining them inside was that they had a little more space as a result. They probably all had small gardens, which among other things solved the sanitary problem to a large degree in the medieval and Tudor town, whereas the well-to-do in the close-built central streets merely had their little enclosed courtyards and their unsalubrious garderobes or close-stools indoors.

At York, the capital city of the north as Exeter was of the west, there was the same long-standing segregation of the richer and the poorer people.[15] The richest parishes lay again in the city centre, stretching in a wide arc from the Minster down to the two main river bridges. Adjoining these, as in Exeter, was a group of mixed parishes, and then, near the walls and beyond the two rivers, lay the poorest.

In Norwich, capital city of eastern England, the picture is much the same. When the city fathers made a census of the poor in 1570 nearly two-thirds of the poor were to be found in the Great Wards of Coslany and Ultra Aquam, with heavy concentrations in particular parishes like St Martin-in-the-Bailey where nearly 83 per cent of the population were listed as poor; other parishes had 40 to 60 per cent so listed. Again the central parishes are the richer and it is generally the outer ones that are filled with wage-earners.[16]

Unfortunately we have no good information about London, the city with the largest number of poor and the most grinding poverty. No detailed tax assessments survive for the 1520s, except for the better-off. We know nothing about the distribution of the richer and the poorer areas except a chance literary reference such as Crowley's remarks in *The Way of Wealth* (published in 1550) about 'whole alleys, whole rents [i.e. rented houses], whole rows, yea whole streets and lanes'

[15] The following remarks are based on David Palliser's unpublished thesis on 'Some aspects of the social and economic history of York in the sixteenth century'.
[16] Pound, 'An Elizabethan census of the poor', *Univ. of Birmingham Hist. Jnl*, VIII, no. 2, 1962, see especially the map, p. 161.

where the immigrant poor faced crippling rents imposed by 'insatiable beasts' of speculators. That London had larger and more concentrated districts of wage-earners and the poor generally than the provincial towns cannot be doubted.

It is possible that in the smaller towns (though evidently not all) the social classes were less sharply segregated from each other, yet even here it is interesting to note that as far back as the early thirteenth century, when the Bishop of Salisbury extended the burghal area of Sherborne (1227–28), he carefully divided the burgages into three classes by size and rent. Rents ranged from 18*d* per annum down to 8*d*, the latter burgages being apparently on the edge of the built-up area. It is not often we can observe such deliberate zoning in action. Even without such deliberate planning from above, however, it is clear that the steady pressure of economic forces over the centuries, notably the rising price of land in urban centres, would produce the same result.

Of the houses of the working class in the first half of the sixteenth century we can say little. They are rarely described in contemporary documents and no structures have survived anywhere, not even in the countryside. Built to house a working population capable of paying only a meagre rent, they probably had a life of less than a hundred years. What little we do know of them suggests they contained only two rooms, a small open-roofed 'hall' and a parlour or 'chamber'. Craftsmen often had a workshop also, and a tiny shop on the street. So, too, did tradesmen such as bakers, butchers and shoe-makers. Very few houses at the artisan or labourer level possessed such an amenity as a kitchen, either in the town or the country. This addition did not become common until much later in the sixteenth century. Many farm-labourers' cottages consisted of only a single room, even as late as the eve of the Civil War. Thus the surveys of the Wiltshire estates of the Earl of Pembroke for 1631–32 show many cottages of one room only (though usually 'lofted over' by that date) and some were even newly built as late as this with only one room, at a rent of 1*s* a year. One such cottage, newly built, measured only 10 feet by 8 and paid a shilling a year rent. Such cottages must have been much more general a hundred years earlier.

In the country, the houses of the wage-earning class must have been specially built by the squire or noble landlord, and less commonly by the bigger farmers, for their work-people. Often, too, a master crafts-man must have built his own cottage. But who built this kind of housing in the towns, houses which can never have seemed an attractive investment? We can rarely envisage employers of labour doing this in order to keep their labour supply. Few employers employed more than a handful of men, and the supply of labour was always greater than the demand except in special cases like the erection of a very large building which might produce temporary shortages. There is no evidence that even the bigger town councils met this need for working-class houses. Yet they existed in great numbers, whole streets of them. Who built them we simply do not know. In towns, large and small, dominated by a wealthy monastic house, or an enterprising bishop, it is likely that they were the chief builders. Rich clothiers were the exception among employers as they needed many work-people, perhaps even competed mildly for them in a district given over to the cloth industry. So Leland tells us (*c.* 1540) that Stumpe, the great cloth merchant who took over Malmesbury Abbey and its buildings for his trade, 'intendith to make a street or two for clothiers in the back vacant ground of the abbey that is within the town walls'. At Trowbridge, Leland also says, the rich clothier Thomas Horton of Bradford-on-Avon nearby, 'made divers fair houses of stone' and 'Old Baylie', another clothier, 'also built lately in the town'. Perhaps we would have found this kind of building by wealthy clothiers in textile towns elsewhere in England, but few towns were so highly specialized or benefited by such rich capitalists. How their houses and streets got themselves built is a subject awaiting a determined explorer of urban history and topography.

CHAPTER SIX

The Plunder of the Church

THE GREAT SACRILEGE

THERE is a pregnant sentence in More's *Utopia*, written when he was a
mature and widely experienced man of thirty-eight, which sums up his
judgment of the realities that lay behind the façade of government and
public attitudes: 'When I consider and weigh in my mind all these
commonwealths which nowadays anywhere do flourish, so God help
me, I can perceive nothing but a certain conspiracy of rich men
procuring their own commodities under the name and title of the
commonwealth.' This profound truth remains undiluted in twentieth-
century Britain, and is equally well disguised from public debate. Had
More lived into the closing years of Henry VIII, he would have seen his
judgment buttressed a thousandfold when the open plunder of the
Church began in earnest.

The net yearly income of the Church was probably not far short of
£400,000 (the *Valor* gives £320,180 in 1535, but there were some
omissions and some undervaluations) at a time when the Crown lands
were yielding some £40,000 at the most. From 1536 onwards a large
proportion of this vast estate, probably at least 60 per cent, passed to
the Crown in the greatest transference of land in English history since
the Norman Conquest; and the greater part of this passed in turn, more
or less rapidly, to the nobility and the gentry, mostly the latter. On
these facts has been erected, chiefly by the Swedish scholar Liljegren, a
whole political analysis culminating in the inevitability of the Civil War
a hundred years later. Whatever truth may still reside in this analysis, it
was greatly oversimplified, not least because Liljegren failed to distinguish between the original grantees of Church property, many of

121

whom were mere agents or speculators, and the men in whose hands the properties finally came to rest.

However this may be, the spoliation of the Church during the greater part of the sixteenth century is one of the most fundamental divides in English history. Some called it the Great Sacrilege (like Sir Henry Spelman a hundred years after); more modern historians refer placidly to the Great Transfer; I prefer to label it the Great Plunder, and to see in it that conspiracy of rich men procuring their own fortunes in the name of the commonwealth, whatever brand of the Christian faith they publicly or privately professed, and however they wriggled from one side to the other when the political wind veered round unexpectedly. The robbery of the Church was nothing new for needy monarchs. Spelman traces these earlier raids on ecclesiastical wealth in the medieval period; but when he reaches the reign of Henry VIII, he opens out with blazing guns:

> I am now come out of the rivers into the ocean of iniquity and sacrilege, where whole thousands of churches and chapels dedicated to the service of God in the same manner that the rest are which remain to us at this day, together with the monasteries and other houses of religion and intended piety, were by King Henry VIII, in a tempest of indignation against the clergy of that time mingled with insatiable avarice, sacked and razed as by an enemy.

Money, or the lack of it, was the continuing problem of the Tudors, as of earlier monarchs; but the vainglorious wars of Henry VIII were steadily draining the whole country. The massive taxation of the 1520s had been soon wasted. Still more revenue was needed despite the rising popular discontent, brought to a climax by the official repudiation in 1529 of the Loan of 1522. The Loan had 'emptied men's purses' said Hall in his *Chronicle*: there were growing demands in 1528 for repayment, with the dearth of corn, a slump in the cloth trade and rising unemployment; but to these Henry gave a pretty rough answer. A bill was introduced in the following year to 'release' all Loan money to the King. It was 'sore argued' in the Commons but eventually assented to. There was widespread fury throughout the country at this barefaced repudiation of an enormous debt, but, as Hall says, 'there was no remedy'.

There still remained the vast wealth of the Church to tempt the plunderers, though the clerical estate had borne a full share of the earlier taxation and the Loan. Not only Henry, but the nobility also, had their eyes on this reservoir, the accumulation of nearly a thousand years of endowments and purchases. Indeed, the first hint of the plunder of the estate of the Church as distinct from straightforward taxation or forced loans comes from the nobility in 1529. In that year the French ambassador (Du Bellay) wrote home in cipher that 'these lords [the Duke of Suffolk is especially named] intend, after [Wolsey] is dead or ruined, to impeach the State of the Church and take all their goods; which it is hardly needful for me to write in cipher, for they proclaim it openly. I expect they will do fine miracles', he adds sardonically.[1]

For a time the Crown was content to exact further heavy sums from the Church under various pretexts. Thus in 1531 the clergy were called on to pay £118,800 in five annual instalments and many of the greater Churchmen were singled out for heavy 'fines' in addition; but already the Venetian Ambassador was reporting back that Henry seemed bent on annexing ecclesiastical revenues completely to the Crown.[2] Early in 1533 the King admitted as much to Chapuys, the Imperial Ambassador in England, and during the following year definite proposals to confiscate most of the episcopal wealth of the kingdom were completed.[3] Ostensibly this confiscation was to finance the next of Henry's wars, but Chapuys reported to the Emperor in November 1534 that total confiscation would be likely to raise a rebellion and it would be 'necessary, to stop the mouths of many people, to give the greater part of those goods to gentlemen and others'.

The predatory governing class of England were hovering in the background for the right moment: it was only two years before the Great Plunder began in earnest.

There is no record that such a bill concerning the bishops was ever introduced and Cromwell compromised for the time being on taking the first fruits of all benefices vacant after 1 January 1535 (the entire first year's income) and the annual tenth of all benefices. This entailed a completely new valuation of every piece of Church property from the greatest monastery down to the poorest chaplain and chantry — the so-called *Valor Ecclesiasticus* — replacing the assessment which had stood since 1291. Such a vast inquiry was an administrative triumph, even though (since the returns were called for within four months) the information is incomplete or sketchy for several counties. However, it

---

[1] *L.P.*, IV, pt iii, no. 6011, dated 17 October 1529.
[2] See Dietz, *English Government Finance 1485–1558*, pp. 110 *et seq.*, on which the following remarks are largely based.
[3] The archbishops and bishops were to become salaried officers (Canterbury at 2,000 marks a year, York £1,000 and all other bishops 1,000 marks).

was massive enough to furnish Henry and Cromwell (not to mention the modern historian) with most of the facts about the total wealth of the Church.[4]

So far as the monasteries were concerned, the *Valor* has been analysed thoroughly by the Russian scholar Alexander Savine in his *English Monasteries on the Eve of the Dissolution* but little or nothing has been said about the wealth of the bishops, deans and chapters, friaries and hospitals, and the remainder of the clerical estate. We are still left in considerable darkness about one-half of the wealth of the Church and its distribution.[5] Further research is needed on many aspects of the *Valor* but in the meantime it is possible to make some useful general observations.

Estimates have been made in the past that the Church owned a quarter to a third of the real property of the country on the eve of the Reformation, but since we do not know the total wealth of the country it remains impossible to verify such statements. The best we can do is to say that when the first of the forced loans was finally closed, the total raised was just over £260,000, of which the Church accounted for rather more than £56,000 − a little over one-fifth of the whole. Hall said the loan had taken 'one-tenth of every man's substance' (except that no one assessed at under £5 paid on this occasion) so that we may perhaps regard this estimate, for all the imperfections of Tudor assessments and arithmetic, as the best we are ever likely to achieve. Its worst feature is that it embraces both landed wealth and personal estate, but this is perhaps a relatively small point compared with the fact that the average of one-fifth for the country as a whole conceals very wide regional variations, certainly so far as ecclesiastical landownership was concerned. In some parts of England the Church owned a relatively small share of the landed and personal estate; in others, notably perhaps in the bishopric of Durham and the ancient monastic estates of eastern England, it dominated the whole countryside.

Two regional studies suggest that an estimate of 20 to 30 per cent is not far wrong if we take real property (excluding personal estate) alone. The work of Dr Swales on Norfolk shows that out of 1,527 manors in

[4] This return was published by the Record Commission in six volumes, 1810−14.
[5] For an important critical analysis of the accuracy of the *Valor* and to some extent of Savine's pioneer work, see Knowles, *The Religious Orders in England*, III, pp. 243−7. A sample of sixty-nine houses (Knowles, p. 312) suggests that the suppression commissioners were able to raise the *Valor* figures by 19.4 per cent; and in Cornwall the average difference for four houses between the *Valor* and a revaluation in 1540 was about 22 per cent (Rowse, *Tudor Cornwall*, p. 195).

that county, the Church in 1535 owned 306: almost exactly one-fifth. In the West Riding, a very different region in geography and social structure, Dr R. B. Smith shows that in 1535 the Church as a whole was taking 27.3 per cent of the temporal freehold income of the region. Though the basis of counting is different, and 'manor' can be a very elastic term, the final results are not far apart and tend to support the conclusion drawn from the Loan.[6]

The other cardinal fact, for what it is worth, is that according to the *Valor*, the total yearly income of the Church as a whole was £320,180 net (after making all allowable deductions). Professor David Knowles considers, however, that the *Valor*, taken by and large, underestimates the monastic income by certainly 15 per cent for the whole country, and by as much as 20 or even 40 per cent in some districts.[7] Thus he is inclined to raise Savine's figure of some £160,000 for the total gross income of monks, canons, nuns, and knights hospitallers to perhaps £200,000, allowing for Savine's omissions and the frequent under-valuations in the record. Whether we have to face similar undervaluations for other Church lands, especially among the greater churchmen, remains for detailed local research to produce an answer. Perhaps the total net income of the Church was nearer £400,000 a year, if we could know all the relevant facts.

EPISCOPAL AND CAPITULAR ESTATES

The estates of bishops, deans and chapters and their fate after the great attack began, have received very little attention and deserve a book to themselves.[8] The *Valor* revealed the immense possibilities for plunder here also. No wonder that in addition to the suppression of the lesser monasteries in 1536, there were further proposals in 1536—37 for the secularization of Church lands in general. Some sees at least were as rich as the wealthiest monasteries. Let us look at the diocese of Exeter, for example, which stretched from the Somerset border down to Land's End. Although when Henry VIII and his sickly son forced the aged

[6] Swales 'The redistribution of the monastic lands in Norfolk at the Dissolution' in *Norfolk Archaeology*, XXXIV, pt i, 43. Smith, *Land and Politics . . . The West Riding of Yorkshire 1530—1546*, p. 73.
[7] Knowles, op. cit., p. 245.
[8] The only detailed book on the earlier period is Hembry, *The Bishops of Bath and Wells 1540—1640*; and there is also Du Boulay, 'Archbishop Cranmer and the Canterbury temporalities' in *E.H.R*, LXVII, 19—36. For the later sixteenth century, there is Hill, *Economic Problems of the Church*, covering the Elizabethan period and after.

Bishop Veysey to alienate most of the episcopal endowments it was described as one of the richest sees in England, this was not strictly so. It was, with a net income of £1,566 14s 6½d, just about the average-sized estate for an English bishopric (see below). The bishop possessed in 1535 twenty-two manors, three boroughs, and fourteen 'well-furnished residences', mostly in Devon and Cornwall, but also some property in London and Middlesex, Sussex, Surrey and Hampshire. Less than one-tenth of his large income was 'spiritual' — the corn tithes of one rectory and the tithes of tin in Devon and Cornwall.

The total net income of the dean and chapter and various dignitaries of Exeter Cathedral came to another £1,726, but here the 'spiritual' income heavily predominated (tithes, glebe and advowsons). The bishop and the cathedral body of Exeter together enjoyed a net income from all sources of some £3,293 a year, nearly as much as Glastonbury, the richest abbey in England outside Westminster.[9] In this comprehensive sense, it is true, Exeter could be said to be one of the richest sees in England. Lincoln, including the dean and chapter, enjoyed £2,863 clear per annum; Bath and Wells £2,573; London £2,100. The Bishop of Bath and Wells possessed twenty-six manors, of which all but five were in Somerset; five boroughs and other properties; as well as the usual London residence necessary to all bishops for their frequent business visits to the capital. He had eight mansion houses, often dignified by the title of palace, as were many of Exeter's fourteen residences.

The 'counting of manors' can be very misleading, and the financial importance of other properties unwittingly overshadowed. Thus a few of the Bishop of Exeter's manors were worth less than £20 a year (say £2,000 to £2,400 today) but there were such fat plums as Paignton (nearly £200 a year), Bishop's Tawton (c. £158), and Crediton (c. £146). Pawton, his richest Cornish manor, was worth well over £100 a year in 1535. Similarly, among the dean and chapter's manors the range in income was from under £4 a year to c. £103. And of the so-called 'spiritual income' many rectorial tithes were worth more than many a manor and were far from spiritual in content. They represented solid commodities such as corn, hay, wool, fish, and a tenth of everything that grew or was dug in the parish. These tithes were often, if not usually, leased to neighbouring gentry, who fed their large households off the produce and sold the surpluses. Such tithes in kind were a

---

[9] The *Valor* gives Glastonbury some £3,642 net, according to Savine. Knowles gives £3,311 net, but considers a sum much nearer £4,000 would be likelier.

perfect hedge against the inflation that lay just ahead. In mineral-bearing areas, the tithes of tin, lead and coal were also of considerable value; and there might be mines owned outright which could be profitably leased. Thus when Wolsey held the bishopric of Durham among his many offices, he leased one coal mine at £180 a year; and the lead mines of Mendip in Somerset brought the Elizabethan Bishops of Bath and Wells, if not their predecessors, a tidy income.

Altogether the seventeen English bishops enjoyed a total net income of some £27,210 a year in 1535, distributed as shown in Table 6.1.

Table 6.1 Episcopal estates in 1535 (net annual income)

Over £3,000	(2) Winchester, Canterbury*	£7,109
£2,000–3,000	(3) Durham, Ely, York	£7,151
£1,000–2,000	(6) Exeter, Wells, Lincoln, Salisbury, Worcester, London	£8,911
Under £1,000	(6) Rochester, Carlisle, Lichfield, Norwich, Hereford, Chichester	£4,039
	Total episcopal income	£27,210

* The *Valor* figure for Canterbury is somewhat confusing. Du Boulay gives £3,005 18s 8¾d as the net income, but he quotes a document of 1546 stating that the revenues of the see then stood at £2,955 17s 9d and had been diminished since the 'exchanges' by £277 1s 0d. This gives an original total of £3,232 18s 9d; but another total in the *Valor* (I, 7) gives £3,223 [sic] 18s 9d. The arithmetic of the *Valor* often presents such minor difficulties; but in the above table, I have accepted the latter figure as the likeliest one.

The average episcopal estate was worth just about £1,600 net per annum, but once again an average figure is to a large degree meaningless. What is more to the point is that the richest see (Winchester £3,885) was worth nearly ten times the poorest (Rochester £411): there was a steep ladder of preferment even within the episcopal hierarchy before the commanding heights of Winchester or Canterbury, York or Durham were attained.

The four Welsh sees were all poorly endowed. Their total net income from all sources was only £919, of which St David's accounted for just about one-half; and the other three were worth less than Rochester between them. The endowments of the cathedral clergy were correspondingly small, and poverty was widespread among the parochial clergy.[10]

[10] *A.H.E.W.*, IV, 381–2.

THE MONASTIC ESTATES

By far the largest share of the total wealth of the Church was owned by the monastic houses: Savine calculated they took as much as 41.5 per cent of the total net income. Though he accounted for 553 houses in all, and the true total was about 650, excluding friaries and hospitals, his sample was so wide that his general conclusions can scarcely be disputed. But if we allow that in general monastic incomes were understated by 15 to 20 per cent, the monastic share rises to just about 50 per cent of the total wealth of the Church. I accept this figure in preference to any other.

We cannot translate monastic incomes from lands (temporal income) into acreages, nor even manors into acreages. There was no such thing as an average manor. What we do know is that three-quarters of monastic income came from temporal sources, and the remainder from 'spiritual' sources, such as tithes and advowsons. But the latter, despite the adjective, consisted of something 'real' which could be valued; great tithes above all could be the most valuable consideration in some parishes.

Taking Savine's figures as they stand, there are several observations to be made. Most notable, perhaps, was the gross inequality between the greater monasteries and the lesser. Westminster and Glastonbury may have enjoyed something like £4,000 a year (the *Valor* gives Westminster £3,912 and Glastonbury £3,642) and at the other extreme more than fifty houses struggled along on less than £20 a year. The gulf between the rich and the poor monasteries was far greater than among the bishops. Among the 553 houses for which Savine gives figures, the distribution of wealth is shown in Table 6.2.

Table 6.2 Net monastic income (temporal and spiritual)

Over £1,000 a year	24 houses
£300–1,000	89 houses
£100–300	199 houses
£20–100	188 houses
Under £20 a year	53 houses
Total	553 houses

The twenty-four richest monasteries took between them more than a quarter of the total income: 4 per cent of the houses enjoyed more than 25 per cent of the wealth. The richest houses were nearly all

Benedictine foundations of ancient origin, when endowments had been on a vast scale in an undeveloped and often scarcely colonized countryside. Monastic wealth was most important in Yorkshire, Middlesex, Somerset, Lincolnshire, Kent and Gloucestershire. Partly this was a matter of the sheer size of the county, and Middlesex was a special case. Its sixteen houses between them enjoyed rather more than £11,500 a year. They were naturally concentrated in London and a high proportion of their wealth (over one-third) came from urban property. For the country as a whole, urban income was only about one-eighth of the whole monastic income, and industrial income was much less. There was an almost entire absence of revenues from mineral wealth. This has led to the belief that the monastic houses were sitting passively on top of untold wealth for later and more commercially-minded owners to develop. To some extent this may be true, but we know from other sources that many houses in the coal-bearing districts like Tyneside, Furness and the Forest of Dean had been digging coal for generations and using it lavishly for their own needs. This valuable 'invisible' income naturally does not appear in the *Valor*.

Even so, the great bulk of monastic income came from purely rural sources. Of the temporal income, a tenth came from demesne lands kept in hand and nine-tenths from tenants of various kinds. The policy of monasteries towards their demesnes varied greatly. Some kept none in hand, but preferred to lease them, usually to neighbouring gentry. Thus Battle had twenty-two whole manors but kept only one demesne in hand for its own needs. And in nineteen of the twenty-one leased out, the demesne was leased as a whole to one person, almost invariably for a term of years, unlike the other tenancies. On the whole, though, the great bulk of rural revenue came from the rents of tenantry everywhere, a large proportion of whom were customary tenants. It was here that the greatest opportunities lay, when secular landlords moved in after the Dissolution, for the maximum development of resources. In so far as monastic tenants were not paying the full economic rents of their lands, the scene was set for what could be called in modern parlance a juicy takeover. But this proved by no means as easy to achieve as it sounds.

Not only were most monastic demesnes leased out as a whole to local gentry and occasionally to rich yeomen, but so too were the tithes. Appropriations of churches were an important part of monastic endowments. This could mean one of two things: either the appropriation of the advowson alone, giving the right to present to the living; or a more complete appropriation which included the tithes of the parish as well. Complete appropriation could take place in two stages centuries apart. Thus Bringhurst Church in Leicestershire was 'given' to Peterborough Abbey *c.* 700, but for centuries the monastery presented to the living and the incumbent (the rector) enjoyed all the tithes great and small. Not until 1496 were the rectorial or great tithes appropriated for the benefit of the monastery, which then proceeded to appoint a vicar instead of a rector, the vicar receiving the so-called small tithes. These were a small fraction of the total tithes of the parish, the balance going to the monastery or to the layman who leased them. The alienation of tithes to laymen preceded the Dissolution, which merely confirmed the process. Rectories farmed out to laymen had become fairly common by the early sixteenth century, so much so that they had virtually become assimilated to lay estates among the neighbouring gentry. With the Dissolution therefore it was usually not difficult for the local magnate to get his lease continued or even sold outright to him. England became a country of alienated tithes — alienated, that is, from the Church and their original purpose. By Elizabethan times the familiar picture had emerged of the more or less well-to-do local squire enjoying the great tithes as lay rector and the underpaid vicar performing the spiritual duties for a fraction of the squire's 'spiritual' income. To take but one example, from Leicestershire again, Sir William Faunt, squire of Foston, had acquired the rectory of Lowesby, once the property of the Hospital of Burton Lazars, and was drawing £130 a year from the great tithes while the vicar got £6 13s 4d yearly for doing all the work, out of which he had to pay tenths, subsidies and official fees. This was by no means an exceptional case.[11]

The monasteries had then to a large degree severed their personal connections with the parishes from which they drew their incomes, especially the larger houses whose estates could be scattered over several counties and often in the form of single manors or advowsons. This was unlike the lay estates which, among the gentry at least, tended to be concentrated in a comparatively small area even if not quite compact. The smaller monastic houses probably had a more personal connection with the local countryside; and sometimes even a wealthy house like Tavistock in south-west Devon had a large block of manors

---

[11] Hill, *Economic Problems of the Church*, pp. 151–2, quotes other glaring examples of such disparities between lay rectors and vicars. A great number of impropriations were granted to the bishops, and to universities and colleges, who were among the worst of the exploiters.

locally and maintained a closer relationship than most with its tenants. Certainly they were not regarded by the peasantry as absentee landlords with no soul, for in the Western Rebellion of 1549 one of the demands of the rebels was that the two largest monasteries at least should be brought back. In Devon this would have meant the resurrection of Tavistock and Plympton.

However, the fact remains that a considerable proportion of monastic demesnes and tithes had been leased out to laymen well before the 1530s; and prominent laymen also proliferated among the officials and administrators of the monasteries, some local magnate frequently being steward to several houses at once and drawing a not inconsiderable income from this source alone. Such an official acquaint-ance with the running of the local monastic estates over the years must have helped greatly when the Dissolution threw much of these lands and tithes into the open market: very like a local councillor or alder-man today sitting on the planning committee and knowing in advance where the best pickings were coming up in a few years' or months' time. In these matters the only true god is Mammon. The sixteenth century showed it abundantly in every decade. Catholic or Protestant, what did it matter when Mammon was sitting in the seat of power? Sir William Petre, who acquired an enormous estate in these decades, was more honest than most of his generation when he wrote in a letter to Cecil in 1551: 'We, which talk much of Christ and His Holy Word, have I fear me used a much contrary way; for we leave fishing for men and fish again in the tempestuous seas of this world for gain and wicked mammon.' To this the historian Pollard adds: 'The confession was unique, but the vice was universal.'[12]

THE ATTACK ON THE MONASTIC LANDS

The attack on the monastic lands began in earnest in 1536, when the lesser houses (those worth under £200 a year clear) were suppressed and their properties confiscated by the Crown. A number of these smaller houses paid over money to be left alone, but it made no differ-ence in the end. In all about 374 of the lesser monasteries went at the first blow, bringing in to the Crown some £32,000 a year, besides the value of the plate, jewels and lead from the crushed communities. The 'great and fat abbots' accepted the bill in Parliament, abandoning the smaller fry to their fate, possibly in the hope of escaping the same fate

[12] Pollard, *England under the Protector Somerset*, p. 315.

but more probably in simple fear of such a King. Yorkshire and Lincolnshire suffered most: ninety monastic houses disappeared in these two counties alone.

In 1539 came the suppression of the larger houses and all those that had previously been allowed to escape. The last to fall was Waltham Abbey in Essex on 23 March 1540. The treasures of Bury St Edmunds had already been looted early in 1538; other shrines followed, including those at Canterbury and Winchester. Cromwell's agent at both was Richard Pollard, a Devonshire man and a younger son of an old family, trained in the law. Like many other lawyers in the same *milieu*, he was able to found a new branch of an old family out of his subsequent favourable purchases of monastic lands. Pollard also did the dirty work at the most venerable of all the monasteries in England – Glastonbury in Somerset – and was finally able to report in November 1539 that the abbot had been strangled on the hill outside the town. The fall of the 186 greater monasteries (Spelman's figure) brought in another £100,000 a year or so to the Crown, though already some of the spoils of 1536 had been disposed of, and Henry therefore never enjoyed the whole of the monastic income at once.

A new ministry was set up in March 1536 to deal with this enormous accession of wealth to the Crown, known as the Court of Augmentations of the King's Revenue. It was part of Thomas Cromwell's administrative revolution in Tudor government and was modelled on the existing court of the Duchy of Lancaster. The principal officers were a chancellor (Sir Richard Rich, the man who had betrayed More a few months earlier), a treasurer (Sir Thomas Pope), an attorney and a solicitor. In addition there were seventeen particular receivers responsible for their own districts, ten auditors, and an army of local bailiffs and collectors. Out in the provinces commissioners were appointed in every county to survey the lands and goods of all the monasteries within their territory; but the bulk of the work was done in the Court of Augmentations itself in London, and the local gentry merely gave a semblance of participation to the proceedings.[13] Most, if not all, of the officers from the chancellor downwards emerged with considerable spoils for themselves. In a corrupt age, it would have taken a saint not to have seized the advantages of being at the centre of plunder.

Rich himself died in 1567, having acquired a peerage and no fewer

[13] For much of what follows, see Knowles, op. cit., esp. Ch. 32, and Dickens, *The English Reformation*, esp. Ch. 7. A useful recent summary is Woodward, *The Dissolution of the Monasteries*.

than fifty-nine manors, thirty-one rectories and twenty-eight vicarages. Of this vast estate, thirty-two manors had formerly been monastic. In point of fact, he had acquired forty-two ex-monastic manors but had sold off ten of them in rounding off his estate. Most of this had been paid for, some at specially favourable rates, and some had been freely granted. Altogether he paid out during his official life nearly £10,000 to the Crown, but he certainly used his official knowledge as Chancellor of the Court of Augmentations to piece together a huge and compact estate, and became the second largest landowner in Essex, next to the Earl of Oxford.[14]

Sir Thomas Pope, born the son of a small Oxfordshire landowner, and, like Rich, trained as a lawyer, died in 1559 leaving some thirty manors or so. Almost all had been monastic property, acquired by royal gift or by purchase. He was said to have made himself one of the richest commoners in England, and founded Trinity College at Oxford in 1555 on the site of Durham College which he had acquired. His post as Treasurer of the Court of Augmentations (he held it until 1541) carried a handsome salary of £120 a year plus large fees and the usual opportunities for skilful acquisitions from the lands of several monasteries: but with no children from his three marriages he left much to churches, charities, prisons and hospitals. All the same, his collateral descendants were still enjoying much of his monastic spoils centuries later.

The Cavendish fortunes (now Dukes of Devonshire) were founded by one William Cavendish, the second son of a Suffolk squire, who became one of the commissioners for taking the surrender of religious houses and thence graduated to the central office as an auditor. His first acquisition of monastic property came in 1540 when he received a grant of three Hertfordshire manors. Then followed many other profitable purchases and exchanges, especially during the time of Edward VI. Like many of his kind, he conformed suitably under Mary. Altogether it would be surprising to find a single officer of the Court of Augmentation who did not warmly feather his own nest; but it is time now to look at the wider scene, of what happened outside these official circles, and at more general questions. Did the Dissolution create a whole class of 'new rich', hard-faced men who treated their acquisitions as commercial investments? How far did the old families, already well rooted

---

[14] These details about Rich and his property are taken with grateful acknowledgement to the author, from M. E. Coyle's unpublished thesis on Rich (Harvard, 1965). Rich also acquired episcopal properties from the see of London in 1550.

in ancestral counties, take part in the Great Plunder? Which class ultimately gained most from this enormous transference of lands — the nobility, the old gentry, the new official class, the rising yeomen? How did the Crown revenues fare in the end?

To complete the legislative picture first, an Act of 1545 gave Henry the power to suppress colleges, hospitals, free chapels and chantries. Spelman reckons that 90 colleges, 110 religious hospitals, and 2,374 chantries and free chapels thus fell into the clutches of the Crown. A few chantries were suppressed before Henry's death in 1547, when the Act lapsed; but Parliament renewed the statute for Edward VI and the great majority of chantries and chapels suffered during his reign. The bishops, deans and chapters were dealt with usually on an *ad hoc* basis. The properties of the see of Norwich were seized by Act of Parliament in 1536 (see below) but in the main the rest were robbed by royal demands for 'exchanges of lands' as and when the King was moved. One species of confiscation usually escapes mention — the suppression of the Irish monasteries, said to have been about 700 in all, by the Act of 33 Henry VIII (1542). And beyond all the lands, and other temporal and spiritual properties of the monasteries everywhere, there was 'a magazine of treasure raised out of the money, plate, jewels, ornaments, and implements of churches, monasteries, and houses' (Spelman), from the richest abbey down to the poorest country church, if it had anything in the way of plate worth grabbing. Many churches took defensive measures and spirited away their special treasures.

But the major impact of the Dissolution was the transference of monastic lands and spiritual possession to the Crown and their subsequent disposal to a select minority of eager subjects. Here a few legends have already been cleared away and there is little need to dwell on them again. Although some of the gifts to grandees like Russell, Rich, the Dukes of Norfolk and Suffolk, Paget and others were on a spectacular scale, they were the lucky few. Only about 2.5 per cent of the spoil was given away; the rest was sold at full market prices after a new valuation and calculated at twenty years' purchase. Moreover the Crown reserved an annual rent even on the 'gifts', equal to one-tenth of the income on all property over 100 marks value granted before 1543. Thus John, Lord Russell, who received an enormous grant of Tavistock Abbey lands in south-west Devon, was eventually saddled with a fixed rent charge, after some recalculation, of £284 5s a year in perpetuity.[15] Still, this charge diminished rapidly in real terms with long-term inflation and was

[15] Finberg, *Tavistock Abbey*, 1951, pp. 269–70.

a mere pinprick in the late nineteenth century when the 22,607 acres of their Devon estate were bringing in nearly £46,000 a year in rents. The Russells could afford to soldier on through such a temporary difficulty. *Che sara sara* was their appropriate family motto.

More serious was the Crown's insistence on making all grants subject to the feudal tenure of knight-service, with its dreadful possibility of prerogative wardship if the inheritance passed at any time to a minor. Wardship meant that the Crown took over the estates — and not only the ex-monastic estates but the entire family estates not hitherto subject to this onerous tenure — and retained them and their income until the heir was married off to a suitable heiress or came of age. The heir's or heiress's marriage was put up for sale in a highly competitive market. Wardship itself was in the hands of a special court, and there were endless opportunities for corruption and plunder here also. As early as 1535 the Venetian ambassador had said, 'England has very bad laws and statutes', citing especially the law relating to wardship. The King was said to distribute wardship lands at pleasure, 'which causes a thousand abuses and improprieties'. Another ambassador, in 1551, said that 'the Wards, on coming of age, find their houses in decay, their woods felled, and their estates despoiled, precisely as if they had been ravaged by an enemy'.[16]

Whatever Henry's or Cromwell's original intentions had been on acquiring the vast addition to the Crown revenues by the confiscation of the monastic lands, the constant need for money, above all in wartime, ensured that sales began almost at once. Nevertheless much of the land was kept out of the market and let on leases for the time being. Rents reached their peak, as receipts in the Court of Augmentations, in 1542; but then the demands of the wars with France and Scotland called for quicker returns and the early 1540s saw a massive unloading on to the market, reaching a peak in 1544—45. Initially, the Dissolution had more than doubled the income of the Crown, but by 1547 more than two-thirds of the monastic lands had been alienated. Out of 1,593

[16] *Cal. S. P. Ven.*, IV, 26 (1535) and V, 356 (1551). For the later period see Hurstfield *The Queen's Wards*, 1958, Chs. 10—15. Contemporaries regarded the Court as a corrupt institution and its Master (Lord Burghley) as a corrupt man. He was Master for nearly forty years, and was succeeded by his son Robert Cecil. The Cecils plundered England well, from monastic lands to the Court of Wards, and achieved two earldoms by 1605 (Exeter and Salisbury). Even in his own lifetime, William Cecil was accused by Spenser of building his palace at Burghley out of the proceeds of official plunder: 'But his owne treasure he increased more/and lifted up his loftie towres thereby.' (Quoted by John Buxton, *Elizabethan Taste*, 1963, p. 58.)

grants of ex-monastic lands in Henry's reign, only 41 were gifts and
another 28 were combinations of gifts with sales or exchanges. The
remainder, some 97.5 per cent, was sold, nearly always at twenty years'
purchase and after a fresh valuation.

Who were the buyers, or rather the final recipients? A number of
detailed local studies points to the answer. Thus in Devon, the mass of
monastic lands passed to moderate-sized local families, mainly well-
rooted in the county, and not to the 'New Rich'. Here, as elsewhere,
the Dissolution did not create 'a new class of profiteer-merchant-
landlords'. Less than 10 per cent went to people outside Devon, and of
this small proportion a great part was represented by the personal grant
to Russell. A few Tudor officials like George Rolle make their appearance on the Devon scene, but the more typical figures were local squires
like the Arscotts and Fulfords rounding off their existing estates with
a convenient monastic manor, or else younger sons with official connections building up new but moderate estates.[17]

Groups of London speculators bought for re-sale, breaking up what
were often job lots of lands scattered about the country so as to find
the right purchasers. There is not much evidence to indicate the rise of
'a novel type of landlord emancipated from the decent usages of rural
society'.

The picture from Lincolnshire is much the same as in Devon, and a
recent study for Norfolk shows once again that though the nobility
gained to some extent, mainly as a result of grants to a few great
families (above all the Duke of Norfolk), it was the gentry, old and
new, who gained by far the most land. The new men were lawyers,
government officials and merchants, and some of these, as in Devon,
were younger sons of old families who had been trained in the law in
default of inheriting the parental estate. Of the £3,000 or so (in annual
income) going to ranks below the nobility, about £1,143 went to the
old gentry, and about £1,090 to the new — roughly half-and-half in this
county, which attracted Londoners more than did distant Devon. Even
so, the figure of £480 for London merchants is largely accounted for by
Sir Thomas Gresham's purchases to the value of £420 a year. The
merchants of Norwich and Lynn took only about £130-worth. This,
too, is rather like Devon: here the bigger merchants of the cloth town
of Totnes showed some interest in monastic lands, but those of the

[17] Youings, ed., *Devon Monastic Lands*, Introduction, esp. pp. xx–xxv. Rowse,
Tudor Cornwall, Ch. IX presents a very similar picture for Cornwall to that in
Devon.

richer city of Exeter showed little, except in picking up urban property
in the city itself.

The final result of the Great Plunder in Norfolk has been well
summarized by Dr Swales[18] in figures based on the counting of manors
(Table 6.3):

Table 6.3 The Great Plunder in Norfolk

Date	Crown	Nobles	Gentry	Church	Monasteries	Others	Total
1535	41.5	143.5	977	43	263	59	1,527
1545	126.5	188	1,093.5	86	–	33	1,527
1555	73.5	174.5	1,151	100	–	28	1,527
1565	67	158.5	1,180.5	91	–	30	1,527

The full rise and fall of the Crown estates is concealed by the fact
that we have no total for the year 1539 or 1540, when they would have
reached their peak. But twenty years after the beginning of the plunder,
the Crown could show a net gain of only thirty-two manors; the
nobility only thirty-one; the Church a gain of fifty-seven.[19] The gentry,
old and new, showed a gain of no fewer than 174 manors. Of the 263
monastic manors, almost exactly two-thirds had passed to the Norfolk
gentry by 1555. As in Devon and Cornwall, it was the moderate-sized
old estates that showed the most general increase. The yeomen, even
the rich and rising families, do not figure at all in these changes for they
bought, if at all, only small parcels – farms rather than whole manors.
Though this was locally important, for the agrarian problem in general
their purchases do not alter the main picture of the Great Plunder.
Many such families were 'rising' from the fifteenth century onwards,
but their social progress was necessarily slow and rarely spectacular.[20]

In Yorkshire too, the disposal of monastic lands followed pretty
much the same pattern. Apart from a very few spectacular examples,
such as Sir Richard Gresham and Fountains, the local gentry were the
main beneficiaries. 'By the end of the sixteenth century most of the
landed property of the Yorkshire monasteries was in the possession of

[18] Swales, 'The redistribution of monastic lands in Norfolk', *Norfolk Archaeology*,
XXXIV, pt i, 1966, 14–44.
[19] Ibid., p. 43. The net gain of the Church was due to the grant of some manors to
the see of Norwich, to the dean and chapter of Ely taking over the Norfolk
manors of the former abbey, and to the endowment of the new cathedral at
Oxford with some ex-monastic manors.
[20] See for example Hoskins, *Essays in Leicestershire History*, pp. 150–9. The
yeomen had to wait two or three generations before ex-monastic lands came their
way to any noticeable extent.

the country gentry ... over one-quarter of the gentle families of 1642 (182 out of 679) owned property which had been seized from the monasteries.'[21] In York itself Gresham engaged in one spectacular trans-action which is worthy of notice. He purchased in 1545 much of the widespread monastic property in the city, a purchase which included no fewer than 464 messuages, tenements, and cottages. It is reckoned that at least a quarter of York's housing changed hands at the Dissolution. The corporation showed no interest in acquiring any of this property, since it was still recovering from its near-bankruptcy in the 1530s. Gresham's 'empire' was sold off piecemeal within a few years of his death, probably to local worthies of the city.[22] It would be interesting to know what happened to house rents afterwards; but we know indeed too little about this anywhere, either in town or country. At Coventry, too, a great deal of the house property had belonged to monastic houses in the city: what happened to that?

Yet we must not forget that all the regions which have been studied in detail are (except Leicestershire) more or less peripheral — Devon and Cornwall, Norfolk, Lincolnshire and Yorkshire — and studies of south-eastern England, within the London influence, might show a much greater influx of new men with more highly developed instincts for the quick returns at any human cost. We do not know.

THE ATTACK ON THE EPISCOPAL ESTATES

The *Valor* had revealed that the seventeen pre-Reformation bishops between them enjoyed rather more than £27,000 a year clear: another tempting target. The first blow seems to have been that aimed at the see of Norwich, one of the less opulent. But the convenient moment came when the aged bishop, Richard Nix, resigned or died late in 1535. An Act dated 27 Henry VIII recited that the see was then void and took all its possessions, temporal and spiritual, into the King's hands. The incoming bishop, William Repps, was the usual pliant tool of the Crown and agreed to take in exchange certain ex-monastic properties, chiefly those of his old monastery (he had been the last abbot) of St Benet's. The King took possession of the important manors of Lynn and Gaywood, thirteen other Norfolk manors, five manors in Suffolk, and two in Essex — twenty-two manors in all. Shortly afterwards the flourishing port of Bishop's Lynn changed its name to King's Lynn,

---

[21] Cliffe, *The Yorkshire Gentry*, pp. 15–16.
[22] Palliser, *The Reformation in York*.

which it bears today. Moreover, the King reserved an annual rent of £33 6s 8d out of the lands handed over to the new bishop. Altogether he had made his usual good bargain. Apart from the reserved rent, Henry had acquired property with a net annual income of about £920 and had given up property worth just under £752. In Norfolk alone he had lost on the deal, but the rich Suffolk and Essex manors more than made up for this.[23] 'Exchanges' under Henry VIII and Edward VI was generally a euphemism for a nice profit by the Crown. According to Sir Henry Spelman, one of the neat dodges was 'giving them [the bishops] racked lands and small things for goodly manors and lordships, and also impropriations for their solid patrimony in finable lands'.

Sir Richard Gresham, lord mayor of London in 1537 and father of the great Sir Thomas, evidently tried to buy some or all of the confiscated Norfolk manors. Like so many successful great London merchants he was descended from an ancient family of gentry in the provinces (Gresham in Norfolk, later settled at Holt) and felt impelled to establish a landed estate in his native county. But, as he wrote to Cromwell, 'the King will not part with any of his lands in Norfolk' and had promised him instead the abbey and certain lands at Fountains, in Yorkshire, though at the full market price of £7,000.[24] Nevertheless, others got what Gresham had been refused: Cromwell got two rich episcopal manors for himself, and William Butts, the King's physician and a Norfolk man, obtained two others of the former bishop's manors. In 1550, however, Edward VI made some redress for his father's expropriation and granted lands worth over £300 to the then bishop.[25]

The attack on the episcopal lands in general was thinly disguised at first by 'exchanges' for ex-monastic property; but the attack on the wealth of the see of Canterbury, which also began in 1536, was further disguised or obscured by preliminary leases, mostly to predatory courtiers and officers of the newly formed Court of Augmentations already skilled in manipulating monastic property in their own interests. The next step followed quickly: a demand from the King that the lands so leased be exchanged for some ex-monastic property. The King then handed over the lands to some officer like Sir Edward North, treasurer of the Court of Augmentations (later promoted chancellor)

[23] Swales, loc. cit., pp. 16–17.
[24] *L.P. Addenda*, no. 1366, letter dated 1538. For the Fountains deal, see also *T.E.D.*, I, 18. The £7,000 of that date would represent about £750,000 today and was one of the largest purchases of the time.
[25] Swales, loc. cit., p. 17.

who promptly resold at a high profit to another predator. It was a shameless land-racket in which, as Cranmer wrote in 1546, it was not even the King who gained but the people who surrounded him.[26]

Cranmer (like Veysey of Exeter whose case we shall examine shortly) has been blamed for acceding to the King's rapacious demands — Otford and Knole, said to be kinder to the royal rheumatism, were notable among them — but in later years Morice, the Archbishop's secretary, defended his master by saying 'men ought to consider with whom he had to do, specially with such a prince as would not be bridled, nor be against-said in any of his requests'. Both Morice and Cranmer were aware that any opposition to the royal will might leave the see of Canterbury totally stripped of its possessions.

The first transaction between the King and the Archbishop took place in 1536 when Cranmer gave up Wimbledon and Mortlake, and shortly afterwards Burstow, all in Surrey, for some monastic property near Dover; and before the end of the year these three manors were in the hands of Thomas Cromwell. Wimbledon was a particularly rich prize, worth in all some £117 a year clear. Cromwell had been born in Wimbledon and had often been taunted by the nobility with his 'base birth': the acquisition of this ample manor must have been peculiarly gratifying to his mind as well as to his pocket.

In the ten years between 1536 and 1546 Cranmer handed over to the King enough for the estates of 1535 to be called 'decimated' by a modern historian, receiving in return a considerable complex of ex-monastic property, mainly in east and south-east Kent. Eventually he had acquired half a dozen monasteries between Canterbury and Dover; but little coherent plan can be detected in the whole complicated mass of exchanges. The financial result after ten years was that the see was worse off by about £277 a year. In 1552 Cranmer complained to Cecil that 'I have more care to live now as an archbishop than I had ... to live like a scholar', and the decline continued long after his death.

The Bishop of Bath and Wells came under attack from 1539[27] onwards, though as early as December 1535 he foresaw the shape of things to come and granted Cromwell an annuity of £20 secured on the manor of Pucklechurch as a sweetener. There were other such propitiations (mostly presentations of livings to laymen in high places) and

---

[26] Du Boulay, loc. cit.
[27] Hembry, *The Bishops of Bath and Wells*, gives a full account of the attack on the estates of Bath and Wells. The following paragraphs are based entirely on this work, but the complete story cannot be dealt with here.

servile letters from the bishop, all to no avail. Dr William Petre, Cromwell's agent, collected an annuity of 40s a year from the dean and chapter, but proceeded promptly to investigate the wealth of the cathedral body, as distinct from the bishop, and to confiscate jewels and plate for the King's use. The list of 'confiscations' is long and follows the familiar pattern. In the summer of 1539 the bishop's London mansion was handed over to William Fitzwilliam, Earl of Southampton; in the autumn the rich Hampshire manor of Dogmersfield, with its palace useful as a halfway house between Wells and London, also passed to the Court of Augmentations and by 1547 was granted to Thomas Wriothesley, the new Earl of Southampton.

But the Protector Somerset was the greatest predator of the estates of Bath and Wells. He had already acquired many of the manors of the Somerset monasteries of Glastonbury (richest in England outside Westminster) and of Muchelney and Athelney. He was evidently trying to build up a vast territorial power in western England, and in due course he got the episcopal manors of Cheddar and Compton Bishop. Later in 1548 he took Wells itself, six other manors, and other properties. Finally he got hold of the manor of Wookey, next door to Cheddar. The bishop was compensated to some degree with certain rectories that had formerly belonged to monastic houses; but after all the political changes and personal vicissitudes of fortune of the next few years most of the old episcopal lands had been lost for ever. After a great deal of chopping and changing the bishop had lost some 55 per cent of his gross income from land between 1539 and 1560, and was left with a mere £975 a year out of which he had to meet the salaries of his principal officers and the expenses of administration.[28]

The see of Exeter suffered much greater devastation in a shorter time. Bishop Veysey had been appointed back in 1519 but he had long neglected his duties, preferring to live in great state at his mansion at Sutton Coldfield in the Midlands, built by him in 1527, probably out of the revenues of his rich western see. He was attacked in 1550 by Latimer, in one of the sermons preached before Edward VI, for continuous non-residence and neglect of duty, and was eventually deprived by the King in the following year. One need waste no sympathy on him: he was allowed a pension for life of £485 9s 3d, but to attain this he had handed over more than two-thirds of the endowments of his see, which by 1551 had become one of the poorest in England. It is true that he had no more choice than any other bishop in resisting the

[28] Ibid., p. 134.

imperious demands of the Crown, and that he was by then an old man; but in his prime he had been a time-server of the worst sort. The Catholic historian of the see rightly says that 'our obsequious prelate went all the lengths of Henry VIII, in the affair of the divorce of Queen Katherine, of the supremacy, and the Dissolution of the monasteries' — but was he any worse in these matters than the Archbishop himself?

When Veysey had come to Exeter he came into possession of twenty-two manors and fourteen 'well-furnished residences'. When he resigned thirty-two years later he left nothing but the palace at Exeter and three manors, and even these were leased out. Henry VIII had made a mild (for him) attack on the lands of the see, when he forced Veysey to make over to Sir Thomas Dennis, chancellor of Anne of Cleves, sheriff of Devon and recorder of Exeter, the episcopal park of Crediton, together with other smaller properties. This was in 1542. The massive attack came under Edward VI, when in 1548 Veysey was required to hand over his London residence and the enormous and rich manor of Crediton, together with the neighbouring manor of Morchard Bishop. These two manors went to Sir Thomas Darcy, reserving an annual rent to the bishop of £40 a year. As the two manors were worth round about £165 clear between them, this was a nice picking. It is needless to trace the handing over of one manor after another between 1548 and 1551, except to say that the great predators got the richest pickings: Paignton, richest of all, some 10,000 acres of fertile land between Torbay and the Dart and worth just under £200 a year clear, came first to Sir Thomas Speke but within a short time was in the hands of William Herbert, Earl of Pembroke and brother-in-law of the new King.

In 1550 the great manor of Bishop's Tawton and the smaller one of Bishop's Clyst were handed over to John, Lord Russell, together with the advowson of the former manor which had belonged to the dean and chapter. The manor and borough of Chudleigh, with the palace, went to Thomas Brydges, esquire, the King's servant; and the manor and borough of Ashburton to Francis Pole, esquire. Sir Andrew Dudley, gentleman of the Privy Chamber, a younger son of the Edmund Dudley who had been beheaded in 1510 (one of Henry's first acts of state) acquired not only the bishop's richest manor in Cornwall (Pawton) but the manors and advowsons of Bishop's Teignton, Lindridge, Radway, and West Teignmouth in Devon also.

When Miles Coverdale took over as bishop in August 1551 he faced the burden of first fruits and tenths based on the old valuation of 1535, and should have paid to the Crown nearly £157 for tenths.

But the revenues are now much diminished by grants of land in fee simple made by John [Veysey] at the King's request and the revenues remaining do not now exceed £500 yearly, so the King exonerates the said bishop from his payment due for first fruits and tenths and wills that the said bishopric shall henceforth be taxed upon £500 yearly.[29]

Other bishoprics suffered severely: Lincoln was reduced from a net income of £1,963 to £828 under Edward VI. In 1550 the newly founded bishopric of Westminster, replacing the abbey, was dissolved and united to the see of London, which then had to sacrifice various manors to the Crown. In 1551 John Ponet, translated from the poorest to the richest see of all (Winchester, worth £3,885 clear in 1535) alienated the whole endowment of the see to the Crown for a fixed stipend of 2,000 marks; in 1552 the see of Gloucester was dissolved, united to Worcester, and its lands annexed to the Crown. Out of all this the Crown profited little: most of the lands and advowsons went pretty quickly to those in and around the court. The most ambitious scheme of all, initiated by the Duke of Northumberland for the division of the too-extensive see of Durham, ultimately failed. Ecclesiastically it was a sensible division but there was inevitably plunder at the back of it; the vast estates of the prince-bishop were to be divided between the King and Northumberland. A bill to this effect passed Parliament in 1553, but the death of the wretched King and the accession of Mary caused it to be stillborn.

The greater part of the pillage of the episcopal estates took place under Edward VI but the see of York was an exception.[30] Here the attack began in 1542 when Archbishop Lee handed over four manors in exchange for some ex-monastic lands and advowsons; and his successor Holgate handed over no fewer than sixty-seven manors in all from 1545 onwards. There were the usual complicated exchanges, the Archbishop getting in return thirty-three impropriations and advowsons (all ex-monastic property).

After this Great Plunder the reign of Edward VI was quiet as far as York was concerned; and under Mary there was a considerable restitution of manors to the see. By that date it was reckoned that York lands still in the hands of the Crown amounted to more than £1,200 a year clear. Even after Mary's restitutions, many manors remained lost to the see for ever. It is almost impossible to calculate the net financial loss to

[29] See *Patent Rolls, Edward VI, passim*, for the details of these and other transactions involving the see of Exeter.
[30] For York, see Claire Cross, 'The economic problems of the see of York', in Thirsk, ed., *Land, Church and People*, pp. 64–83.

the see of York (though Miss Cross makes a valiant attempt to do so) as Tudor accounting and arithmetic are at times bewildering. All one can say is that whereas the see had been valued at £2,195 clear in 1535, Archbishop Grindal (1570–76) in Elizabethan times declared that taking one year with another his clear annual income was only about £1,300. By the end of the century there had been some apparent recovery: in 1597 the total temporal income of the see was some £60 more than it had been in 1535,[31] but this makes no allowance for the more than threefold inflation in these sixty years. Even with Mary's restitutions, then, the see of York had lost heavily as a result of Henry VIII's savage attack in the late 1540s. Nor can we say who were the gainers by the whole complicated series of transactions, for the confiscated manors seem to have passed through so many hands in a short space of time. Thus Southwell in Nottinghamshire was annexed by Henry VIII, and granted by his son in 1550 to the Earl of Warwick, later Duke of Northumberland. In 1551 the latter had sold it to John Beaumont, the infamous Master of the Rolls who in May 1552 forfeited all his lands and goods to the Crown for gross corruption and other causes while in office. Within a few months Edward VI had regranted the manor to Sir Henry Sidney but he, in the autumn of 1553, was compelled to surrender it back to Mary, who four years later handed it back to the see of York.

It is abundantly clear that many if not most of the English sees lost heavily as a result of this plunder by Henry and Edward. Without the most elaborate analysis it is impossible to say with any degree of precision who were the ultimate gainers, but contemporary and later opinion seems to be agreed that most of the plunder finished up in the hands of the courtiers and their friends, above all in those of the junta who ruled the country under Edward VI. As we have seen, the biggest plums of the see of Exeter went to Russells and Dudleys and Herberts, and to lesser men in and around the Court. Seymour (Somerset) gained heavily from the see of Bath and Wells and from the see of Lincoln, whose rich Oxfordshire manors (Thame, Dorchester, Banbury and other lands) passed to him in 1548. The Pagets had their share of both Exeter and Lichfield; the Darcys took episcopal lands from London and Exeter; the Paulets did well out of Winchester when the incoming Bishop Ponet — 'who is more of an astrologer than a theologian', wrote the Spanish ambassador from England — took a fixed stipend from the

[31] Ibid., p. 83.

Crown some £2,550 a year less than the old revenues. The Spanish ambassador wrote in 1551 that the King had taken over all the temporalities of the see and 'the castles and lands have already been distributed among some of the Lords of the Council'. Cromwell too had profited greatly out of Canterbury while he lasted. Unlike the monastic lands, most of the confiscated episcopal estates were given away under Edward VI. Jordan calculates that one hundred manors were taken, of which only five were sold, the rest given away by the boy-King. The total value of these manors was put at £54,760 17s 0d,[32] which at twenty years' purchase represents some £2,700 a year. Clearly this cannot be the full story as Exeter alone had lost £1,067 a year, Lincoln well over £1,100, Bath and Wells some £900, to name only three.

They were nearly all the 'new men', these massive plunderers, and some of them did not live long enough to found great families and estates. They lost their heads and their lands in the political confusion of these decades (1540—58) but there was always another vulture waiting to snap up the pieces. Even so, many a noble landowner of the eighteenth and nineteenth centuries owed his opulence to an ancestor of these years who, like Paulet and Petre, bent before the storms, from whatever quarter they blew, like pliant willows. Their roots shook now and then, but they kept their heads.

It is hard to estimate the total permanent loss to the pre-Reformation sees. A detailed document, drawn up apparently in 1552 after the worst of the plundering was over, put the wealth of all the English and Welsh bishoprics at some £30,325 a year,[33] but the figures are useless as a guide to the wealth of the bishoprics at that date. For the pre-Reformation sees they merely repeat, with minute variations if any, the old *Valor* incomes, though by this date many of them had been more or less seriously denuded. It is indeed difficult to see the purpose of this document beyond the fact that it includes the six new sees created between 1540 and 1545 out of ex-monastic revenues. These were Westminster (1540, suppressed and merged with London ten years later); and Peterborough, Gloucester, Bristol, Chester and Oxford.[34] Most of these had been monastic houses and the changeover necessarily involved extensive boundary changes in the older dioceses.[35] Some

[32] Jordan, *Edward VI: the Young King*, p. 119.
[33] Jordan, *Edward VI: The Threshold of Power*, p. 377.
[34] The new see of Oseney (1541) was transferred to Oxford in 1545.
[35] A useful map of the old dioceses and the new, showing the boundary changes, is to be found at the end of Gairdner, *The English Church in the Sixteenth Century*, 1902.

monastic wealth was therefore carried over and injected into episcopal estates; but the new sees were in fact endowed with a miserably small fraction of the old wealth as part of the policy of cutting down all bishops to size. Thus Peterborough Abbey had enjoyed a net income of some £1,979 but the new bishop's income was £411 (it had started by being about £333 in 1541). Westminster's £3,912 was reduced to £573; and Gloucester's £1,745 became £315. Some of the difference is accounted for by the endowments of the new deans and chapters, but if Peterborough is anything to go by these too were fiercely reduced. The total stipends of the dean and chapter seem to have been round about £310 a year in 1541, so altogether the new see was founded on the cheap: about a third of the old monastic revenues went to the new see.[36] Most of the wealth of these old monasteries disappeared after all into the royal exchequer, temporarily at least, and the creation of six new sees was by no means such a generous gesture as it appeared at first sight.

The bishops lost heavily in both status and income in the generation after 1535. They had once been, most of them, feudal potentates and powerful landowners. By Elizabethan days they had become mere hangers-on of the Court, scarcely better than civil servants; and in their social origins too they were 'new men' often with no particular family connections.[37] Yet they still retained in one way and another enough wealth to make them a special target for spoliation by Elizabeth, as the monasteries had been for her monstrous father.

What was the net effect of the plunder of the Church after the initial years of turmoil, of multifarious sales and exchanges? Spelman, in his *History of Sacrilege*, written in 1632, sought to demonstrate that most of those who had acquired monastic property came to a bad end in one way or another. About the year 1615 or 1616 he described with a pair of compasses a circle of twelve-mile radius round Rougham in Norfolk. This enclosed the mansion houses of twenty-four families of gentlemen and the sites of as many monasteries. All had been standing together at the time of the Dissolution; but whereas the former continued in the same old families, the latter 'had flung out their owners with their names and families (all of them save two) thrice at least, and some of them four or five or six times, not only by fail of issue, or ordinary sale, but very often by grievous accidents and misfortunes'. Elsewhere he

[36] Mellows, 'The foundation of Peterborough Cathedral', *Northants Record Soc.*, XIII, xx—xxi.
[37] Hill, *Economic Problems of the Church*, esp. Chs. 1—3.

found much the same story. Waverley Abbey in Surrey began its secular history in the hands of the Earl of Southampton in 1537. In the following 225 years (the story is brought up to date by a later editor) it had nineteen owners, or eight different families, an average tenure per family of less than thirty years. The rich abbey of Chertsey in Surrey also, not sold by the Crown until 1610, ended up by being sold to a stockbroker in 1809, who pulled it down. In these two hundred years there were fourteen owners and nine families, an average tenure of twenty-one and a half years. Merton priory passed through no fewer than eighteen families in two hundred years. These statistics, some of them Spelman's own and some those of later editors of his work, are striking to the historian, not so much as a demonstration of the fate of sacrilege but as showing the remarkable mobility of the land market at this high level.

On the other hand, the 1895 edition of Spelman reveals that of the 570 peers who composed the aristocracy at that date, about 470 'are more or less implicated in Sacrilege', that is, they retained some parts of former Church lands in their estates. It is difficult to strike a balance between these conflicting views when one thinks of the great estates and families surviving in the latter part of the nineteenth century whose fortunes had been well and truly laid in the two or three decades after the Dissolution. Think, for example, of the Russells, the Howards, the Cecils, the Cavendishes, the Petres, the Thynnes and the Pagets. Their estates had been in most cases vastly enlarged since that date by judicious marriages, but they still held the solid core their ancestors had acquired, by fair means and foul, at the Great Plunder. And despite the statistics of mobility among moderate-sized estates, those of the gentry, few counties in Victorian days could not show a tidy number of old gentry who still possessed the manors acquired between 1536 and 1600. The Great Plunder had a permanent effect on the pattern of land-ownership in England, but much further research requires to be done before we can make other generalizations.

What is certain is that the gentry were the greatest gainers from the transfer. Even the so-called 'new gentry' were not, as we have seen, always non-gentry in social origins. Many were younger sons who had been trained in the law in default of any inheritance at home. They were of 'good family', though perhaps our criterion should be that they were not strictly 'gentry' until they had acquired an independent landed estate. The point is important because such men tended to acquire their lands in their native county: to rejoin, as it were, the ancestral society from which they sprang. To this extent they were more than likely to conform to the social and economic usages of their fathers' class. The example of Sir John Gostwick in Bedfordshire has been cited as an example of a good conservative landlord. He was already the owner of a manor bought from the Duke of Norfolk in 1529 and became eventually one of Thomas Cromwell's most trusted assistants. He left behind a book of advice for his heir (written *c.* 1540) urging him to treat tenants fairly, not to enchance their entry fines or to raise their rents unless he saw them making undue profits by sub-leasing.[38] To have credit in the county, to be known as a good landlord with a satisfied tenantry, was far more important to many gentry than screwing the ultimate penny from the estate. Even a new gentleman without this kind of start might well feel his way cautiously when he entered on his estate, anxious to stand well in the social class he was seeking to enter.

We cannot be sure how many such good landlords there were, or how many there were who sought to extract the utmost farthing as soon as they could. Legal records are plentiful which show bitter disputes between landlords and tenants on hundreds of manors, but legal records are the pathology of society, a symptom of its breakdown; whereas the good landlord (who rarely put his practice down in writing as Sir John Gostwick did) has left few documents to make the other side of the case. Probably the Great Plunder brought little change to the great mass of English people, like that other great act of plunder, the Norman Conquest. The mass of toiling peasants went on tilling their fields and tending their stock without interruption. It was a matter of pure chance whether the new Norman was a better or a worse landlord than the old Saxon. The state of the harvest was a much more vital concern. So it was, too, in the mid-sixteenth century. There had been harsh monastic landlords (or so the tenantry thought) as well as easygoing; and the local squire who took over in most cases anywhere in England was not likely suddenly to become more voracious: not until the coming age of inflation forced even the most conservative landowner to look more carefully into ancestral and inherited practices.

[38] Dickens, 'Estate and household management in Bedfordshire, *c.* 1540', *Beds. Hist. Record Soc.*, XXXVI, 38—45.

CHAPTER SEVEN

Industry

ENGLAND, and even more so the rest of Britain, was grossly under-populated and underdeveloped at the beginning of the sixteenth century. The rich mineral resources of the country, above all in tin, lead and coal, had scarcely been scratched, and of these only a tiny fraction entered into foreign trade. It was almost a colonial economy, awaiting the discovery, and in some things the rediscovery, of its resources and possibilities, for the Romans had pioneered some exploitation of Britain's resources and their works were then forgotten.

We know little about the scale and distribution of industrial activity except in so far as a product entered into foreign trade and so generated, in some cases, customs and other records for the later historian to study. Farming was far and away the major economic activity of the mass of the working population, but in many places it was carried on in conjunction with some more obviously industrial activity such as textile processes, mining or open-cast working of minerals, and with small-scale metal trades such as nail-making in the West Midlands and round Sheffield. Most families lived in such a 'dual economy': part farming, part industrial. This was not a matter of house-holds 'ekeing out a living' as modern urban-minded economic historians so unthinkingly assume, with the implicit conclusion that such families were failures at both occupations. On the contrary, it was an economy in the truest sense, making the maximum use of the natural seasons of the year and of the labour of all the members of the family capable of holding a tool or performing some more trivial task. This dual, and in some cases even more versatile, economy survived well into the nine-teenth century as the printed directories of Victorian times reveal, in the countryside above all; and indeed it survived in some families until well within living memory.

Such a marked element in the pre-industrial economy of the country is fundamental to the understanding of its history, above all in an age of inflation such as the sixteenth century pre-eminently was, and in an age, too, of a growing specialization of industrial processes and products. Partly as a consequence of this specialization there came in some regions an increasing dependence on overseas markets which were subject to forces beyond any local control in the exporting country. So developed the phenomenon of unemployment as an institutional, an inbuilt, feature of economic life rather than as a purely personal event arising from age, accident or sickness.

In earlier periods unemployment had been more or less a family affair and was coped with by the family, a family which often extended over three generations and in which all helped out. Such a family did not necessarily all live in the same house, but they lived only a street or so away from each other. By the time of Henry VIII institutional un-employment was already making its appearance in the most highly industrialized part of Britain, namely along the Essex—Suffolk border and in parts of inland Suffolk centred on Sudbury. It was unemploy-ment irrespective of age and illness. That it was not a more serious and widespread feature of economic life elsewhere in Britain was due largely to the dual economy in which most families lived. How ancient this kind of life was we do not know. In some sense it is as old as the human race, probably oldest of all where farming and fishing were involved. Medieval Cornwall had developed this economy to a high degree; but it was well developed also in mining and open-cast working of minerals and stone, and in the metal trades, well before the sixteenth century dawned.

Medieval Cornwall indeed illustrates another aspect of the English economy which was well developed by about 1500, and that was the wide range of major industries that gave employment. Farming was, as ever, the basic occupation, but medieval Cornishmen could also be engaged in cloth manufacture, tin-working, shipbuilding, the victualling of ships, fishing, and building and quarrying. It was a very varied regional economy and the industrial and commercial population, even in this relatively poor county, had grown to an extent which already necessitated large-scale imports of foodstuffs.[1] There can be little doubt that if we had detailed studies of the scores of regional economies of

[1] Cf. John Hatcher, 'A diversified economy: later medieval Cornwall', *Econ. H.R.*, sec. ser., XXII, no. 2, 1969, and the same author's *Rural Economy and Society in the Duchy of Cornwall: 1300—1500*.

late medieval England they would show a similar diversity of major occupations, naturally with local variations according to the particular resources of the region. In the towns there might be fifty to a hundred different occupations: in the larger villages a score or more. This, too, helped considerably to mitigate short-term trends in some major industry such as cloth-making. We tend to take a too simplistic view of the late medieval economy, extending it into Henry VIII's reign and later, and to overweight our view with the ancient cliches of cloth and wool. Nevertheless, any account of industry during the reign of Henry VIII is bound to begin with cloth-making, not least because so much farming was directed towards it — much more in some regions than others; also because it generated surplus wealth and important subsidiary occupations. There is the obvious connection in many regions of England between the wealth of the cloth and wool trades and the intense building activity that was fed by it, chiefly in hundreds of noble parish churches and monastic houses which might occupy teams of masons and carpenters for a decade or two at a time, before they moved on to a new long-term job.

THE CLOTH INDUSTRY

The cloth industry employed many thousands of workers, some full-time in a few highly industrialized areas, and beyond these tens of thousands as part-time workers (mostly women and children, but by no means all) in the less specialized regions. But all attempts to estimate even roughly the total number of workers engaged in the cloth industry are fruitless. In large towns such as Coventry and Norwich, and even in smaller towns like Sudbury, about a third of the whole occupied population worked in the textile trades, and if we included all those in the clothing trades (the manufacture of clothing as distinct from cloth) the proportion rises to something like 40 to 50 per cent even in the 1520s. In other towns, though we have no comparable figures for the West Country and the West Riding, the proportion may have been somewhat lower. And then we think of the multitude of cloth-workers scattered over the English countryside in farmhouses, hamlets and villages from Cumberland down to Cornwall, and from Worcestershire across to Kent, and we envisage a veritable army which must surely prove that cloth-making was the largest single industry in Henry VIII's England. Yet it was far from evenly distributed.

The great days of the wool export trade were over by 1500: more and more since the late fourteenth century English wool was being made up into cloth and exported as such: though it is certain (see Chapter Eight) that the great bulk of cloth of all kinds went into the home market. Thus, though we get some idea of the magnitude of the cloth industry from the customs accounts, a great deal goes unrecorded except in the aulnagers' accounts which covered all cloths. These come to an end as early as 1478; and more than that they have been criticized for their accuracy, or lack of it, by both Heaton and Carus-Wilson. Despite this, the figures for *c*. 1470 do reveal such a strongly contrasted picture of cloth production as between the different regions that we can certainly take them as a rough indication of the distribution of the cloth industry during the next generation. Unless we are prepared to do this, we have no information at all except Leland's haphazard comments on particular towns.

In the 1470s the leading areas of cloth production were Suffolk, Somerset, Yorkshire, Gloucestershire and Wiltshire, in that order, all producing more than 4,000 cloths a year. Rather more than a third of the national total came from the West Country (Gloucestershire, Wiltshire and Somerset): just about a half of the country's production came from the west of England if we extend the region to include Devon and Cornwall, the former being by far the more important of the two. The best broadcloth (mainly for export) came from Wiltshire; Cornish cloths were of poor quality and probably went almost entirely into the home market.

A quarter of the total production came from East Anglia, including Essex, where Suffolk was easily the largest producer. The remainder of the nation's cloth came from the West Riding, extending up as far as Kendal in Westmorland, and from Wales and the Welsh border. But even within the thirty years between the 1470s and the early 1500s important changes in the distribution of the industry were taking place within particular regions. Thus whereas York had been the important centre of the cloth industry in the north, the Halifax–Huddersfield district and the Leeds–Bradford area were rapidly overtaking it as centres of production.[2] Leland, writing *c*. 1540, speaks of Leeds, Wakefield and Bradford as standing most by clothing, Wakefield entirely so (but this cannot be totally true: only that it was by far the most important single occupation). In the West Country the cloth trade centred on Exeter

---

[2] Thus at York in the early sixteenth century the textile workers numbered only 8.5 per cent of the occupied population as against 30 to 33 per cent at Norwich and Coventry (see Table 4.1).

began to rise rapidly in the 1490s, judging by the volume of cloth exports,[3] and the same would be true of smaller Devonshire towns like Totnes, Cullompton and Tiverton, which were all well endowed with rich cloth merchants by the first decades of the sixteenth century. Among these the name of John Lane of Cullompton is commemorated visibly in the magnificent south aisle of the parish church, and those of the two John Greenways, father and son, in the beautiful aisle, completed in 1517, in Tiverton Church. Altogether there must have been a marked increase in the proportion of cloths manufactured in Devon over the lowly figures of a generation earlier. The port of Exeter drew some of its cloth exports from as far away as Taunton, where again the church of St Mary Magdalen, with its superb tower, stands as a landmark (mostly built between 1490 and 1510) to the new wealth of south-west Somerset as distinct from that of the older cloth towns towards the Wiltshire border.

Even so, the richest cloth merchants of south-western England were not in the same class as those of Suffolk; and those of west Yorkshire were less important again. In Suffolk the industry was already organized on a strongly capitalistic basis by the late 1400s. Of the Suffolk clothing towns, Lavenham was easily the richest, largely (but not entirely) owing to the three generations of the Spring family. There were several other rich clothier families, but the Springs have captured the historical imagination. Thomas Spring I had died in 1440. His son, also Thomas, died in 1486, and his will gives us some idea of the magnitude of his business. He left the sum of 100 marks (probably some £7,000 or £8,000 in today's values) to his fullers and tenters, who were clearly a considerable body. He also left 300 marks towards the building of the splendid tower of Lavenham Church, and no less than 200 marks towards the repair of the roads around Lavenham on which he depended for the carriage of a great part of his cloth-producers in neighbouring towns and villages. The importance of road traffic in late medieval England has long been seriously underestimated (see Chapter Eight). His son, Thomas Spring III, dying in 1523, was the richest man in England outside London and the greater peerage. He bought land on a grand scale, dying possessed of no fewer than twenty-six whole manors, all in eastern England, and he left money for masses to be said for the repose of his soul in every one of the 130 churches in whose parishes he possessed lands. Part of this great estate, which a nobleman might have envied, seems to have been dispersed at his death, for his

[3] See Carus-Wilson, *The Expansion of Exeter*, esp. p. 35.

son John Spring died in 1549 leaving only eleven manors, but with a knighthood as compensation. Three generations in a medieval and Tudor business was exceptional,[4] but the transition to the landed gentry for the successful merchant family was traditional.

That the Suffolk cloth industry was already well established on a capitalistic basis is made clear by the organized and strong resistance in the clothing districts to the proposed war taxation of 1525, coming on top of the swingeing taxation of the year before. All branches of the industry depended on the capitalist entrepreneur, who depended largely in turn on the foreign market, either directly or through the London merchants. Not only did Henry's savage taxation deplete the industry of working capital, but his wars and threats of wars were equally disrupting. Trade could be stopped and men thrown out of work by even rumours of war, especially any threat to free intercourse with Flanders. Early in March 1528 the Duke of Norfolk, the almost royal power in Suffolk, wrote to Wolsey informing him of the steps he had taken to deal with the 'discontent' he had found brewing at Bury St Edmunds. A few days later he called before him at his great house at Stoke forty of the most substantial clothiers, to exhort them to keep their employees in work. The clothiers had already put men off but were persuaded to take them back: even the duke feared the onset of a deputation of two or three hundred women asking him to see that their husbands and children got work. But two months later, in May 1528, there was further trouble: the clothiers blamed the London merchants through whom they sold for withholding their orders. The duke proposed to Wolsey that pressure be put on the London merchants to resume buying under pain of the King's 'high displeasure'. If that were not enough the King was prepared to take the cloth trade into his own hands. This might, in Henry's hands, have proved to be the kiss of death.

The cloth industry of the 1500s, like the building industry today, covered a wide range of industrial organization, from the great 'contractors' like the Springs of Lavenham, Thomas Paycocke of Coggeshall in Essex, or the almost legendary John Winchcombe — 'Jack of Newbury', who is said to have supplied a hundred of his men at the Battle of Flodden in 1513 (some said 250 men) — down to the single household on some lonely northern farm which spun wool and wove cloth, but then had to hand over to the bigger men for the finishing

---

[4] For the Springs, see McClenaghan, *The Springs of Lavenham and the Suffolk Cloth Trade.*

processes for which only they had the facilities. So there was a wide range of organization in the cloth trade from the capitalist 'putter-out' of wool and yarn down to the cottage spinner and weaver.

The grip of the capitalist clothier on the weavers dependent on his local power is well illustrated in the petition of the weavers of Suffolk and Essex in 1539. They complained to the Lord Privy Seal that 'the Richmen the clothiers' had their looms and weavers and also their fullers daily working within their own houses while they, the small men working at home, were many times 'destitute of work' and the longer they lived the more likely they were to grow to extreme poverty. Moreover, the richmen — note the naive word to describe the new class — had agreed among themselves to fix one price for the weaving of cloths at such a level that the poor weavers could not make a living even working incessantly day and night, holy days as well as workdays, and because of the unequal struggle were glad 'to become other men's servants'. Even allowing for the extreme language of all petitions on whatever subject, we can see clearly here the onward march of the capitalist clothier, gradually extending his economic power and breaking the independent producer into servitude: another very characteristic step in the evolution of modern capitalism.[5]

With this very wide range of organization in the cloth industry, from the single household owning its own spinning wheel and loom on some moorland farm to the entrepreneur employing dozens of workers in what was virtually a factory, like William Stumpe at Malmesbury where he had converted the 'vast houses of office' that had belonged to the abbey and filled them with looms, the question arises why some districts became highly industrialized and others remained placidly in the age-old domestic system.[6] Much naturally depended on the major raw material of wool, but this could be carried considerable distances from the sheep pastures to the manufacturing districts, either by water or by road, and was not, therefore, a primary consideration. Thus Suffolk depended largely on Midland wools.[7]

[5] *T.E.D.*, I, 177–8.
[6] Stumpe did not defame the great abbey church, but was the prime mover in getting it made into the parish church we see today. Leland also tells us that he was intending to make a street or two for his work people in the 'back vacant ground' of the abbey site. By this date Malmesbury alone was turning out some 3,000 cloths a year, whereas in the 1470s a whole county was doing well to produce 4,000 odd.
[7] Thirsk, 'Industries in the countryside' in Fisher, ed., *Essays in the Economic and Social History of Tudor and Stuart England*, p. 71. Dr Thirsk gives several examples of this long-range movement of wool to the manufacturing areas and

More important was the available labour supply, and to some extent proximity to a major exporting centre like London, Exeter or Southampton. This was not important for cloths destined for the home market, but it explains in part the industrialization of the Stour valley along the Essex—Suffolk border, and of the adjacent cloth towns such as Sudbury, Hadleigh and Lavenham. The map (Fig. 1) shows the chief cloth-manufacturing areas to be densely populated and some had been so since early medieval times. This was particularly true of East Anglia. It seems likely that while there is an obvious connection with density of population in the 1520s (see Fig. 1), since the industry attracted workers from the land over a wide area, the original impulse had been in fact the reverse. Early overpopulation on a limited supply of land, extending over generations and indeed centuries, gave rise to a surplus of labour seeking employment and induced men of enterprise with capital to settle their businesses in those places. It was probably a combination of surplus labour and the accident of an enterprising man or family that led to the early industrialization of a given district. It was men like the Springs, the Winchcombes, Stumpe, the Paycockes and the Hortons who were the prime movers in establishing a local cloth industry in a big way, seeing their opportunity in the surplus labour for whom no land was available as farmers, however small.

The custom of partible inheritance or gavelkind in many areas made it impossible eventually to live off the small parcels that were produced by such a system operating over many generations. Dr Thirsk quotes a contemporary phrase 'scratch a weaver and find a parcener'. She also shows that the custom of Borough English, by which the land went to the youngest son, might have worked in the same way as partible inheritance in that the elder sons would not have been left landless but might well have been provided for during the father's lifetime. That partible inheritance at least produced large populations who tended to stay in their own village or parish where their land lay is amply demonstrated from the remote dales of Garsdale and Dentdale, high up in the West Riding, where an early knitting industry developed to eke out the meagre rewards of farming an inadequate holding. In the Westmorland dales, too, there were remarkably high populations, and a corresponding development of the textile industry in and around Kendal. The combination of farming and industry was nearly always associated with a pastoral economy which required far less labour than arable farming:

---

concludes that the wool supply 'can never have been the factor which made or marred a nascent industry'.

so both partible inheritance and a particular kind of farming together produced a local overpopulation and hence a local industry based on the major farming product, mostly either wool or leather, in the Midlands above all. The extent to which the custom of partible inheritance prevailed in England is still unknown. It was certainly much more widespread than we have hitherto imagined and more examples are likely to turn up as research is pursued.

Basically, then, it was a growing population on a fixed supply of land, relative overpopulation in other words, that led to early industrialization, though it still needed men of rare business genius to see the larger possibilities and it was they, aided by access to good river and road transport,[8] and above all proximity to London or some other large urban centre, who slowly transferred the industrial system from a purely domestic economy, a household affair, into workshops filled with looms working largely for an overseas market.

There may have been yet another factor at work in producing local overpopulation, and that was whether a village was a closed or an open one. Where the land was monopolized by one, two or three men there might be little opportunity for the smaller farmer to acquire a farm of his own. This is yet another aspect of Tudor industrial history that calls for further exploration.

Thus labour supply was the major factor in the development of the cloth industry, preferably a poor, hard-pressed labouring population at that. The strange disappearance of Hertfordshire cloth-making early in the sixteenth century, with the major advantage of a large river (the Lea) heading for London, may have been due to a radical change in the type of farming. Much of the county had been reclaimed from wood and pasture in medieval times and provided the stimulus for an early cloth industry. But by the early sixteenth century it was rapidly becoming a corn-producing county — one of the granaries of London — and even children were needed at the plough and for weeding, gleaning and other necessary farming occupations. When an attempt was made to establish the New Draperies in the county in James I's reign it was resisted on the grounds that arable farming gave full employment and better employment than 'this new invention'.

---

[8] The concentration of the Suffolk cloth industry in the southern part of the county rather than spreading generally over the whole of the wood-pasture region may well have been due to the faster-flowing estuaries of the Orwell, the Stour, and the Deben as against the slow-moving Waveney in the north. A great deal of Suffolk cloth went to London via Ipswich (Thirsk).

THE BUILDING INDUSTRY

The overall size of the building industry in Henry VIII's England is even more difficult to estimate than that of the cloth-making industry. It was scattered all over the country in small units which kept no records (except where a magnate was building a country house) and did not enter at all into overseas trade. If there was any concentration it would have been on or near the oolitic limestone belt which crossed almost the whole of England diagonally from the Dorset coast to the Yorkshire coast, and the associated belts of building stone like the magnesian limestone, which furnished generally the finest building stones in the country. Possibly England, because of its complicated geology, furnished a wider range of building materials than any other country in Europe, from certain kinds of mud (used in cottages and smaller farmhouses) to chalk and granite. The variety of building materials was infinite.[9] So too was the colour, the texture, and the durability; even the mud from suitable earths could last, and has indeed lasted, for some four hundred years, acquiring the hardness of brass as time goes by.

If we include quarrying in the scope of the building industry, then in numbers employed it cannot have fallen far short of the cloth industry. And it was possibly as important in terms of capital employed as the cloth industry, when one thinks of the thousands of local quarries alone, some of them worked for centuries. Successful freemasons were men of considerable local importance, often rising to be mayors of their native town, though nowhere of course did they rival the individual wealth of the greater cloth merchants.

Though building activity may have fallen off during the worst decades of the fifteenth century, it was always active.[10] Nevertheless there is little doubt from the surviving amount of architectural evidence that there was a tremendous resurgence of parish church building (more strictly, rebuilding) from the 1480s onwards, lasting for two generations or so until about 1540, a period which rivalled the great wave of ecclesiastical building of the twelfth to fourteenth centuries. It has been rightly said that 'never before or since has so much money been spent

[9] For the best modern and comprehensive treatment of this subject, see Clifton-Taylor, *The Pattern of English Building*.
[10] See, for example, Hoskins, 'The wealth of medieval Devon' in Hoskins and Finberg, *Devonshire Studies*, where there is abundant evidence of church building all through the fifteenth century. Suffolk also seems to have been extremely active in even grander churches at the same period.

on the parish churches of England as in the half-century before the last bad years of Henry VIII'.[11] England became a country, almost from end to end, of churches 'bright-shining with the resin of the Faith', gleaming with new stone: what a marvellous landscape Leland must have travelled around in those days, the 1530s and 1540s, when so much had been made new. And not only the structures themselves, but inside there were coloured chancel screens, carved bench ends, and gorgeous coloured roofs, often enriched with flights of angels' wings: and the glorious windows, like those of St Neot, on the very edge of Bodmin Moor in Cornwall, which survive almost intact to show us today what an apparently poor parish in a relatively 'backward' county could manage to pay for in the 1520s. Fifteen windows contain rich stained glass paid for by what one might almost call rival groups for the greater glory of God: 'the young men of this parish' (1528), 'the sisters [of the young men]' (1529), 'the wives of the western part of this parish' (1523). What a wonderful parochial world it must have been where even the different parts of the old parish subscribed to outdo the others if they could: the human real world of English life and faith as distinct from the greed, brutality and power politics of a mercifully faraway London where the King fulminated and postured and created meaningless havoc all around him. At St Neot some of the windows were paid for by single freeholder families like the Kelways, the Muttons, and others; and other families banded together to raise the money for a single window. One of the most notable windows is the so-called Borlase window, which depicts Nicholas Borlase and his wife Katherine, together with their four sons and eight daughters: not least a salutary reminder of the size of some late medieval households. Such works of art in a remote moorland parish tell us more about the economy as well as the piety of a farming community.

Of another type than little St Neot there is the glory of Fairford in Gloucestershire, almost completely rebuilt *c.* 1490–1500 by John Tame, a wool merchant, and completed by his son Sir Edmund Tame. Here too survive miraculously a complete set of stained glass windows. We can only imagine the riches that were destroyed by the iconoclasts

---

[11] Wickham, *Churches of Somerset*, p. 34. Somerset is especially rich in grand churches of this period. In Devon and Cornwall, too, nearly every parish church was rebuilt and/or refurnished in these generations, though less splendidly except in the rich little textile towns. There was scarcely a county in England, except perhaps in the far North, that did not undergo this transformation during these years. For details, see especially the volumes of Pevsner's *The Buildings of England.*

and bigots of the seventeenth century (above all perhaps the splendid glass of Henry VII's chapel at Westminster) and by the educated barbarians of the nineteenth century — Victorian squires and clergy — with their excessive wealth and their horror of 'superstition'. England in Henry VIII's time must have been a blaze of colour, of which shreds now remain only in East Anglia, the West Country, and other 'backward' parts.

Often parish churches were more or less rebuilt by the money of the whole farming community, down to the halfpenny contributed by one poor widow to the rebuilding of Bodmin Church in Cornwall. Sometimes however they were built entirely at the cost of the local squire or lord of the manor, and sometimes by a group of three or four leading gentry associated with the parish. The greater monasteries, too, were rebuilding 'their' churches grandly during the last decades before they themselves fell to the Great Predator: in the Somerset Levels, Glastonbury Abbey was responsible for such superb churches as Weston Zoyland and many others. Not only this, but the monasteries all over England were building and rebuilding their own inheritances in the last fifty years or so before their final doom. Almost the whole of Bath Abbey as we see it today was the work of the last priors and remained unfinished at the Dissolution[12] and much of Canterbury Cathedral gleamed anew from the 1490s onwards. At Winchcombe, Evesham and Gloucester great building activity was going on; at Peterborough, on the other side of England, the 'new building' was completed c. 1528. Sherborne, in Dorset, was completed in 1504, and Ford, not far away, was completed by Abbot Chard c. 1528: he was one of the greatest builders of his day. Glastonbury was building extensively, adding to what Professor Knowles has called 'one of the most magnificent complex of purely monastic buildings in England, if not in Europe'. Here the great builder was Richard Bere, whose initials appear on so many of the Glastonbury churches on and around the rich Somerset Levels where their lands stretched as far as the eye could see. And up in the far north, Abbot Huby's grand western tower still dominates every view of Fountains. Many of the smaller houses were also rebuilt or extensively repaired. All over England the monasteries, large and small, were building as though their world was going to last for ever and ever. So many besides Bath remained unfinished when the crash came: the western towers of Furness and Bolton Abbeys were never completed; and in

[12] For the spate of monastic building in this period I have drawn heavily on Knowles, *The Religious Orders in England*, III, esp. pp. 21—4.

deepest Leicestershire, Ulverscroft and Owston remained unfinished.

Not only did the monasteries, out of their vast wealth, build or re-build their own fabrics, and build or rebuild so many of their churches, but they also seem to have done much house-building in towns and villages where they were the lords, as Glastonbury did in the little Somerset town of Mells, and Walsingham in the adjacent town of Little Walsingham in Norfolk. Walsingham was a great place of pilgrimage in medieval times, and doubtless new streets were needed to accommodate the growing flood of pilgrims. At Sherborne Abbot Ramsun, so Leland reports, had built the New Inn and divers new houses in the northern part of the town, probably for the same reason. Bishops, too, were great builders: at Wells, Thomas Beckington (1443—65) built twelve 'right exceding fair houses al uniforme of stone high and fair windoid' on the north side of the marketplace, and had intended before his death to have built twelve more on the south side.

So much building was being financed out of ecclesiastical wealth from the late fifteenth century onwards (until the Great Plunder put a stop to it), in one form or another, that one is tempted at times to say that the building industry might well have rivalled the cloth industry in importance. Nor is this the whole of the story, for from the closing years of the fifteenth century the country house was making its appear-ance in the English landscape. It is difficult to define a country house accurately: rich abbots and priors had had their country residences for generations before this time. But if one defines the true country house as one built by laymen for show and comfort, not to say ostentation, without thought of defence, then we can put the beginning of this new culture again in the 1490s. In Leicestershire, the Marquis of Dorset must have begun Bradgate just about then for it was well advanced when he died in 1501. Compton Wynyates, that perfect redbrick country house in Warwickshire, had been completed when Sir William Compton died in 1528. Barrington Court in Somerset was begun for Henry Daubeny in 1514—15; and Hengrave Hall in Suffolk was begun *c.* 1525. Perhaps a score of such houses had been completed by the 1520s. Thereafter the pace quickened rapidly in the 1530s, and accelerated yet again when the downfall of the monasteries in 1536—39 released not only a flood of lands but also mountains of valuable materials in the form of lead, stone and timber.

Few magnates attempted the difficult task of converting monastic buildings directly into a new country house: most acquired the sites and demolished the buildings in order to start again. And as Knowles sadly observes, many of the very craftsmen and workmen who had been putting up monastic buildings in the 1520s and 1530s could have assisted in pulling them down a decade or two later. So the fall of the monasteries brought little or no recession in the building trades. The founders of country houses took over the monastic civilization but perhaps built more slowly as they were rarely so rich as the culture they had pillaged. It is not until the second half of the century that, apart from the gigantic buildings of Wolsey and the King, the magnates were able to build on a truly regal scale such palaces as Longleat, Burghley and Holdenby, and Somerset House in London.

Wolsey, at the height of his power, had begun Hampton Court in 1515 but handed it over years later to Henry as the signs of royal disfavour grew. From 1529 onwards Henry became obsessed with building royal palaces. Five years later a worried Thomas Cromwell complained: 'What a great charge it is to the king to continue his buildings in so many places at once . . . if the king would spare for one year, how profitable it would be to him.' Henry was building simultaneously at Hampton Court and at Whitehall Palace, both buildings begun by Wolsey years earlier; and St James's Palace was going up between 1532 and 1540. In November 1538, fortified by the first flow of funds from the dissolved smaller monasteries, he began an even more grandiose project in Nonsuch Palace, emulating perhaps his rival Francis I's château of Chambord. By 1545 he had spent £23,000 on it, but it remained unfinished at the time of his death – a little poetic justice when one thinks of what he had done to monastic culture – and it was eventually demolished about the year 1670, too absurd for even the richest magnate to live in. Finally, so far as royal building went, Henry's string of fortresses all along the south coast from Sandgate, Deal and Walmer in Kent to St Mawes and Pendennis in faraway Cornwall, were all going up in the years 1539–40 as a precaution against his two great continental rivals, Charles V and Francis I; and there were further works at Dover and Calais. All this cost came out of the ex-monastic revenues before they were frittered away in other directions. Between 1536 and 1539 Henry's non-military building cost just under £60,000.

Magnates, the King, great abbots and priors, were not the only builders in Henrician England, though their remaining works are the most conspicuous and a vast amount has also been destroyed. But in addition to all this large-scale building, thousands of the gentry and larger freeholders were rebuilding their own houses at this period. Kent and Sussex and Surrey are still full of houses of this period (say 1450 to

1550), but so too is Devon, where they are more disguised by later changes. They are nevertheless basically work of the same century. All over Suffolk too thousands of good houses of the large yeoman and the small gentry class abound. There is no doubt that a systematic search of every county in England, certainly south of the Trent, would show abundant evidence of house-building at this social level. Of the towns it is more difficult to speak categorically. Leland frequently reports both sadly decayed towns, their houses clean fallen in street after street (such as Bridgwater and Leominster), and towns with much new building. The legislation on the decay of towns passed between 1532 and 1540 suggests that some eighty English towns were in need of widespread repair. It looks from the surviving evidence of such town houses as have escaped the ravages of the twentieth century as if there was much substance in this legislation, and that the great period of rebuilding in towns as well as countryside came during the second half of the century. All the same the building trades ranked high among occupations. An analysis of the recorded occupations shows that some 9 to 10 per cent of the employed population were engaged in these trades at Norwich and York about 7.5 per cent at Northampton, but fewer (about 4 or 5 per cent) at Coventry and Leicester. If we remember that these figures are drawn chiefly from the freemen's lists of these towns, from which the labouring class was virtually excluded, the actual proportion would have been appreciably higher, as most casual labour would have been employed in the various building trades.

MINING AND METAL-WORKING

It has already been said that, by the early sixteenth century, the rich mineral resources of this country had scarcely been scratched, but this bald statement calls for closer examination. Nef has shown that the export of coal was a trivial few thousand tons in this period. But it may well be that we underestimate the total amount of coal being worked and mined. Coal went mostly to the home market, and probably localized markets at that. We depend for most of our knowledge of coal-working on casual references in records and to some extent on visible remains of bell-pits and other archaeological signs. The very extensive complex of bell-pits on Catherton Common in Shropshire shows what is probably widespread medieval mining, possibly still being practised in the sixteenth century; and a systematic search of other commons in various parts of the Midlands and northern

163

England might well produce more widespread evidence. We know that coal was found on a west Leicestershire common at Swannington in the thirteenth century and that pits were being worked here and elsewhere in the county in Henry VIII's time. There is indeed one interesting reference to a coal mine in west Leicestershire which burnt for many years on end and was unusable. Most coal-working and mining seem to have been developed on common land and waste for the simple reason that the minerals all belonged to the lord of the manor, and he was generally in a financial position to mobilize labour in cottages around the edge of the common, as at Lubberland in Shropshire, and to exploit the full possibilities in a way that the small freeholder could not, even though he might know that there was coal beneath his own farm.

A great proportion of the land of England belonged to the Church, largely the bishops and monastic houses, and it has often been said that these landlords showed little or no interest in exploiting their minerals: that not until the great transfer of church lands to laymen was any substantial exploitation undertaken. But one must not minimize the economic activities of the Church. Much went unrecorded, or is recorded incidentally in some other context.[13] Thus the monks of Finchale derived an income of about £30 a year from their coal mines, which is not recorded for some reason in the *Valor*, possibly because all was consumed on the premises. The outstanding example is that of the coal-mining along the south bank of the Tyne where the princely bishops of Durham owned miles of the riverbank, with access to both coal and water transport. When Wolsey was Bishop of Durham, in addition to many other high offices, he was letting one single mine for as much as £180 a year. Durham had many other mines, but none of these is mentioned in the *Valor Ecclesiasticus*. The prior of Tynemouth leased one mine in 1530 for £20 a year. Again there is no mention in the *Valor*; but the Ministers' Accounts which came into existence to handle the monastic revenues after the Dissolution reveal that coal mines and saltworks produced rather more than £100 a year for the Crown. There can be little doubt that the coal mines and open workings of Durham and Northumberland were numerous and lucrative. The monks of Furness in north Lancashire exploited their own coal; so too did Newminster, and Flaxley in the Forest of Dean. It is possible that nearly all the coal-bearing lands known in eighteenth-century England

[13] Much of what follows is based upon Hay, 'The dissolution of the monasteries in the diocese of Durham', *Archaeologia Aeliana*, XV, fourth ser., 1938, pp. 69–114.

were being exploited to some extent in the time of Henry VIII, if only
we had the record evidence. No doubt much of the evidence still lies in
the financial accounts of lay families, exploiting either their own lands
or land leased from monastic houses.

So in the extreme north of England the Percies were getting an
income from coal in the fifteenth century and had potentially lucrative
mines in Northumberland. But early sixteenth-century private accounts
are rare; coal mines were often leased out so that we do not know anything about total production. The clearest evidence we have of large-
scale exploitation of coal at this period comes from a valor of the
possessions of Thomas, Lord Darcy, made in 1526.[14] His total revenues
were put at the enormous figure of £1,834, less fees, etc., of £330, bringing his net income to somewhere round about £1,500 a year. Apart
from being a great landlord with estates in many counties, he had considerable financial interests in coal mines round Leeds (at Temple
Newsam and Roundhay), in charcoal and ironstone at Silkstone (also in
west Yorkshire), lead mines at Ashford in Derbyshire, and in addition a
valuable fishery at Berwick let out at some £130 a year. He also had an
appreciable income from sales of wood from various of his estates. His
Yorkshire coal mines were especially valuable, but the figures are mixed
to some extent with agricultural rents and are not precisely ascertain-
able. There must have been a few great landowners in northern England
who were exploiting their mineral resources successfully, almost if not
entirely for the home market, such as the metal trades in and around
Sheffield. In the West Midlands, Leland, who is rarely interested in
giving any industrial information other than cloth-making, tells us that
the metal trades of Birmingham got their iron out of Staffordshire and
Warwickshire and 'sea coal out of Staffordshire', in other words what
later became the Black Country. There was, too, a certain amount of
coal-mining in West and North Wales. Taken all in all the production of
coal for domestic consumption, a large part going to local industries,
must have been far more substantial than we imagine. We must not be
deceived by the minute amount going overseas during the first half of
the sixteenth century.

Together with coal-mining to some extent went salt works. The
northern monasteries such as Tynemouth derived a considerable income
from salt-making; but beyond that there is abundant archaeological
evidence along almost the entire length of the east coast from
Northumberland to Essex that salt-making was carried on in hundreds

[14] See *L.P.*, IV, no. 2527.

of seashore places. Numerous 'salt ways' then carried the finished product over a wide inland area. Of Droitwich, one of the largest sources for inland salt, Leland makes the specially interesting comment that the town was poor because the gentry had all the profit from the trade. The town itself had but one street and many lanes, and a 'mean church'.

In the same way the tin industry of Cornwall and Devon, which had been active for centuries, had got increasingly into the hands of the rich men. The equipment needed for tin-working was simple: a pick, a shovel and a bucket. The industry was therefore pre-eminently suited to the small farmer, and so no doubt it began. But no tin could be sold until it had been weighed and stamped for quality at one of the official coinage towns and this stamping took place only twice a year. Hence the smaller tin-workers fell into the hands of capitalist 'adventurers' and tin-dealers. As early as the thirteenth century we hear of wage-earners in the trade working for others, and by the early sixteenth century many landed families, including the Earl of Devon himself, were acquiring and investing in tin works. So, too, were the richer town merchants: the small man needed his money quickly and inevitably sold his unstamped tin to those with larger resources. Many a small man still worked away in the moorland solitude, adding a little to his meagre income from a small farm; but the big capitalist had already appeared on the scene.[15]

Cornwall was always more important as a source of tin than Devon, but both counties showed a remarkable increase in output in the 1490s. From 1450 to 1490 the Cornish output fluctuated round about 700 to 800 thousandweight a year (500 thousandweight was roughly equivalent to 275 tons); in the early 1500s it doubled to some 1,200 to 1,400 thousandweight a year. In Devon too output more than doubled, reaching a maximum in 1515 at some 470 thousandweight and continuing at nearly the same level during the early 1520s. There were considerable annual fluctuations in both counties, but by the 1540s Devon production had fallen sharply[16] to some 300 or so thousandweight, while Cornish production on the whole showed an upward trend, reaching a peak in 1547 of some 1,413 thousandweight. The marked rise in tin production in the two counties in the late fifteenth century is almost certainly attributable to the development of shaft mining beyond the ancient method of open-cast working of the

---

[15] Hoskins, *Devon*, p. 135.
[16] See Lewis, *The Stannaries*, Appendix J.

surface. Problems of drainage must have early become apparent. Leland makes a distinction between wet and dry tin works, which is probably to be explained in this way. Obviously, the development of shaft mining involved more expensive capital equipment and the industry became increasingly organized on a capitalistic basis: hence the appearance of rich town merchants and enterprising landowners by the early sixteenth century.

English tin was one of the most important sources of supply in Europe. Much of it was distributed to the home market for the pewter manufacture and for bell-casting. The pewter trade was concentrated in London, which came to dominate the import and export of tin. This came by coast from the southern ports of Devon and Cornwall, though a little seems to have been exported direct overseas; and much of the London imports was sent overseas to the Continent. Much of the trade in tin was illicit and few accounts survive, so that it is almost impossible to give figures for tin exports.

As with tin, English lead was one of the most valuable products in European markets. Some had been mined even in Roman times, the chief sources being in the hills of Shropshire, in Cumberland, the Peak, and the Mendip Hills in north Somerset. The bulk of the world's supply in the sixteenth century came from England and Spain. Indeed, until the development of German mining in the second half of the century England had acquired a monopoly of all the lead used in western Europe.[17] Its main use was as a roofing material for churches, monastic buildings, castles and other important private dwellings. The demand must have been almost insatiable. Once again it is not true to say that the Church sat on its mineral resources without thought of gain. On the Mendip Hills, the Bishop of Wells, the Carthusian priories of Witham and Hinton Charterhouse, and St Augustine's Abbey at Bristol, all derived a useful income from their lead-bearing lands.[18]

As with tin, production was fluctuating and unstable from year to year (probably because so much depended on accidental discoveries of the mineral-bearing deposits) but curiously enough there was a marked recovery of production here also in the 1490s, and the Mendip mines were certainly very active throughout the early sixteenth century. Again, no reliable figures survive for output in any one of the lead-bearing regions of England, but the boom from the 1490s onwards

[17] Richardson, 'Some financial expedients of Henry VIII', *Econ. H.R.*, sec. ser., VII, no. 1, 1954, 39.
[18] See Gough, *The Mines of Mendip*.

must surely have been due to the incessant rebuilding of parish churches and monastic houses above all. Even supposing that some of the old lead was re-used, the new churches and new monastic buildings were larger and grander than the old, and the demand for lead roofing was consequently greatly enhanced. Some Mendip lead was exported overseas from Bristol, and some lead from the Peak was actually bought at Bristol for repairs to the church roof at Wookey at the foot of the Mendips.

Much of the northern lead was carried over the fells to the east coast at Newcastle, whence some went coastwise to London and much went directly overseas. Although most if not all of the larger Newcastle merchants were interested in the coal trade, it is still surprising to find as late as 1558 that a rich merchant like Henry Anderson had nearly as much lead in his warehouses (£493) as he had coal at the pits and in the staithes (£595).[19] Of the important Peak mines and pits we know too little; but the lead-mining of the West Riding moors was important enough to be the subject of a bitter dispute between the lead-miners and the merchants of York over weights and measures in 1499.[20] Lead was being mined on these high moorlands as early as the twelfth century and carried down the Yorkshire rivers to York for tranship-ment to London and so overseas.

It is highly likely that down to the mid-1530s the English lead industry enjoyed an unprecedented boom as a direct consequence of the tremendous activity in the building industry. All this came to an abrupt stop with the dissolution of the monasteries which threw on to the market such vast quantities that one writer to Thomas Cromwell in May 1539 reported that lead-mining in England was 'dead'. This was basically true, though a great deal of lead was still needed for Henry's futile wars and for the repair of castles and other buildings on the royal estates. But still the stocks piled up in the royal store-houses[21] and there was periodic talk of organizing shipments to the Continent. The major scheme failed because the King was unwilling to hoard his supplies for a few years. Short-term expediency prevailed, as always in Tudor finance, and the unloading of such quantities abroad merely brought the price down. At home, lead production must have come pretty well to a standstill, for a few years at least.

On the Mendips it seems that the lead production was largely

[19] Surtees Society, II, *Wills and Inventories*, pp. 166–8.
[20] *T.E.D.*, I, 229–30.
[21] Richardson, loc. cit., pp. 37–9.

financed by small peasants and Bristol merchants, but the smelting was in the hands of the Lords Royal, the owners of the four chief manors in the lead districts. These landowners seem to have been content to take a 10 per cent royalty. In Derbyshire it was otherwise. The smelting works were financed and operated by the local nobility and greater gentry. It was they who bought the ore from the miners (small miner/farmers as in Cornish tin), processed it in their own mills, transported the refined lead to Hull, and negotiated with the London importers.[22] And it was they who reaped by far the greater profit, like the local gentry in the salt-mining of Droitwich.

Various metal trades were of considerable antiquity in England, and a few notable concentrations had developed by the beginning of the sixteenth century. The nailers and other makers of small metal gear were well established in the region later to become famous as the Black Country, in and around Dudley. Here the dual economy of metal-worker/farmer was well developed, helped out not a little by the great extent of heaths and commons that characterised this part of England: it was an example of Cobbett's 'cottage economy' *par excellence*. More-over, these heaths and commons were the visible signs of the underlying Coal Measures, so that the nailers and others had all they needed on the spot, not to mention also cottages built hurriedly on the 'waste'.[23] The Sheffield district was similarly endowed and had its variety of metal trades (mostly small articles that could be made in a home workshop); and Birmingham resounded in Leland's ears to the noise of smiths making knives and all manner of cutting tools, many lorimers making bits for horses, and a great many nailers. Deritend, now well inside modern Birmingham, he noted as having an entire street of smiths and cutlers. But though these made all the noise, they were mostly small manufacturers: the real money of Birmingham was in the hands of the butchers and the tanners, as their wills and inventories show.

The iron works of the Weald had been known to the Romans and medieval references are copious. It was all on a small scale, however, until the early years of the sixteenth century when Henry VIII's almost incessant wars created a great demand. Iron-working, in the south of England especially, waxed and waned according to the alternations of

---

[22] Stone, *The Crisis of the Aristocracy*, p. 343.
[23] See *inter alia* Court, *The Rise of the Midland Industries*, esp. Ch. 8 on Domestic Capitalism in the Nail Industry, though the evidence is mostly from a somewhat later period. However, the nail-making industry must have gone back well into medieval times as a domestic trade.

war and peace. Thus in 1513 Robert Scarer of Hartfield, in the Sussex Weald, supplied 9 tons of iron 'gunstones'; another manufacturer at Hartfield also supplied some. Cannon were also made, but they were of forged and not cast iron. From the early 1540s onwards two events led to a rapid expansion of the Wealden industry. One was the transference of monastic lands into secular hands; the other was the successful casting of the first iron cannon in this country, at Buxted in the Weald, by a French founder of brass cannon in the King's service. Henceforth the Weald enjoyed an almost complete monopoly of iron gun-casting for two centuries. Iron works proliferated in the 1540s, many of them manned by Frenchmen. There were said to be fifty or more in Sussex alone by 1548.[24]

The other cause of expansion was not technical but purely economic. Changes in land-ownership in these parts stimulated the more enterprising of the local gentry and even the nobility. Thus the lands of Robertsbridge Abbey came to Sir Henry Sidney, who as early as 1541 erected a furnace and a forge near the abbey, and a year later a furnace at Penningridge. The third Duke of Norfolk set up an Ordnance factory in the early 1540s. Seymour, the Lord Protector, had many furnaces among his possessions at the time of his downfall in 1549. The foundations of the Wealden iron industry had been firmly laid by the time of Henry's death in 1547, but the great age of expansion still lay ahead. From its very nature it was in the hands of the great and the rich from the beginning of this new phase.

SHIPBUILDING AND FISHING

Shipbuilding, like the building industry in general, was so widely distributed and almost invariably on a small and local scale, that its overall importance tends to be underestimated. Dr Scammell has rectified this view to a considerable extent[25] and has expressed the view that merchant shipping was 'one of the biggest employers of wage-labour along the east coast'. A survey of the able-bodied men made at Newcastle in 1547 showed that no fewer than 10 per cent were classed as seamen, and to this must be added the ancillary trades of shipbuilding, cargo handling, and the provision of sails, tackle, and stores. 'At all

[24] The standard work is Straker, *Wealden Iron*, but see also Crossley, 'The management of a sixteenth-century iron works', *Econ. H.R.*, sec. ser., XIX, no. 2, 1966, 273–88.
[25] Scammell, 'English merchant shipping at the end of the Middle Ages . . .', *Econ. H.R.*, sec. ser., XIII, no. 3, 1961, 327–40.

times shipping has been of far greater consequence than either its capital value or the size of its labour force would suggest.' The same observation could be made precisely of the building industry in general.

Burwash has said that shipbuilding was carried on in most of the busier seaports from Berwick round to Bristol[26] but this still under-estimates the actual extent of the industry, for every 'head port' had scores of creeks and small harbours and along most of these the smaller ships, which constituted the greater part of the fishing and merchant fleet, could be built by almost any well-trained carpenter. It was again mostly a small man's industry (with certain notable exceptions), and gilds of shipwrights are few; hence there is a great lack of records. At Newcastle a list of crafts made in 1516 includes the company of ship-wrights: curiously enough the long list of City companies drawn up for the City of London in 23 Henry VIII does not include such a company but this may be because ships were built further down-river at places like Deptford where there was more space. At any rate the English herald in the famous Debate of the Heralds in 1549 boasts of England's wealth for shipbuilding in timber and iron. 'And as touching ship-wrights, there be as good in England as in any other realm', though he cites only war vessels particularly.

Under Henry VII the navy had been very small. He had inherited only four ships, and added six more during his reign. These included the *Regent*, of 600 tons, the largest ship built till then, built in Reding Creek on the Rother and launched in 1489 or 1490. Another large ship, the *Sovereign*, was built at Southampton. Henry's policy was to encourage home shipbuilding by means of bounties, the first bounties going to Bristol men in 1488 and 1491, the latter for a ship of 400 tons. He also built the first dry dock at Portsmouth in 1495–97. This was the sum total of naval shipbuilding when Henry VIII came to the throne. Bristol had no doubt been chosen for the first bounties because it already had become an established centre for shipbuilding under William Canynges the younger (*d.* 1474). William of Worcester tells us that he kept 800 men employed for eight years in his ships, and had a hundred workmen, carpenters, and masons engaged in their construc-tion. Altogether he owned about 3,000 tons of shipping, about a quarter of the total for Bristol. His ship, the *George* (511 tons), carried the goods of sixty-three merchants, who tended to spread their risks by distributing their cargoes over several vessels. Canynges had ten ships,

---

[26] Burwash, *English Merchant Shipping.*

which voyaged to Iceland, the Baltic, Spain, Portugal, France and the Netherlands. His career marks a new era in Bristol trade: the emergence of the shipowner, more wealthy and influential even than the merchant. Hitherto merchants had used shipmasters to take their goods overseas. Somewhat later (1480) another Bristol man owned twelve ships, and others were building their own ships on a smaller scale. Many merchants still preferred, however, to purchase their ships abroad, especially in Prussia.

Early in his reign Henry VIII hired Spanish ships, and later Hanseatic, but he too pursued the policy of getting merchant ships with bounties, at Lynn (1521) and Topsham on the Exe (1530), not to mention London and Bristol.

He pursued more actively the establishment of naval dockyards, beginning with Deptford in 1513 where the famous *Henry Grâce à Dieu* (1,000 tons) was built with the aid of shipwrights and caulkers pressed into service from all over England. Devon alone produced men from Otterton, Beer, Dartmouth, Exeter and Plymouth. More men came from Dartmouth and Ipswich than from any other port, but the inclusion of such small coastal villages as Otterton and Beer gives some indication of the number of places where ships could be built for coastal and other local use. Henry also put Erith dock into use, but Deptford (1517) became the most important of the naval dockyards by the end of his reign, and Portsmouth declined rapidly. Leland comments, about the late 1530s, that 'there is much vacant ground within the town wall' (which was indeed only a mud wall reinforced with timber) and further that 'the town of Portsmouth is bare and little occupied [i.e. employed] in time of peece'.

The wealthier English merchants had their ships built for them. Thus Henry Tooley, one of the richest merchants of Ipswich, bought his own ship, the *Mary Walsingham*, in 1522, presumably from a local shipbuilder; and the same may be true of Henry Anderson, a Newcastle merchant at a somewhat later date, who when he died had shares (usually a half or three-quarters) in six different ships, besides owning two keels, half a lighter, and a boat. It was apparently common practice in the Tudor period to own shares in one ship or in several, so as to spread the risks of navigation, just as merchants distributed their cargoes over several ships at a time.

Early surveys of English shipping are so defective or exclusive in some way that they afford little information about the total amount of English tonnage. The first comprehensive survey does not appear until

1582: a brief survey of 1560 shows that there were still only about eighty ships of 100 tons and more. Indeed, the bigger ships were found to be uneconomic in anything but the most distant trades: slow, difficult to fill, requiring a large crew, and a great risk in the absence of a developed system of marine insurance. In the later fifteenth century, the smaller ships came into their own: those under a hundred tons had most of the advantages, easy to load and man, quick to turn round, and able to get into all but the most awkward places.

A large proportion of English tonnage must have gone into the fishing fleets, the long-distance fleets that reached out to Iceland, and the short-distance that covered the coasts or fished as far as the Dogger Bank in the middle of the North Sea (see Chapter Eight).

THE LEATHER INDUSTRY

It has been truly said that 'the leather industry is one of the forgotten occupations in English industrial history'.[27] It may be, as some historians have pointed out, that the leather industry was more important than the metal crafts in England, France, and even Germany, before the eighteenth century. Macpherson, in his *Annals of Commerce* thought the value of leather goods in the late eighteenth century second only to that of woollen cloth. They had a wide variety of uses, not only in footwear and other clothing, but in farming and even in the iron-working industry in belts, buckets, and bellows for the blast furnaces. The trade also attracted a large body of legislation during the Tudor period.

In London, where the Leathersellers Company had been incorporated in Richard II's time, the industry was well established as a result of the immense supplies of animals needed for the food market. The tanneries were centred on the river in Bermondsey and Southwark, as ample supplies of water were needed. Outside London, the leather industry was concentrated notably in the Midlands. The wealthiest men in Birmingham were butchers and tanners, though the metal trades made more stir and noise. At Northampton the leather and allied trades occupied the largest single group of the population in the subsidy list of 1524, and the admissions to the freedom at Leicester between 1510 and 1540 show butchers and shoe-makers well at the head of the list,

[27] Clarkson, 'The organization of the English leather industry in the late sixteenth and seventeenth centuries', *Econ. H.R.*, sec. ser., XIII, 1960, 245–56. Much of this section is based on Dr Clarkson's work. See also Clarkson, 'The leather crafts in Tudor and Stuart England', *A.H.R.*, XIV, pt i, 1966, 25–39.

with tanners and glovers also in the leading dozen trades. Even at Coventry, so noted for its cloth industry, butchers, shoe-makers, and tanners all come into the first dozen trades in numbers.

All this we should expect in a countryside in which large areas were being enclosed and converted to grass at this time, and in what was basically a pastoral country in any event. The butchers and tanners were on the whole wealthy men and prominent members of their local governing bodies. A great deal of early Tudor enclosure was for cattle-grazing and not so much for sheep, though the latter attracted the popular imagination and contemporary attacks. A great many of the Midland cattle were driven up to the insatiable meat market of London along the green drove roads which still survive for mile after mile in the now empty countryside, but all the important provincial towns had their own meat markets and leather industries, especially the distant towns of the west, such as Bristol, Gloucester and Exeter. The western side of England, with more pastoral farming, was naturally more important than most for its leather industries; but even Norwich was a notable leather town. Further north, both Lincolnshire and west Yorkshire were also strong in this field. Tanning was also important in the Wealden parishes of Kent and Sussex, where the extensive felling of timber for the iron industry left masses of bark as a valuable byproduct. The bark of Sussex was reckoned especially suitable as it had a high tanning content. Since the Weald was predominantly a wood-pasture region there was a good local supply of cattle, hides and skins. The same happy combination of metal trades and the leather industry could be seen in the West Midlands, the Forest of Dean, and in south Yorkshire.

Apart from these local concentrations, most conspicuous in the pastoral regions of England, every village and small town necessarily had its quota of leather trades, based on leather bought from a larger local market, though many a village may have had its own small tanyard. In all, the leather industry and its allied trades, just like the building industry, must have added up to one of the leading half-dozen industries of England, to put it at its lowest. We fail to recognize its overall importance partly perhaps because it was a humdrum activity, but mainly because it was widely scattered and, apart from the large tanners, in the hands of a multitude of small men.

BREWING AND OTHER INDUSTRIES

Like so much of English industrial activity, brewing depended directly on the produce of the land. Again, London was the largest single centre of the industry, with its huge labouring population, to whom ale and beer were food as well as drink. On the whole the brewers were not big men, the wealthiest in the 1522 Loan Book being assessed at £50, £70, and £100, about the same as a well-to-do yeoman in the provinces. All the larger towns naturally had their own breweries and in the grain regions of England, above all in the east, most small towns also. Brewing, more than most industries, was the subject of much legislation or at least of local infighting with the authorities, as the quality of the drink was a very frequent source of complaint. At Leicester there were five different grades of ale, with different prices, so that the product lent itself readily to fraud and anguished complaints. Taken altogether this, too, must have been a substantial industry, but once again it was widely scattered all over the country and in the hands generally of small men. The main exception to this observation, and an important one, was the trade in barley and malt, centred in the counties to the north of London; much of this went to the London brewers but much also to local brewers who were above the average in wealth. The demand of the brewers for bread corn was a periodic cause for bitter complaints, especially as it lent itself to direct and private trading, diverting corn from the open market. The brewers' demand was almost insatiable, like the national thirst in a country where no tolerable wine could be grown, and where a considerable part of the working population were paid partly in food and drink.

Finally, there were local pottery, tile, and brick industries scattered up and down the country, of little national importance but vital to their neighbourhood, and occasionally to a wider market. Sometimes these produced small but remarkable concentrations of wage-earners, as at Brill, the hill-top village in Buckinghamshire, where the lay subsidy of 1524 reveals that no fewer than 60 per cent of the recorded payers were assessed on 'wages'. In so far as a proportion of any population escaped even this comprehensive tax, as we know they did by reason of poverty rather than downright evasion (the prerogative of the rich), the actual size of the wage-earning population may have been as high as three-quarters of the whole. Brill had been for many generations a centre for pottery, and tile- and brick-making; all over England some unusual local natural resources would produce such 'industrial' villages.

CHAPTER EIGHT

The Trade of England

THE interpretation of English economic history has been bedevilled and indeed distorted by an excessive concentration on overseas trade, merely because it is in this field that documents abound. The coastal trades have scarcely been treated at all, and then usually only as an adjunct of foreign trade; and of the vast inland trade by rivers and roads almost nothing is known, certainly in the sixteenth century. Perhaps the greatest distortion has been the belief, based largely on the partial evidence of the customs accounts, that the Port of London was steadily absorbing the trade of the outports from the reign of Henry VII onwards, and that what happened to London's export trade reflected the state of the English economy as a whole. This metropolitan illusion persists strongly to this day; yet even in the late twentieth century the provinces remain the industrial and agricultural strength of Britain, and London largely a grey and inflated parasite on them.

It is probable that the coastal and inland trades were worth at least ten times as much as all the overseas trades put together, and very likely considerably more in the first half of the sixteenth century. We have no statistical evidence in this field before Gregory King's analysis of the English economy in the late seventeenth century, when he estimated the total national product at £50.8 million and exports at £4.3 million, or about 8.5 per cent of total production. In other words, only one-twelfth of the total production of the country entered into foreign trade even at this date. One would be guessing if, in view of the growth of foreign trade in the latter part of the seventeenth century, one put the proportion as low as one-twentieth in the early sixteenth century; but after all the largest industry by far, in terms of numbers and capital employed, and of gross output, was agriculture; and only a minute proportion of this immense output of foodstuffs and raw materials of all kinds entered into overseas trade. Only wool (and later cloth) was of any appreciable significance in this respect. The great bulk of agricultural produce was consumed in the home market. As for the other industries, except for some coal and a little lead and tin, they too produced largely for a home market.

The statistics of shipping registered in all the ports of the kingdom provide a much more reliable guide to the trading activity of various ports than the enrolled customs accounts. Here the alleged dominance of London is sharply cut down to size. The first comprehensive shipping survey comes late, in 1582. It excludes ships of under 10 tons, which means virtually all fishing craft and these were largely based on provincial ports and creeks. Even so, the total tonnage of English shipping was 66,714, of which London accounted for just under 19 per cent and the outports for some 81 per cent. The shipping of Norfolk and Suffolk alone far surpassed that of London. If we include the smaller craft, engaged in local coasting and fishing, the provinces may well have possessed five times as much shipping tonnage as London in Henry VIII's time. Some comparative evidence as to foreign (customable goods) and coastal trades comes from Newcastle: in 1543 and 1544 the local Trinity House Books record 754 sailings altogether. In the same period the customs books record only thirty-eight sailings — about 5 per cent of the total.[1]

With all this we have not counted the multitude of barges, lighters, keels and other craft that plied up and down the navigable rivers of England, mostly carrying commodities for local consumption but occasionally feeding the overseas trade through a larger port nearer the sea. It is in the light of all this (mostly undocumented) trading, coastal and purely internal, that we now consider England's foreign trade during the reigns of Henry VII and Henry VIII.

OVERSEAS TRADE

Despite what has been said above, England's overseas trade was of indirect importance in other ways. It was the easiest source of revenue for the Crown by way of customs duties. Moreover, the richest men in England other than the greatest landowners were merchants who

---

[1] Newcastle may have had a heavier coastal trade than the average port (though this remains to be proved) and the customs record may have been 'light' on certain transactions. Even so, it is abundantly clear that the coastal trade was vastly more important than the overseas. See Scammell, loc. cit.

engaged in foreign trade, such men as the Springs of Lavenham, the Marlers of Coventry, the Canynges of Bristol, and the great merchants of London too numerous to mention. None of these would have been a tenth as rich from inland trade alone. Their wealth, too, was more liquid than that of landed magnates. Hence they became important sources of loans to the importunate Tudor monarchs with their futile and costly wars. At first the Crown borrowed from foreign bankers, but by the mid-century it was turning to organized groups of English merchants such as the Merchants of the Staple, the Merchant Adventurers, and the City of London direct.

The customs accounts for the period 1485 to 1547 reveal the bare outlines of England's overseas trade.[2] Cloth exports boomed at the expense of wool exports, the latter falling rapidly as a result of heavy taxation and the demands of home industry. Most of the cloth went out through London; most of the wine came back to it. In the years 1510–15, for example, cloth exports ranged from 76,000 to 93,000 cloths a year, wool exports from 5,100 to 8,600 sacks. The average value of both cloth and wool exports in these sample years was about £104,000 per annum. London handled 70 per cent of the trade, the outports 30 per cent. Foreign merchants had a large hold in the trade, taking between 40 and 50 per cent at different times, English merchants the remainder. By the early sixteenth century, cloth and wool accounted for four-fifths of all English exports.

Although it is unreal to divide the customs figures between the two reigns, to do so reveals some long-term trends in overseas trade and in the prosperity of the different ports.

Though no growth in foreign trade can be seen in these figures, they conceal considerable changes within themselves. Thus there was a boom in cloth exports from 1500 onwards until well into the reign of Henry VIII which more than offset the fall in wool exports.[3] On the whole, though, no overall growth. Imports show a marked rise, especially of wine, a purely luxury commodity; and beginning in the first year of Henry VIII came a number of statutes which reflected concern at the increase of foreign imports, especially of this kind. Yet the balance of trade remained generally favourable throughout Henry's reign.

London handled half the total customable overseas trade during the

[2] The standard source is Schanz, *Englische Handelspolitik gegen Ende des Mittelalters*, supplemented by P. Ramsey, 'Overseas trade in the reign of Henry VII: the evidence of customs accounts', *Econ. H.R.*, VI, no. 2, 1953.
[3] Ramsey, loc. cit., pp. 178–9.

Table 7.1 Customs duties 1485—1509 and 1509—47

Port	Annual average customs duties 1485—1509 (£)	Per-centage of total	Port	Annual average customs duties 1509—47 (£)	Per-centage of total
London	18,528	49.5	London	24,990	66.1
Southampton	7,095	18.9	Southampton	3,626	9.1
Boston	2,400	6.4	Newcastle	1,886	5.0
Newcastle	1,908	5.1	Boston	1,294	3.4
Ipswich	1,682	4.5	Bristol	1,079	2.9
Bristol	1,273	3.4	Exeter	1,024	2.7
Exeter	1,178	3.1	Hull	928	2.5
Hull	1,039	2.6	Ipswich	773	2.0
Others	2,337	6.5	Others	2,204	6.3
Total	37,440	100	Totai	37,804	100

reign of Henry VII. Since Southampton was primarily an outport for London the proportion was nearer to two-thirds. Boston was the leading provincial port: the town still drew on a rich hinterland and above all the wool of the limestone uplands and the Midlands behind. The three principal outlets for English wool during the years 1485 to 1509 were London, Boston, and Ipswich, which handled nearly 95 per cent between them. Cloth exports were not so concentrated as wool, even though here London and Southampton between them handled more than two-thirds of the trade.

Though there was no marked growth of foreign trade by the 1540s, a number of changes nevertheless become evident in the different ports. One was the apparent expansion of London at the expense of all the outports except such distant places as Newcastle and Exeter, Bristol and Hull. London's share now averaged two-thirds of all customable goods, three-quarters if we include Southampton. Secondly, there were marked signs of collapse at Southampton. Its average customs receipts were nearly halved during the reign of Henry VIII, and the detailed figures show an even worse position. Whereas the average receipts had been well over £7,000 a year in the time of Henry VII, by 1535—40 the average was down to £2,033 and by 1540—45 to as low as £633 a year.[4]

This spectacular decline resulted largely from the withdrawal of

[4] See Ruddock, 'London capitalists and the decline of Southampton in the early Tudor period', *Econ. H.R.*, II, no. 2, 1949.

London merchants and trade from Southampton. Southampton's high position among outports in the reign of Henry VII had been due to London participation in a port that saved a long and hazardous journey up the Channel and round the Kent coast. With improvements in ship-building and rigging the longer voyage became less hazardous, above all when the organization of a gild of experienced pilots (Trinity House was founded at Deptford in 1512) made the navigation of the Thames estuary safer. There were, too, changes of fortune in the wide hinter-land of Southampton when the collection of wool for export dwindled in favour of local cloth industries in the Cotswolds, Wiltshire and Berkshire, which marketed largely through London.

This changeover from wool to manufactured cloths affected the port of Boston similarly, together with its major inland collecting centre at Stamford. At Boston the customs receipts nearly halved, and it was not a natural centre for a compensating cloth industry. The river was neglected and became difficult to navigate: the town then blamed its slow decline on natural forces, but the real reason was the more funda-mental one that English wool was now being manufactured at home. Even so, Boston remained one of the three leading wool ports until about 1520, when a sharp decline set in.[5] By the 1540s wool exports had fallen to well under one-third of their volume in the first decade of the century.

The changeover from wool to cloth exports had repercussions all over England, and not only in the ports. Salisbury was a notable casualty, dropping from sixth place among provincial towns in the 1520s to thirteenth or so fifty years later. Stamford went into deep decay by the 1540s; and even as far back as Leicester the wind of change was felt: the wool merchants and mercers who had ruled the town and its economy gave way over the middle decades of the century to a new class of rich tanners and butchers. The Port of Ipswich too was a casualty. Under Henry VIII its average customs receipts more than halved. Nearly all of this was due to a massive decline in wool exports which set in about 1500. By the 1530s fewer than a hundred sacks were leaving the port annually, and after 1539 the trade dried up completely. The most vigorous and advanced cloth-manufacturing region in Britain lay immediately behind it, but even so Ipswich did not benefit appreci-ably from the export of Suffolk cloths. Most went out via London. Ipswich cloth exports increased to some extent after 1500 but never

[5] The detailed figures are given in Carus-Wilson and Coleman, *England's Export Trade 1275–1547*.

achieved the level of the half-century between 1420 and 1470.

The more distant outports held their ground or only fell back slightly; Newcastle took the place of Ipswich as a wool port for a while, yet even here wool exports fell almost to zero in the 1540s, and cloth exports were always negligible. Yet Newcastle's customs receipts remained the most stable of all the outports. Exports consisted chiefly of coal, grindstones, canvas, sheepskins, lamb fells, rough and tanned leather, and lead. The Merchants' Company were still general dealers rather than specialists, which probably explains the stability of the local economy.

Exeter enjoyed a remarkable boom in cloth exports from 1500 onwards which lasted, though on a somewhat reduced level, well into the 1540s; but at Hull there was no spectacular rise until the second half of the century. Bristol, another distant outport, had never exported raw wool, and cloth exports during Henry VIII's reign were far below the boom level of the 1490s. We do not know what was happening to the Bristol wine trade in these years, but it may well have been buoyant, as the port lost relatively little ground so far as customs receipts were concerned.

The conflated customs figures already quoted show no overall growth between 1500 and 1550; but again this broad statement conceals a good deal of the truth of what was happening to English overseas trade in this half-century. To put it simply, Henry VIII inherited a healthy trading position from his father, besides an immense personal fortune, and squandered all his inheritance in foreign wars and madly extravagant building at home. He was, apart from all else, an economic disaster for his country.

During the first ten years of his father's reign, the average revenue from customs was just under £33,000 a year.[6] Thanks largely to Henry VII's vigorous commercial policy, combined with a remarkable boom in cloth exports, the average annual figure for the rest of the reign rose to just over £40,000 — a jump of more than 20 per cent. This improvement continued into the first decade of his son's reign: the annual yield averaged £42,643 in these years. But it was the peak. Then followed some twenty years of falling revenue, reflecting the shrinkage of trade as a consequence of Henry VIII's wars. Not only open warfare, but incessant rumours of wars and fears of impending closure of overseas markets equally brought trade to a standstill at times, notably in the

[6] These and other customs figures are taken from Schanz, op. cit., II, pp. 12, 46, 59.

early 1520s. From 1521 to 1529 the average annual yield of the customs fell to £35,305; then from 1530 to 1538 down to a little over £32,000. This decrease was due largely to a fall in the wool subsidy (as exports dwindled) by an average of nearly £10,000 a year between Henry's first decade and the 1530s. Other customs, thanks to buoyant cloth exports, showed a slight rise and this continued vigorously into the 1540s. Even so, the annual average of customs revenue in the last nine years of the reign was under £39,000: rather less than it had been in the latter half of Henry VII's reign some fifty years earlier (Fig. 4).

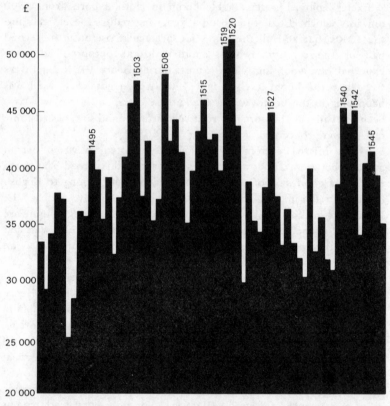

Fig. 4 Annual customs revenue 1485–1547
(based on Schanz)

The economic achievement of Henry VII, considering his formidable political problems, was remarkable. His lust for personal wealth enriched his country also. In many ways he can be regarded as the greatest of the Tudors and his son as the most disastrous. With the *Intercursus Magnus* (1496) he stabilized the important trade with Flanders, though its direct contribution to growth was perhaps little: the trade would have grown anyway through economic forces. The Anglo—Spanish alliance of the 1490s opened up for English merchants one of their most profitable trades during the next thirty years or so; and he eventually brought the merchants of Venice and the Hanse (especially the latter) under sufficient control to benefit both English merchants and English shipping. Even so, his success with the Hanse was far from total, and at the end of his reign foreign merchants still carried nearly half the Anglo—Flemish trade, the most important English overseas connection. The Hanse merchants still took about a quarter of this trade, and other aliens the rest.

Henry's Navigation Acts of 1485 and 1489 encouraged native shipping and seamen in the wine and woad trades from south-western France, and even more directly he encouraged shipbuilding at home by means of bounties in order to lessen the dependence on foreign ships and hence the invisible drain of money from the economy through freight charges. On top of all this, he actively encouraged the exploration of the 'New World' across the Atlantic, notably by the larger Bristol merchants of whom John Cabot was the best known. It was significant, however, that when Sebastian Cabot, one of John's sons, returned to England after a voyage that probably penetrated into Hudson Bay, he found his royal patron dead and the new King intent only on military glory in Europe. Cabot thereupon left England and entered the service of Spain. He returned only at long intervals, came back for good in 1547 (by which time he was seventy-three years old) and was still active at a great age. In 1551 he settled the dispute between the London merchants and the Hanse; he was still interested in the north-west passage to China, and he supervised trading expeditions to Russia when he was in his eighties. But the services of this far-seeing man were lost to England during the whole of Henry VIII's reign: one of the many prices England paid for royal megalomania. A few other small expeditions at long intervals also failed: the exploration of the New World was left to Spain and Portugal for the next fifty years.

As to the effect of Henry's wars and generally bellicose policy on English industry and trade, there is much evidence. The Suffolk cloth industry, more dependent than any other on foreign markets, was particularly resistant to the heavy war taxation of 1523—25. There were complaints of lack of work and above all of a shortage of ready money, for the comprehensive subsidy of 1523–25 had drained all classes except perhaps the richer landowners pretty dry. The so-called Amicable Grant of 1525 for the prolongation of the French War roused even fiercer opposition all over the kingdom. In East Anglia some 20,000 men of Suffolk and Essex, supported by the scholars of Cambridge, assembled in May. The Dukes of Norfolk and Suffolk quelled the rising, and arrested the leaders; but the proposal for a grant was dropped. The King took it 'unkindly'; it was very rare for him to be frustrated, but in this case the whole country was solidly against him. Overseas trade indeed suffered: before the outbreak of war in 1522 the customs revenue had begun to exceed £50,000 a year (1518–20): during the war it dropped to £34,000 to £38,000.

In 1528 there was further trouble, this time over the mere rumour of war. The year had opened with a general shortage of foodstuffs, for the preceding harvest had been a disaster. Corn prices reached their highest level within living memory, and the prices of dairy produce were the highest for thirty years.[7] Commercial war had broken out with the Netherlands, Wolsey was believed to want open war, and the clothiers of Suffolk and merchants of London were holding back for fear of the immediate future. It was rumoured that English merchants were being detained in Flanders. The Suffolk clothiers were turning off men: there was growing unrest in East Anglia by the end of February. The Duke of Norfolk (the great power in Suffolk) summoned before him at Stoke-by-Nayland forty of the most substantial clothiers of the region, exhorted them to keep their employees in work, and assured them that reports of English merchants being detained in Flanders and Spain were unfounded. This was in early March. But in May the clothiers complained to the duke that the London merchants were refusing to buy their cloths and they would have to turn off workpeople again in two or three weeks. The duke suggested to Wolsey that pressure should be brought to bear on the London merchants. A great number were duly summoned before the cardinal, who informed them that unless they resumed buying they would incur the King's 'high displeasure'. And if that threat were not enough, the King would take the cloth trade into his own hands: a pretty thought for the future of the economy. The cloth trade was the worst affected because of its foreign markets, but

[7] See Hoskins, 'Harvest fluctuations . . .', *A.H.R.*, XII, pt i, Appendix II. Also Harrison, 'Grain price analysis', loc. cit., and the price tables in *A.H.E.W.*, IV, 815–62.

the eastern counties complained more generally that they were deprived of their foreign markets also for butter and cheese, red herrings and sprats. Thus though there was no open war, but only persistent rumours, the dislocation of trade was real enough. The customs revenue, which had recovered immediately after the ending of the French War of 1522–25, reaching well over £44,000 in 1526–27, slumped in 1528–29 to under £33,000 (a drop of 25 per cent) and took ten years to get back to the old level.

There were other side-effects of war. The third French War of 1542–44 saw the growth of uncontrolled privateering on a large scale, and honest merchants on both sides of the Channel found themselves ruined by the seizure and pillage of their ships at sea. Occasionally there were glimpses of sanity amid this turmoil. In October 1542, the fishermen on both sides arranged a truce 'during herring time', and letters to this effect went from Dieppe and Calais to the King in London.[8] The food supply was much too valuable to both sides to be jeopardized by bellicose magnates who never went hungry themselves.

Several export trades escaped the customs system and hence any measurable record. These were mainly coal, tin, lead, grain and fish. Such exports were relatively small during the first half of the sixteenth century, and some (like grain) were intermittent. As to coal, Nef has reckoned that perhaps 2,000 to 7,000 tons a year went overseas to ports from Dieppe along to Lübeck. Vastly more went down the coast to East Anglian ports like Lynn (and thence up-river to Cambridge and elsewhere) and Aldeburgh. Most disappeared into the maw of London. Even in a boom year for exports like 1564–65 the sea-coal sent overseas was worth only £4,310 out of total exports amounting to £1,088,000 (i.e. about 0.04 per cent). In the 1590s Newcastle was still sending four times as much coal coastwise as overseas. As for tin and lead, exports amounted in 1564–65 (there are no earlier figures) to about £25,400 and about £26,200 respectively – some £50,000 altogether or a little under 5 per cent of all exports. Small though this is, these two valuable minerals were the most important exports after cloths of all kinds, wool, and wool fells. The tin came from Cornwall and Devon and was carried coastwise, to start with at least; probably most was absorbed by the London pewterers and went no further.

How far fish entered into overseas trade is hard to say. It was largely a coastal and river trade for the home market, but some had a wider field. Cod from Norway and stockfish (dried fish) from Iceland were

[8] *A.P.C.*, I, 1542–47, pp. 41–2.

reaching English markets, above all, London, from the fifteenth century onwards. Though the first English boats to reach Icelandic waters came from Norfolk ports like Cromer and Blakeney as early as 1412, Hull had an immense trade in stockfish and partly other fish also. The De la Poles owed their great wealth to the Hull fishing industry in Richard II's time; and Leland records that since the burden of stockfish was light, in stormy waters, the Hull ships were ballasted with 'great coble stone' out of Iceland which over a long period gradually paved the whole town.

London, far more than Hull, had long been the greatest market for fish. There had been a Fish Street and Fish Market here as early as the twelfth century, and doubtless since pre-Conquest times, since fish was the cheapest and commonest food for the immense army of the poor. The stockfish mongers were far more important than the wetfish mongers, for obvious reasons of carriage over wide areas. In the great days of the trade, Stow relates, they produced no fewer than six mayors of London out of twenty-four in the period 1350–74, all 'jolly citizens'. The fishmongers had six separate halls in the city. In an official list of the order of precedence of some sixty companies at the Lord Mayor's Feast (1532) the fishmongers came fourth after the mercers, grocers and drapers, and above the goldsmiths, skinners and merchant tailors. And in the Loan Book of 1522, where we find them still highly localized in St Margaret's parish, the richest stockfish mongers were assessed at £400 to nearly £500, more than most top merchants in the largest provincial towns. At Lynn, too, the richer fishmongers appear among the aldermen and councillors. The drying of fish was in itself a considerable industry here, as it must have been at all the bigger landing-places up and down the east coast. Some of the fish fairs and markets were famous over a wide area, above all the international herring fair at Yarmouth. Lynn had its great 'February mart'. On its open fields, acquired by the council when it obtained the fee-farm in 1536, three kinds of industrial workers used the large space available for their own purposes: the clothworkers who needed to dry their cloths after fulling, the rope-makers who needed long narrow grounds to lay out their ropes, and the fisher men (probably fishmongers rather than the actual fishermen) who used the open ground for washing and drying their fish.[9]

[9] For Lynn, see Parker, *The Making of King's Lynn*, esp. p. 131, where the process of drying the fish is fully described. The process used at Lynn in the sixteenth century is still practised at Overy Staithe on the north Norfolk coast.

Most important of all, and certainly the most ancient, was the herring fishery of the North Sea, an immense reservoir of food for all the countries bordering it. Its history has never been written from the English standpoint. Most of the herrings landed came in to Great Yarmouth and Hull, but some were landed at a hundred lesser ports up and down the east coast. To a considerable extent, too, the herring entered into overseas trade. John Johnson and his partners, for example, had a continued interest in the herring trade from Dunkirk and Calais down to Dieppe and other Normandy ports, and they suffered greatly from the attacks of privateers in the 1540s. Calais and Dunkirk were both well entrenched in the herring trade. In 1549 forty or fifty hoys and other ships 'bound with herrings into France' were intercepted by English privateers. The whole eastern and southern coasts of England furnished nests for these pests. Their lawless actions brought reprisals on honest merchants: the stopping of the herring boats in 1549 provoked 'the general restraint or rather arrest in Antwerp of all our English merchants' bodies and goods'. The French and Imperial ambassadors in London protested in vain against the continual depredations of the English pirates.[10]

Off the south-west of England, the pilchard was caught in millions during the season. 'The commodity that ariseth of this silly small fish is wonderful', wrote Norden in his description of Cornwall (*c.* 1605), both in the home market and abroad. Well back in the fifteenth century, Cornish exports of fish were second only to those of tin, but the export of pilchards to the Catholic countries of southern Europe did not develop on a large scale until the early years of Elizabeth's reign. Both Devon and Cornwall shared in this valuable trade. When Nicholas Ball, merchant of Totnes (a rich little cloth town in Devon), died comparatively young in March 1586, he had made his fortune not in cloth but mainly in exporting pilchards to Portugal and the Mediterranean. Within four months his widow married Thomas Bodley, son of an Exeter merchant but already a trusted servant of the Crown. Marrying a rich widow, preferably young as Ann Ball was, provided one of the quickest roads to advancement for able men. Bodley won her (he was then aged forty-one) by a neat trick: Manningham's *Diary* records in 1602–03:

Mr Bodly, the author, promoter, the perfecter, of a goodly library in Oxford, won a riche widdowe by these means. Coming to the place where the widdowe

[10] Winchester, *Tudor Family Portrait*, esp. pp. 240, 250, 287–8.

was [the very house in Totnes which still stands in the High Street] with one
whoe is reported to have bin sure of hir, as occasion happened the widdowe
was absent; while he was in game, he, finding this opportunity, entreated the
surmised assured gent. to hold his cards till he returned, in which tyme he
found the widdowe in a garden, courted, and obteined his desyre; so he played
his game, while an other held his cardes.

With her wealth he began bringing together the Bodleian Library in
1598: the noblest foundation ever to be built upon a humble little fish.

As for grain, England had long since ceased to be a provider for
Europe, though in good years there might be a small export trade.
Much more likely, in bad or deficient years — and the sixteenth century
saw many of these — there was a heavy import from the Baltic coast-
lands. The largest corn exporters were on the east coast: Lynn,
Yarmouth, and Ipswich, with some from Boston after an abundant
harvest. But there were not many years when corn exports reached, say,
2,000 quarters, though at Lynn in 1530–31 nearly 20,000 quarters went
out, and the late 1540s also saw considerable exports. John Johnson
exported much through Lynn, barley and malt going to Flanders, with
mixed cargoes in return for sweet wine, claret, iron, pitch, tar, canvas,
paper, glass, salt, raisins and dyestuffs. Occasionally, the export of corn
was prohibited after a particularly bad harvest, but it was not until the
Act of 1555 that a serious attempt was made to control the export of
corn and other victuals, and this was largely prompted by the continued
price-rise at home, above all of foodstuffs. In general, the bulk of East
Anglian corn went coastwise (see below), northwards to Newcastle and
Scotland and southwards to ever-hungry London.

Of imports we know very little before the Elizabethan period, except
what we discover incidentally from the surviving account books of
Henrician merchants. Thomas Howell, a prosperous London draper,
spent over thirty years in the Anglo–Spanish trade, one of a number of
prosperous English merchants who lived more or less permanently in
Seville. He exported cloths of all kinds, and sent back dyestuffs, oil,
soap, alum and woad for the English textile industry. He also had
factors in northern Spain, through whom he exported considerable
quantities of iron. Spanish iron was in great demand because of the
bellicose policy of Henry VIII. It was, for example, by far the largest
import into Bristol from at least 1517 onwards. Howell's business was
not in luxuries, such as wine, but in industrial raw materials; this was
true of the Spanish trade as a whole. Henry Tooley, who became the
richest merchant of Ipswich, also had a factor in the Biscayan ports,

bringing back iron. Tooley sent out Suffolk cloths and also brought back woad, but wine seems to have been his principal import. Iron also came into England as a re-export from Flanders, together with ship-building materials like pitch and canvas. Probably wine was the most valuable of all the imports into England and since it was a luxury trade it was the one that occasioned the greatest concern. Imports fluctuated widely but tended to grow.[11] On the other hand, the fussy concern over wine imports probably conceals the fact that a considerable proportion of England's imports were necessary raw materials for industry, above all the cloth industry, the iron trades and shipbuilding.

Foreign trade was organized through two privileged companies, who regulated the trade of member merchants and partnerships. Most important in the early part of the century were the Merchants of the Staple of Calais, who had a monopoly of the export not only of tin and lead, hides, butter and cheese, but also of raw wool and fleeces. Both in London and in the provinces the Merchants of the Staple were among the wealthiest men in the kingdom. Profits were high in successful ventures, but the risks were also high. We see this in the level of 'desperate debts' recorded in merchant inventories, such as that of William Wigston, a Leicester merchant of the Staple, who died in 1536 with more than £3,500 owing to him (say about £400,000 today) of which more than two-thirds were written off, at least temporarily, as 'desperate'. This was money owed by foreign merchants in Antwerp, Malines, Bruges, and Delft. In other inventories the desperate debts range from less than a tenth of the whole money due to as high as two-thirds, the higher figures being almost certainly the result of war or rumours of war overseas or some other interruption of trade; but a diligent executor might eventually recover something over the years.

The other great company was that of the Merchant Adventurers, who had their separate companies in the greater ports such as York, Bristol, Newcastle but pre-eminently in London. They were mainly engaged in exporting unfinished and undyed cloth to the great mart of Antwerp,

[11] Schanz, op. cit., II, 22, gives the annual average for wine imports under Henry VIII as follows:

anno	1–2 to 5–6	7,726 tuns
	6–7 to 12–13	13,027 tuns
	13–14 to 16–17	6,509 tuns
	17–18 to 23–24	10,418 tuns
	24–25 to 33–34	11,613 tuns
	34–35 to 1 Ed. VI	7,456 tuns

Annual average for 1509–47: 10,060 tuns.

and some grew immensely rich, forming almost patrician families such as the Greshams, the Holleses, and the Osbornes. The early years of the Merchant Adventurers saw them trying to break into the European cloth market through Zeeland and Brabant. In their search for a single cloth mart they tried Antwerp for a time, and Utrecht, and considered Middelburg also. In the last decade of the fifteenth century they finally fixed on Antwerp where the merchants of Cologne, the main distributors of English cloth in Germany, could be found. As a result of this choice Antwerp became the commercial hub of Europe for the next two or three generations. And here most of the cloths from England were dyed and finished.[12] It has been said, with considerable exaggeration, that 'the economy of England during the first half of the sixteenth century was concentrated to an increasing degree upon a single product, handled through a single port, and directed along a single trade route' — meaning the export of cloth from London to Antwerp, which in turn yielded manufactured goods for the English market. The Merchant Adventurers had not a complete monopoly of cloth exports. The Hanse, a federation of north German trading cities, kept the whole of the Baltic trade in its own hands, or tried to, and consequently handled about one-fifth of English cloth exports at its trading station in London known as the Steelyard, and to a much smaller extent from its depot at King's Lynn.

The general commercial trend of the first fifty years of the sixteenth century has been well summarized by Professor Fisher:[13]

> Together they formed, especially in contrast with the years that followed, one of the great free trade periods of modern English history. They were preceded by the famous statute of 1497 which temporarily curtailed the power of the Merchant Adventurers; they were marked by the collapse of the usury laws, the relaxation of the restrictions upon the export of unfinished cloth, and by the virtual cessation of attacks upon the Hanseatic merchants; there was a period in the 'thirties and 'forties when the differential duties imposed on aliens were abolished; and none of the spasmodic efforts of the Government to interfere in commercial affairs seems to have been more than half-hearted.

The reasons for this 'liberalism' were mainly, according to Fisher, political and economic combined. The international situation was delicate: the English could not afford to antagonize the Emperor by imposing trading restrictions on his subjects. He could in the event of

---

[12] Ramsay, 'The Antwerp Mart' in Ramsay, ed., *English Overseas Trade*, 1957.
[13] Fisher, 'Commercial trends and policy in sixteenth-century England', *Econ. H.R.*, X, 1940.

economic warfare close the Antwerp market to English goods (a far more powerful weapon than any that we possessed) and penalize our flourishing trade with Spain. Nor was there much, if any, pressure at home for the Government to interfere in commercial affairs. The growing import of wines was a special grievance, but a very limited one. In minor slumps the mercantile interests obtained legislation to ease their complaints, as they thought; but it is not true (as Fisher says) that the fundamental cause of the general indifference was that 'trade was so continuously growing'. It was not, as we have seen; but perhaps we can concede that after each slump the trading figures revived in time to lead the mercantile interest to believe that long-term growth was setting in at last. They deceived themselves in this, but how were they to know better? We are all deceived, even modern economists, by the short-term trends in the economy at any given time.

THE COASTAL TRADES

Foreign trade generated a good deal of coastwise trade. The primary cargo from abroad might enter any one of a dozen or so of the larger ports, but there a good deal of it was broken up for distribution up and down the local coast and up the larger rivers. Conversely, a good deal of foreign trade was fed by small vessels that beat up and down the long English coastline from a hundred little ports and creeks with cargoes that were eventually concentrated into larger vessels for shipment overseas. Even so most of the coastal trade lived off its own, so to speak. Each region fed other regions with its own specialities, and brought back their local surpluses in return: it went no further. This inter-regional trade appears only in local port records (such as the petty customs accounts at Exeter and at Great Yarmouth) and these are still almost totally unexplored. Many other provincial ports possess town customs records. Such purely local trade goes a long way to explain the discrepancy between London men paying some two-thirds of the national customs dues while owning only about a fifth, if that, of English shipping tonnage.

In the absence of any examination of these local customs and other records the evidence for a substantial coasting trade must be largely circumstantial. A survey of shipping at Great Yarmouth in January 1513 of vessels of 10 tons and over reveals that there were 167 ships in the main port and its 'creeks'. The jurisdiction of the main port ranged from Blakeney on the north Norfolk coast round to Woodbridge in

Suffolk: altogether no fewer than nineteen creeks, or more strictly minor ports, are named. Many of these are today hardly accessible by a rowing boat, such as Salthouse not far from Blakeney: several others have to be sought for on a large-scale map. All had their home-based ships. Thus Cley, Blakeney and Wells had eighteen ships between them in 1536 (181 tons); and in 1550 they had grown to no fewer than forty-six ships (1,950 tons). These figures of shipping fluctuated sometimes inexplicably in the same port in different years, but there seems to have been a general tendency for the size of local fleets to grow. So Aldeburgh's twenty ships in about 1520 fell to nine in the 1540s but by 1550 had reached twenty-five, and the total tonnage had more than doubled in a few years. Even the bigger ports like Lynn and Yarmouth, as foreign trade fell away in the 1540s, found ample compensation in developing the active coastal trades in coal and grain.[14]

The overseas trading of Henry Tooley of Ipswich has been referred to, but he had also considerable coasting trade along the coasts of Suffolk and Norfolk, even going as far as Norwich. He seems to have employed smaller shippers for this local distribution, among whom was one John Humphrey who during the reign of Henry VIII had what was almost a regular sea service to London.[15]

Serving London with local produce of all kinds must have employed a great number of small ships along the east and south coasts. A survey of an Essex manor, Woodham Ferrers, in 1582 shows that this little place had wharves on two creeks that led off the river Crouch: Clements Green Creek and Woodham Fen Creek. From these now-deserted waterside places salt, oysters, cheese, butter, corn and wood were shipped to London. The coast of Essex was honeycombed with creeks, some of them reaching far inland, all dotted with wharves which were chiefly notable, according to Norden, for shipping wood to the metropolis. Indeed, they were simply called woodwharves.[16]

When we get the first comprehensive survey of English shipping (in 1582) the East Anglian ports owned some 27 per cent of the total, London rather less than 19 per cent, and the south-east some 16 per cent. The south-west owned just about one-fifth, from Dorset round to

[14] Scammell, 'English merchant shipping . . .', pp. 338–9. Some of the small ships made long overseas voyages (see Burwash, Ch. 5) but the majority, especially the under-10 tonners must have been purely coastal.
[15] Webb, *Great Tooley*, pp. 102–3.
[16] Emmison, 'Survey of the Manor of Woodham Ferrers, 1582', *Trans. Essex Arch. Soc.*, XXIV, 1951.

Bristol: the north-east from Lincolnshire up to the Scottish Border about 15 per cent, much of this concentrated in Newcastle and Hull. London was the biggest single port for tonnage (12,300 tons) as might be expected, with Newcastle and Yarmouth equal second (6,800 tons), but Yarmouth's tonnage at least was swollen by the ships of a score of subsidiary ports, as we have seen.

Much of the shipping of the south-east coast plied to and from London, but as one went westwards beyond Poole in Dorset the hundreds of little seaside and riverside ports traded very much with each other, especially as the much indented coastline of Devon and Cornwall harboured ports scarcely heard of today. Some of these tiny ports with their small ships made overseas voyages (one can only admire their courage and skill when one sees where they went), but most were probably purely coastal. In Devon, for example, much local stone and slate was carried from local quarries well along the coasts for inland distribution. But the biggest single trades by far were the coal trade from Newcastle southwards, and the grain trade from Yarmouth north-wards: a reciprocal exchange for months in the year, though at times the problem of ballast for empty coal ships was a real problem at the Newcastle end. The northern bank of the Tyne was increasingly piled up with such ballast, so much so that in 1549 the town obtained an Act to extend its boundaries eastwards to take in the manor of Byker. This was chiefly to give more land for casting out ballast, but also for ship-building and repair, and for limekilns. Other towns had such problems, but not all could be solved in such a large manner.

The history of the coasting trade in the sixteenth century has yet to be written. It probably became increasingly important as the century went on. Not only in England but also in north Germany and the Low Countries there was a phenomenal rise in shipping tonnage. According to a Venetian report in 1551 England was then 'very powerful at sea' and could fit out more than three times as many ships as she could have done twenty years earlier. As overseas trade had shown no particular increase in these years, we must assume that a great deal of this increased tonnage went into the coastal trades. We might expect this, with the long indented coastline of England. Wales shared to some extent in the increase, probably in coal ships, but the north-west of England was of very little account. From Aberystwyth northwards to the Scottish Border, shipping tonnage in 1582 was only one-fiftieth of the whole for England and Wales. Liverpool had only 400 tons, less than many a Norfolk 'creek'.

INLAND TRADE: THE RIVERS

The subject of inland trade before the seventeenth century, by rivers and roads, has been almost completely neglected. The sources are few, but they suggest altogether that the major rivers of England carried a very considerable trade from medieval times onwards, and that through their tributaries (many of them insignificant streams today) they reached far inland and gave rise to a multitude of busy little river-ports.[17]

The major river systems were the Thames, the Great Ouse, the Severn, and the Trent. The Thames was navigable in the sixteenth century for craft of one sort or another from the sea up to Burcot Wharf, near Dorchester: then came a virtually impassable stretch to Oxford which required transhipment to carts: and finally the river became navigable again from Oxford to well above Lechlade. Not until 1605 was there sufficient pressure to secure an Act for the improvement of the difficult stretch, and even then the work went on too slowly. Throughout the sixteenth century the Thames below Burcot carried a considerable proportion of London's grain supply, as it did up-river from the coast of Kent.

The Great Ouse, flowing into the sea below King's Lynn, was probably the second largest river system in economic terms, possibly even the greatest because of its ramifications. Though not as long as Trent or Severn, it drained with its navigable tributaries some eight counties, and those among the richest in England. A writer in Edward VI's time speaks of it as 'the milky way, by reason of those accommodations of merchandize, food, and necessary provision, which are constantly carried up and down it; and Lynn fits at the door of this river, as it were the turnkey of it'.[18]

The Great Ouse itself was navigable right up to Bedford for ships of 15 tons, and its tributary the Cam up to Cambridge. The Lynn–Cambridge traffic was especially important to both towns, and they were frequently at loggerheads. From Lynn wine, fish, salt, and coal went up to Cambridge by keels and lighters, which returned with corn,

---

[17] Willan, *River Navigation in England, 1600–1750*, is naturally sketchy on the sixteenth century; but it should be said that the frontispiece map of navigable rivers 1600–60 calls for detailed amendment in several places. The fifteenth and sixteenth centuries would repay a special study: what is said in this section is a mere beginning.

[18] Quoted by Williams, 'The maritime trade of the East Anglian ports, 1550–1590'. Most of what follows about the Great Ouse system is drawn from this thesis, with grateful acknowledgement to the author.

butter and cheese. This was a regular trade throughout the year, greatly enhanced in September by the Stourbridge Fair at Cambridge, by now the most famous fair in all England and notable, besides all else, for the quantities of raw materials from the Baltic countries. Some Cambridge ships traded as far as London (via Lynn), as did some from York and Lincoln, though in general the majority of craft kept to the Fenland rivers. Lynn aimed at a monopoly of this teeming river traffic. As early as 1535 a Star Chamber decree was obtained to compel the authorities at Lynn to give full harbour facilities to all craft belonging to Cambridge merchants, which were also to be allowed to pass without tolls of any kind. In the time of Edward VI there was further trouble. The Mayor of Cambridge complained that Lynn merchants prevented Cambridge men from passing through the haven and refused to allow them to unload there. The Lynn council had passed a resolution that no stranger to Lynn should rent any warehouse, yard or chamber in the town: but again Cambridge won the case.

Less important, but still busy, were the Little Ouse and the Lark, where Brandon (on the Little Ouse) and Mildenhall (on the Lark) were river-ports at which cargoes were transferred to keels. Thetford was the head of navigation on the Little Ouse, where cargoes were transferred to the main London to Norwich road (now the A11).

Lynn also controlled to some extent the river traffic on the Nene and Welland. It is not certain how far the Nene was navigable,[19] but Yaxley (in Hunts) was the scene of a bitter dispute in 1528 between 'the poor inhabitants' of Yaxley and a merchant of Lynn who was loading his keel with peas to take away, while the local people starved: the harvests of 1527 and 1528 had been very bad. In the previous year (1527) the Lynn men had collected all the local pease crop for export to Scotland.[20] In the early fourteenth century, ships or boats could get as far as Yaxley, Holme, Glatton, and Ramsey; and 'divers lodes and trenches' brought water traffic as far up as Walton, Sawtrey, and Connington.[21] Several of these little river-ports lay on or very near the

---

[19] This would be the Old Nene, whose course was very different from that of the present river. The major changes seem to have taken place in the eighteenth century.

[20] *T.E.D.*, I, 144—6.

[21] Gras, *Evolution of the English Corn Market*, p. 62. The medieval references are dated 1331—42. There is no reason to think these small ports had been abandoned by the sixteenth century: we know that Yaxley was still active. Similarly, the Cam developed a number of river-ports reached by artificial cuts or lodes from the main river. Of these, Burwell is the best example where the

Old North Road (the present A1) and it seems most likely that they were deliberately chosen to be transhipment points from water to a great through road. Indeed, we can generalize and say that everywhere east of the Old North Road rivers and lodes were the normal means of carriage for goods.

The Welland and its trade are rather more obscure. At one time it had probably been navigable up to Stamford, an important wool-collecting centre and the scene of a medieval fair of international reputation. Here again the river navigation met the Old North Road. That Stamford had once been the head of navigation is implied by the petition of the town authorities and the commonalty which resulted in the Act of 13 Elizabeth (1570). 'The town had formerly been inhabited by many opulent merchants, whose wealth had been advanced by the navigation of the River Welland, and its connexion with Boston, Lynn, and other ports.' It had since gone into great ruin and decay (this was certainly so after the 1540s), partly at least because the navigation from Stamford to Market Deeping had been impeded by the erection of mills, with a consequent blocking of the river. The Act was intended to make the Welland navigable from Stamford to the sea, but not until the early 1620s was the work complete. The failure to implement the first Act was apparently due to a desperate shortage of cash in a town already decayed, a not uncommon cause in the sixteenth century of failure to keep a navigable river open.

Less is known about the Severn and its traffic. It was navigable as far up as Welshpool,[22] on the borders of Wales, and undoubtedly carried a vast traffic up and down. Even as large a river as this, however, could be rendered unnavigable for up to five months in the year through low water. Two Acts (1503–04 and 1542–43) concerning the river show how important it was. The earlier Act (19 Henry VII, c.18) recited that the free navigation of the river was interrupted by various people and authorities on or near its banks, and it cites an Act of 9 Henry VI which had tried to deal with earlier troubles. Among other frictions, the officers of Gloucester, Worcester and other riverside places imposed

[22] Mendenhall, *The Shrewsbury Drapers and the Welsh Wool Trade*, p. 36. Between Welshpool and Shrewsbury barges were used, but they were subject to low water in summer and floods in winter. The bargemen were therefore as undependable as the road-carriers. There was a small trade in Welsh cottons down the Severn from Shrewsbury to Bristol from the last quarter of the sixteenth century, but it was not fully established until 1605 (op. cit., p. 68).

numerous docks can still be traced behind the houses on the main street. Another old river-port was Reach, anciently a market town.

tolls on all river traffic. The Act provided that all persons making such impositions should be penalized unless they could produce an ancient title to levy such duties. The Act of 34–35 Henry VIII (1542–43) reveals something of the kind of trade the river carried and the problems that arose. 'Boats and vessells' came down the Severn with cargoes of corn and grain, which were transferred to large vessels waiting in the river about 5 miles north of the Avon mouth. The latter then discharged their ballast of stones and other rubble into the river to make room for the Midland corn, to the detriment of the navigation. The Act stated that ballast was only to be unloaded above high-water mark in future. Another considerable trade down the Severn had been in wool down to Bristol, though this was perhaps declining in favour of cloth by Henry VIII's time. Coal also became an important riverborne trade from Shropshire downwards: the first barge-load is said to have come down the Severn in 1520. Gradually it became the most important commodity carried on the river.

The busy port of Ipswich continually had trouble with barge-masters who threw ballast into the Orwell to lighten their load in shallow water, or simply to make room for a paying cargo.[23] Above Ipswich, the Orwell (now called the Gipping) had been navigable up to Stowmarket, in the very heart of Suffolk and some 15 miles further upstream, 'to the great profit and commodity of all the inhabitants of the said country and to the common wealth of the same'. But by the 1530s this stretch had been blocked by the erection of mills at Ipswich, which occasioned a suit in the Star Chamber. In the eleventh century, indeed, it was said that Caen stone for the abbey church at Bury St Edmunds had been carried by water as high up as Rattlesden, 5 miles beyond Stowmarket along this now tiny stream, to be carted the last 8 or 9 miles by road.[24]

The Stour, which joins the Orwell near Harwich in a wide estuary, tapped the richest cloth-making region in England, up past Manningtree to Nayland, Bures and Sudbury, with Lavenham, Kersey and Hadleigh not far away. It is inconceivable that it was not used for many miles as a route to London. We know it was used up to Manningtree at least, though much Suffolk cloth went to London directly by road.

The Act of 23 Henry VIII (1530–31) relating to the Yorkshire Ouse and Humber, passed at the instigation of the city of York, reveals

---

[23] Bacon, *Annals of Ipswich*, pp. 164, 195, 207, 209, 261. As early as 1492 ships throwing ballast into the river were to be fined 12*d* per ton thrown out, but the nuisance continued at least until the 1530s.
[24] Webb, *Great Tooley*, pp. 101, 102.

another common kind of riverine obstacle besides mills and ballast, and that was fishgarths, piles, stakes, and weirs, which had apparently multiplied in the two great rivers to the detriment of the river trade between York and Hull. Silting of a navigable river was another common cause of the decay of waterborne traffic, as at both York and Boston. In bad times towns tended to neglect the expensive outlay required to keep their river clear, and later, when the river became clogged, blamed their decay on the forces of nature. The Yorkshire Ouse had in medieval times been described as 'a highway and the greatest of all the king's rivers within this kingdom of England'. It was then navigable as far up as Boroughbridge — again the familiar river terminus on the Great North Road — and the Wharfe carried traffic up to Tadcaster, and the Don to Doncaster. The relatively small river Hull was navigable for no less than 20 or so miles up to Wansford, near Great Driffield. It is possible that the Ouse waterways carried less traffic by the early sixteenth century than in medieval times,[25] but Beverley was still actively disputing with Kingston-upon-Hull in the 1550s about tolls and harbour facilities: and even in the seventeenth century it was still possible to reach Wansford, though the way was then hazardous.

The river traffic on the Trent is singularly ill-documented. Willan shows the river navigable only up to Nottingham *c*. 1600, but there must have been lighter vessels going much further upstream. 'Navigable' in any event is a relative term. There were ships, boats, keels and lighters, all of varying draught, and rivers were more navigable at some seasons than others.

In Norfolk, the Yare, Waveney and Bure were all used for river traffic, a small but busy river system that converged on Great Yarmouth as the Great Ouse, Nene and Welland all converged on Lynn. In early medieval times, Norwich (on the Yare) could be reached by seagoing ships. By the time of Henry VIII the river had become too shallow (or perhaps ships had grown larger) and incoming cargoes were transferred at Yarmouth to lighters, which were sailing-craft and not horsedrawn barges.[26] Most were owned by Norwich men, and a great deal of Norwich trade went down the river, to be transferred at Yarmouth. As an indication of the relative costs of water- and land-carriage, merchants had to pay eighteen times as much by road as by water when the Yare froze over in the hard winter of 1607—08. All the

---

[25] Duckham, *Navigable Rivers of Yorkshire*, p. 11. Most of the material on the Yorkshire Ouse system is drawn from this source.
[26] Williams, op. cit., for information about these three rivers.

rivers of England froze over for ten weeks, laden carts could move on the ice, and mills froze so that they could not grind any corn. The whole pre-industrial economy was, at times, at the mercy of the weather.

The Bure was navigable for lighters of up to 30 tons as far as Aylsham; and the Waveney could take 20-ton barges or keels as far up as Bungay. A survey of Mettingham Castle, just outside Bungay, in 1562 says that timber growing locally could be sold at high prices because it could be conveyed to London by water.[27]

Far away in the Somerset Levels was another active river system, though not a single river is of any notable size today. Barges could reach Langport in the middle of the county, and indeed continued to do so until within living memory. In the thirteenth century there was a network of streams serving Glastonbury Abbey, reaching up as far as Steanbow where an important road took over. Similarly, the Abbots of Athelney used the Yeo right up to Ilchester on the Fosse Way. It is hard to believe that the rich monastic houses of mid-Somerset had allowed these useful waterways to decay before the Dissolution, though there may well have been neglect afterwards.

Enough has been said to show that river traffic formed a large proportion of internal trade; that some large rivers formed an intricate system with wide ramifications; that even minor rivers could have their own locally important systems; and that in many places river traffic tied up at critical points with the old through-roads of the country, often Roman in origin.

During the sixteenth century eight Acts were passed dealing with the improvement or maintenance of rivers already in use as navigations. Of these, five were passed between 1504 and 1543, but we do not know with what result; three related to the clearing of Severn, Humber, and Yorkshire Ouse of manmade obstructions.

The Act of 6 Henry VIII empowered the deepening and clearing of the Kentish Stour from Canterbury to Fordwich. The river had apparently been navigable at one time up to Canterbury, which was now alleged to be in 'great ruin and decay', but mills and dams had blocked the channel. Apparently, too, it was intended to deepen, cleanse, and scour the river all the way up to Great Chart (above Ashford) for lighters and boats. This would have taken river traffic to and from the heart of Kent, but it seems that nothing was done. We do know, however, that the Act of 1540 for clearing the channel of the Exe in

[27] I am indebted to Mr John Ridgard for this reference.

Devon up to Exeter produced results after nearly thirty years. Exeter had been reached by seagoing vessels from Roman if not pre-Roman times, but the river had been blocked by weirs in the thirteenth century (the work of the Earls and Countesses of Devon). With the downfall of the Courtenays in 1538 the city of Exeter obtained powers to remove these medieval obstructions. This immediate effort failed, so in 1564 a new cut was made around the impassable stretch: this, the first ship canal in England, and the first to employ the foreign device of the pound lock, was opened to traffic in the autumn of 1567. It was largely paid for by the confiscation and sale of plate from the city's score of medieval churches. Exeter was prosperous, it had a city council composed almost exclusively of merchants, and once the right idea dawned the money was found and the canal was born.

INLAND TRADE: THE ROADS

Road traffic is even less documented than riverborne, but the survival of the unique brokage books at Southampton gives us a remarkable picture of the extent of such traffic in the half-century between the 1440s and the 1490s.[28] They are not a complete record, for various reasons, yet even so they show no fewer than 6,689 laden carts leaving the town in four years between 1439 and 1451, and 223 laden packhorses. A great deal of this traffic served the Hampshire region (Winchester and Salisbury were both important destinations), but much went to London and as far afield as Oxford, Gloucester, Worcester and Coventry. Much of the long-distance trade was in materials for the cloth industry, the woad traffic from Southampton to Coventry being especially notable. Later books (for the 1490s) show that this trade had dwindled greatly, but the wine trade to London, Salisbury, and Winchester remained important. The trade in woad and alum for the Salisbury cloth trade had also fallen greatly by the 1490s.

The record is far less complete for inward traffic, but the overall picture of commercial traffic by road destroys any notion that roads were 'bad' and dangerous. A wide range of goods left Southampton for places as far away as Manchester, Yeovil, Kendal and Sandwich.

Southampton was a busy port and perhaps not wholly typical, yet there are plenty of hints that many other roads of England carried a

---

[28] The broker sat at the Bargate and took toll from all merchants or carters leaving or entering the city. Three volumes of these records have been published: Bunyard, ed., *Brokage Book of Southampton 1439–40*, 1941, and Olive Coleman, ed., *The Brokage Book of Southampton 1443–44*, 2 vols, 1960, 1961.

regular well-established traffic. The major port of Newcastle had in 1504 a monopoly, among other commodities, of the export of lead, wool, and wool fells from Cumberland and Westmorland,[29] all of which must have come across the Pennine moors by carts, wagons, and pack-horses. There was also the considerable traffic in wool and wool fells from the hinterland counties of Northumberland and Durham.

Other towns with good water communications made considerable use of roads. Thus, though Norwich used the Yare a good deal, the river was taking in the 1560s and 1570s only 5 to 10 per cent of the total cloth output. Most went to meet the local demand and to fairs and markets all over England. Norwich had two great fairs a year — the Tombland Fair beginning on Good Friday, and the Whitsun Fair — and fairs and markets were served by roads rather than rivers.[30]

Then, too, the seaports and river-ports of England were the distribu-tion centres for a wide hinterland. Most of this trade went by road. We only discover the range of a merchant's inland trade from the chance survival of his account books or a probate inventory. So the inventory of John Broke, mercer of London, who died in 1533, lists 'doubtful debts' in twenty-nine different places, most of which could only be reached by road. Such were Coventry, Kings Norton (near Birming-ham), Bedford, Atherstone, Leicester, Loughborough, several places in Kent and elsewhere.[31] The list is probably far from complete as 'sperat debts' are not itemized. Robert Tooley, the Ipswich merchant, was distributing goods to at least eighty different places in the 1520s and 1530s, most of them within a 30-mile radius of the port but some-times as far away as Newmarket and Bury St Edmunds, Maldon and Thetford. He confined himself to his own county of Suffolk, rarely going over the border into Norfolk except to Yarmouth (and hence Norwich) which he could reach by sea.[32] It is unfortunate that we do not possess the probate inventories of the greater merchants of Norwich. At Exeter, Harry Maunder (d. 1564) had customers in thirty-odd different places, the most distant being Dorchester. Most were within a 20-mile radius.

Coventry, still one of the richest cities in England though decaying by the 1520s, must have been the focus of road traffic from every point of the compass. It figures in Southampton records and in London

[29] Welford, *History of Newcastle and Gateshead*, 1885, II, pp. 19, 23.
[30] Williams, pp. 364—5.
[31] Devon Record Office, Broke Papers, FY.36 (1533).
[32] Webb, op. cit., p. 99.

merchants' books, and it had a regular traffic in fish from the east coast. Its valuable cloth trade must have left the city entirely by road, but of this we know nothing; nor do we at Norwich.

One busy road trade we hear of, as usual, by accident. This was the trade in corn, malt and other grain from five counties to the north which regularly supplied the bakers and brewers of London: Hertford, Middlesex, Cambridgeshire, Bedfordshire, and Essex. It comes to light only because of a battle over the proposal to clear the channel of the Lea from Ware, 20 miles out, into London in 1571. At Ware the Old North Road had met the navigable river, the familiar conjunction in medieval England. Barges were carrying corn from Ware to London in the early thirteenth century. They still used the river in the 1420s, but it was deteriorating. Various petitions for clearing the channel followed, but meanwhile corn and malt were carried by road as far as Enfield before being loaded into barges. Indeed, much malt (lighter and more valuable than corn) was carried all the way into London by road. One reliable witness (who died in 1573) recalled he had counted no fewer than 2,200 pack-horses in one morning on the road between Shoreditch and Enfield.

The reopening of the river to Ware in the early 1570s produced petitions to Burghley and direct action from the Enfield 'loaders'. The new locks were damaged, barges were attacked with gunpowder. One petition reveals incidentally that laden barges drew only 16 inches of water, which throws light on the potential extent of navigable water-ways in Tudor England. A petition to Burghley in 1581 recites that 'many thousands' of people in the five corn-growing counties were now 'utterly decayed' by the waterborne traffic down the Lea to London: but a counterpetition says that the London to Ware road is now more tolerable for other users than when 'it was pestered with malt horses besides very many other commodities'. By 1588 there were forty-four barges plying on the river, employing 123 men. As to relative costs, a baker reckoned that by road his ten horses had cost him at least £100 a year to feed: now he could have as much meal by boat for £30. Corn and malt went down-river to London, and coal and iron made the return journey up to Ware and even Hertford.[33]

Another regular trade was that in Welsh cloth from Oswestry to navigable water at Shrewsbury, 18 miles away; but much went on by regular carriers all the way to London for general sale and export

[33] Hunt, *The History of Ware*, 1949, pp. 17–19. Also Pam, *Tudor Enfield*, for a more detailed and scholarly account of the struggle over the navigation.

abroad. Carriers averaged 20 miles a day, each horse carrying four pieces of cloth.[34]

Other established routes were the ancient saltways which criss-crossed the country from the producing areas of the east coast and the West Midlands; but more important were the long through routes known as drove roads, used for centuries by herds of cattle and to a lesser extent by sheep. The cattle trade from Wales into the fattening pastures of the heart of England already existed in the thirteenth century; and from here the animals went on later to their doom at Smithfield and other large urban centres. Other drove roads crossed the Anglo–Scottish frontier, and yet others were internal routes that led eventually to the specialist cattle fairs and markets. We read of Welsh cattle being fattened as far away as Romney Marsh even in the 1520s. Altogether there must have been thousands of miles of drove roads in England, Wales, and Scotland, the greatest mileage being in England with its multitude of markets, fairs, and urban centres of consumption.

Despite the marked growth of private trading as the sixteenth century went on, the bulk of inland trade still passed through weekly markets and periodic fairs.[35] Altogether there were about 760 market towns in England (some had more than one market a week) and fifty in Wales. Most were of ancient origin: very few were added in the six-teenth century. It is possible that the bulk of agricultural produce never reached any market. Even so, much of the larger and more valuable commodities such as cattle, corn, sheep and wool came by road to markets and fairs, some of which were already highly specialized. It has been reckoned that out of some 800 market towns in England and Wales, rather more than 300 tended to specialize in a particular product by 1640. Possibly this specialization had become more marked with the expansion of marketing in general as the sixteenth century went on and also with the growing specialization of agriculture. But the pages of Leland (in the 1530s) bear ample witness to the existence of lively market towns famed for one thing above all, and in general to the dominant part played by the weekly market in the whole economy and life of a town. It was not only the market itself, but the multitude of handicrafts that a large market naturally engendered. The withdrawal or decay of a market could ruin a whole town. Leland notes particularly

[34] Mendenhall, op. cit., pp. 34–5.
[35] Alan Everitt, 'The marketing of agricultural produce', in *A.H.E.W.*, IV, 466–592, on which the following section is based. It is difficult to overpraise this pioneer essay.

the town of Leominster, which had formerly had a flourishing Saturday market greatly frequented by a wide countryside to the annoyance of both Hereford and Worcester men who, more powerful in high places, caused the day of Leominster market to be changed to Friday. The mere change of day was enough to ruin the market and send the town into decay. Clearly, Saturday was the best day of the week to hold a market, when a whole countryside came in and enjoyed the end of a working week. But apart from changes of day, markets could decay for purely geographical reasons. Leland often refers to places where this had happened. Trade had gone elsewhere.

Market towns were far from evenly distributed over the countryside. The average market area in England was 70 square miles; in Wales more than twice as large, as we might expect. But averages are quite misleading: Hertfordshire's twenty market towns each carved up 20,000 acres of a prosperous countryside: Northumberland's eight markets as many as 161,000 acres each. It is not a simple equation between acreage and relative prosperity. Much depended on the nature of the product; nor did the bigger markets necessarily draw only on the average acreage — far from it. They might well overlap, but on different days. A biggish farmer might patronize several markets.

More to the point as regards the degree to which roads were used in early Tudor England: how far did people travel to market each week? This varied widely in different regions, and for different products. On average, people travelled 7 miles each way. This represented a day's walk with butter, eggs, poultry and light-weight provisions, with time to sell and talk; but at the other extreme the usual cattle-market area was an 11-mile radius, and to the larger sheep marts of the north and Midlands it might be 40 or 50 miles and more: clearly a week's undertaking with animals on the hoof. Corn was a less extensive commodity: in East Anglia few sellers came from more than 10 miles, most about 5.

The mere fact that there were some 800 markets every week and innumerable fairs throughout the year generated a constant traffic by road. Not all fairs by any means were held in market towns, though the two generally went together.[36] Somerset had thirty-nine market towns and no fewer than 180 fairs. A writer in 1572 lists 352 'principal fairs' in England as a whole, but the 1602 edition of his work lists 494. Fairs tended to be more specialized perhaps than markets. The most important were cattle-fairs, some of them of great size; sheep- and horse-fairs

[36] Everitt, loc. cit., pp. 532–43.

were also notable. At the other extreme for variety was Stourbridge Fair which was a vast emporium for eastern England and even further afield. Leland, for all his special addiction to fairs and markets, does not even mention it, though it was already ancient and important. By 1516 it had grown to a duration of over five weeks, from 24 August to 29 September, laid out on so grand a scale that it had its own 'street-names'. In 1549 the proclamation of the fair mentioned particularly various ales and wines, bread, fish (salted and fresh), flax, yarn, cloth (woollen and linen), silk, pitch, tar, coal, charcoal, faggots, salt, hay and grain. This was probably only a small sample of the wares on show, for medieval records mention yet others. Already by the fifteenth century, Stourbridge Fair had become a mart for London importers and producers, and for more distant towns. Much of this enormous assembly of goods reached Cambridge by road from all directions, but a great deal came up the Great Ouse and the Cam: hence the bitter disputes over the waterway between the authorities of Lynn and Cambridge. For the consumer, from noble households down to peasant families, the fair was a grand stocking-up for the year ahead.

In addition to organized markets and fairs, private trading between sellers and buyers was beginning to develop, more so in some regions and in some commodities than others. It was a growing practice that was viewed with suspicion by the government and by the mass of conservatively-minded people for it escaped the regulations of the marketplace, disregarded as antiquated such notions as 'the just price', led to forestalling and engrossing, and thence to higher prices generally to the consumer. The malt and grain trade through Ware and Enfield seems to have been entirely in the hands of the private trader and was based largely on credit. The maltmen were a wealthy class by the closing decades of the fifteenth century and became more so in the Tudor period, buying from farmers and maltsters on credit and extending credit to the larger brewers and bakers of London. Hundreds of pounds in credit might be involved (several thousands today): it was not a trade for small, timid men, who quickly went to the wall. Gradually, private trading extended, especially during the second half of the century and especially in corn, cattle, sheep and wool. Yet such was the expansion of inland trade in general after 1550 that markets and fairs also expanded in volume. There was room for all.

The revival of inland trade may have begun well back in the 1400s. Several rivers were being improved by the second quarter of the century. The evidence for road traffic is mainly that of bridges, where

205

we find old timber bridges being replaced by stone, and stone bridges being repaired or completely rebuilt. In the diocese of Exeter (the counties of Cornwall and Devon), not the most advanced part of England economically, the bishops' registers are strewn with references to indulgences for bridge-building for a century or so.[37] Scarcely a minor river lacked its new bridge (many still stand), and major rivers like the Tamar had no fewer than half a dozen new stone bridges built between 1437 and 1500. Many of these magnificent bridges, like those of Bideford and Barnstaple in north Devon, Wadebridge in Cornwall, Staverton and Holne over the Dart in south Devon, Greyston and New Bridge linking Devon and Cornwall, survive, and many still carry heavy modern traffic. We may know too little about the roads they carried in those generations, but it is inconceivable that such masterpieces of bridge-building, as some of them are, were made for the benefit of miserably bad roads. They were made because there was a pressing need with the renewal of road traffic after the post-1350 decline. Bishop Redman of Exeter could average nearly 60 miles a day when riding to London in the 1490s — a feat of endurance. Ordinary traffic was much more leisurely, but the fact that it was possible to move at this pace should end once for all the idea that English roads were of little consequence in the century between 1450 and 1550. They must have teemed with traffic, more so in some regions than others; though in the depths of winter they subsided into a muddy quiet for weeks on end, a not unwelcome calm when the vast majority of people lived in a rhythm dictated by the seasons.

[37] Hoskins, 'The wealth of medieval Devon', pp. 236–7, 240–1; and Henderson, *Old Cornish Bridges*, generally.

CHAPTER NINE

The End of an Age

_____

WAR

AM ID the complicated political, economic and other changes during Henry's long reign, it is often the intelligent foreign observers who see the wood rather than the overcrowded trees of facts. They were not invariably right in their conclusions, as witness the so-called *Italian Relation of England*, but occasionally they clear a swathe through the jungle. The best of these reports are those of the Venetian ambassadors. A considerable part of the reign, and even more of its economic resources, was devoted by Henry to fighting futile and vainglorious wars on various pretexts. Of the second war with France (1522–25) the ambassador reported back to Venice as early as August 1522 (the war had only begun in May of that year) that 'the whole population is dissatisfied with the war because they are made to pay and do not approve of these affairs'. And Barbaro's report made nearly thirty years later (May 1551) adds some significant observations about the state of the economy four years after Henry's unlamented death. After observing that Henry had made himself 'master of all the gold and silver of his realm, which was the cause of its ruin' he goes on to make a point which has never been fully explored. 'Considering', he says, 'how very many persons who had the management of the war have become immensely wealthy, and how recklessly the money is spent, and how many appetites his late Majesty had to gratify', very little of the vast sums levied by the King was left in the coffers.

Thanks to Postan, we know far more about the economics of the Hundred Years' War, and the financial and commercial magnates involved, than we do about those who ran Henry's wars on the financial and supply side.[1]

Apart from this lust for military glory, from 1511 onwards (the first French war), rising to a positive mania during the last twenty-five years of the reign, Thomas Cromwell was worried by Henry's growing obsession with building new palaces and purchases of new manors. By 1534 he was writing: 'What a great charge it is to the king to continue his buildings in so many places at once ... if the king would spare [i.e. save] for one year how profitable it would be to him.'[2]

In 1525 Wolsey, the richest and most powerful magnate in the kingdom, had passed over his uncompleted palace at Hampton Court, begun ten years earlier, to the King. Wolsey finally fell in 1529; within two years Henry began work on the Great Hall, completed in 1536. Wolsey, too, had begun Whitehall Palace (called York Place to begin with), but Henry took it over and completed the building in 1530–36. Simultaneously Henry was building St James's Palace from 1532 to 1540; and among the lesser works was the superb screen in King's College chapel at Cambridge. Finally he began work on the monstrous palace of Nonsuch (in 1538) which Summerson suggests may have been an attempt to rival Francis I's Château of Chambord begun in 1526. Nonsuch was still unfinished when Henry died, and was sold by his daughter Mary into private hands. It was a spectacular waste of money. The total amount of money spent by Henry on building is not known, but at the time of his death he had accumulated over forty houses in various parts of the country and the expenditure on them – apart from such major works as Hampton Court and Nonsuch – was very considerable.[3] No wonder Cromwell was complaining so bitterly by the early 1530s about the King's waste of his resources.

As well as these great civil buildings, Henry also caused to be built a chain of fortresses (about 1539–40) along the south coast, from Sandwich in Kent right along to St Mawes and Pendennis in distant Cornwall, as well as castles in the Thames estuary and on the Isle of Wight. These were purely military structures, a protection against the possibility of invasion by the Emperor Charles and Francis I. Many

---

[1] The only study I know is by Davies, 'Provisions for armies, 1509–50', *Econ. H.R.*, sec. ser., XVII, no. 2, 1964.

[2] Dietz, *English Government Finance*, I, p. 104.

[3] Personal letter from Mr H. M. Colvin of St John's College, Oxford. Volume IV of the *King's Works*, edited by Mr Colvin is not yet completed, but will eventually provide the individual figures for Henry's houses and hence the total for his reign.

remain to this day as tourist attractions. Their total cost, according to Dietz, was something over £200,000.[4]

It was Henry's almost incessant wars that not only bedevilled his own finances but also impoverished the whole country except the usual small class of those who always profit in more or less obscure ways from war, and always will.

Within two years of assuming the throne Henry began his ill-fated first war with France, lasting from 1511 to 1514 and achieving precisely nothing. It cost just under £900,000 but if we add the aids and subsidies to the Emperor and other payments the total was not far short of a million pounds. Such figures are admittedly meaningless unless we can translate them into modern terms by a credible multiplier, and above all relate them to the total national income at the time, which we have no means of knowing. France was the principal enemy, the major cause of mad expenditure, but Scotland, and to a lesser extent Ireland, also involved war and money. The second French war, lasting from 1522 to 1525, cannot be costed with any accuracy over the whole period: all we can say is that as a start more than £350,000 was raised by forced loans in 1522−23, and this with further taxation brings the total to some £400,000 by the end of the 1523 campaign. Nor does this take account of the unprecedented yields from the subsidies of 1523−27. The 'scarcity of money' and the popular unrest all over the country is a feature of English economic history in the early 1520s.

The rich, of course, could always evade a substantial part of their tax obligations. The subject has been touched on earlier (see pp. 21−2, 41). But the unprecedented taxation of this period stimulated them greatly. So at York in 1498 the Bishop of Carlisle and Lord Surrey reported that the subsidy is being levied on the poor 'while the Lord Mayor and his brethren [i.e. the council] and other persons in favour are but little charged towards the said duty and subsidy. The collectors are feeble and decrepit and not of power to gather the tax.' The city fathers seem tacitly to have accepted the charge. And at Norwich, the great Wolsey himself, with his eye even for local detail, queried the assessments of 1525 of the rich in the city and in the county.[5] The point might be thought to be hardly worth making but for the fact that the most

[4] These and the following figures relating to the cost of Henry's wars are taken from Dietz. Though Dietz has been criticized often enough, the fact remains that his work remains by far the most authoritative we have, and anyone who has toiled over Tudor accounts and arithmetic owes him a vast debt.

[5] For York, see *York Civic Records*, II, 136−7; for Norwich, see *L.P.*, IV, pt 3, Appendix, no. 36.

effective weapon for diminishing the gap between rich and poor is a swingeing taxation policy, and this, despite the brave words and figures on Tudor paper, and a somewhat tightened administration, was simply not being achieved.

Perhaps it is best to sum it up by saying that Dietz reckons that the total cost of the wars with France and Scotland between 1511 and 1547 amounted to £2,134,784, Scotland alone costing some £350,000. And still nothing was solved by this egomaniac. Even his so-called 'victories' proved to be nonsense: the capture of Boulogne in 1544 cost nearly £600,000 and hanging on to it afterwards another £400,000 odd – a million pounds expended on one useless military endeavour.

Wars were now costing far more than in the recent past, due not only to a slight monetary inflation but also to their growing scale. When another war loomed up, that of 1542–46, Cromwell knew beforehand that it would surpass all previous wars in costs: and so it did.

The country's finances were already in a critical position and usual methods of taxation were running pretty dry. Henry spent another £1,300,000 in 1544–45, but the subsidy and the Benevolence only brought in some £300,000 between them. Hence the beginning of the outright selling-off of ecclesiastical lands, while the confiscated church plate was melted down and turned into coins. The war had been estimated (by Henry) to cost about £250,000 altogether, but was costing £600,000 to £700,000 a year before it was over. Since the nation had been bled dry, a wholesale exploitation of Crown property was decided on: not only lands, but the mountains of confiscated lead from dismantled roofs, and wardships and marriages (both feudal 'incidents' from land held by knight service), all were sold. The lead had been held in reserve and the bulk of the world supply came from England and Spain. Indeed England had almost a monopoly in western Europe, not only in monastic spoil but also in her own lead mines. The lead sales proved disappointing. Most of the £1½ million from the sale of monastic movables went on the French war: Henry was forced by his own policy to be a financial opportunist and the Court of Augmentations had no hope of husbanding the new resources as part of the future regular income of the Crown.[6]

[6] This paragraph is based entirely on Richardson, 'Some financial expedients of Henry VIII', *Econ. H.R.*, sec. ser., VII, 1954. Yet Richardson makes the extraordinary statement that 'economically the country was stable and prosperous, well able to carry the war burden'. I come to a totally different conclusion, even allowing for the fact that the rich had by now learnt how to evade the worst of their burden by faking their own assessments.

Not only did Henry drain the economy of nearly all its money but his armies drew heavily on the meagre population of able-bodied men. Armies of 15,000 to 20,000 men were frequently sent to France or to the Scottish border; in the largest campaign of all he led an army of some 48,000 men into northern France in 1544, with 20,000 horses. Such an army was equivalent to about two-thirds of the total population of London, or three times that of Norwich. Many of these men were foreign mercenaries, but all had to be paid. Ireland was also a running sore in the 1530s, consuming men and money and providing an additional source of worry to the Exchequer and Cromwell. Despite the increase of revenues from the suppression of the Irish monasteries in 1538 and 1539, the army in Ireland at times became mutinous and was in danger of breaking up for lack of pay.[7]

Henry was not only continually short of ready money for his wars but also short of men. In later years William Harrison remarked that 'King Henry the Eighth ... lamented oft that he was constrained to hire foreign aid, for want of a competent store of soldiers here at home', contrasting his lack with foreign princes who could each summon up 30,000 or 40,000 men out of their own dominions. The so-called Debate of the Heralds (1549) has already been quoted as evidence of the tacit admission by the English speaker that England was greatly underpopulated as compared with France. Even in the mid-century this was still so. There is no convincing evidence for a substantial rise in population before the last quarter of the sixteenth century, long after Henry had ceased to fulminate. The great muster and valuation of 1522 — half financial in purpose, half to comb every town, village, and hamlet for 'able men' — produced some impressive figures of able-bodied men on paper, but only a fraction got as far as the field of battle. Kenyon has remarked in passing that the apparently small armies of this period 'represented an enormous expenditure of national effort'. France was perhaps overpopulated by the fifteenth century, and the wars of the sixteenth may have been a salutary bloodletting, but England certainly could not afford to lose men on anything like this scale. That wars cost England much in manpower despite the extensive use of foreign mercenaries was made clear when English observers in the 1580s attributed the rise of population in their time to the absence of large-scale plague during the preceding decades and to the prolonged peace of Elizabeth's reign. In the campaign of 1513 Henry took abroad about 31,000 men, of whom 24,000 were English and the rest mostly

[7] Dietz, pp. 141—2.

Germans. Such an army represented in Englishmen alone the combined male populations of about seven Coventrys or four Norwiches (assuming that males formed roughly half the total population). These are only approximate calculations, but they serve to show the comparative magnitude of small armies in relation to total human resources; and if we exclude the children and the elderly the impact is that much worse. Small wonder that Elizabeth, with her father's dreadful record in mind, hated war. 'She hated it not merely because it involved killing, but because it almost invariably taxed the state beyond its strength.'[8]

Old-established industries which might well have grown (above all the cloth industry and building) were starved of capital investment. It is possible too that the decay of some eighty named towns, the subject of various acts for rebuilding between 1534 and 1543, may have been due not a little to the sheer lack of money in the country as well as to better investment opportunities in trade.[9]

On the credit side, if such an ambiguous word may be used, the many years of warfare must have stimulated the metal industries, above all the making of cannon in the Sussex and Kentish Weald. Henry had inherited the old organization of army and armaments based on medieval practice. There was no standing army and scarcely any cavalry. The foot soldiers fought with bow and bill, despised by professional soldiers abroad. Henry was slow to see the necessary changes: even in the great war of 1523 no Englishmen were equipped with firearms. The army of 1544 was double that of 1522—23 but still there was very little use of small firearms though more of the larger. Gun foundries were already known and used intermittently but became 'permanent and important establishments' during the 1520s, both for the growing navy and on shore. Buying cannon from abroad became exceptional, so that there was a saving on imports and an increase in home employment. In the 1540s two German specialists were brought over to the arsenal at Greenwich. The new fortifications all along the southern coast, and elsewhere, were made at an unprecedented expense and also gave skilled employment, though artillery was of little use and not decisive until the Battle of Pinkie against the Scots in 1547, after Henry was dead.

---

[8] Johnson, *Elizabeth I*, p. 99.
[9] In *Provincial England*, pp. 77—8, I said that the failure to repair and rebuild even the most important towns was due primarily to the greater profitability of both external and internal trading, so that investment in houses had little or no appeal; but the continual references about this time to the shortage of money must have been a major factor also, which I then overlooked.

It is possible that in addition to the increasing development of furnaces and forges in the Weald, in the countryside which provided iron ore, water-power, and timber as a fuel, the metal industries of the area north-west of Birmingham, now called the Black Country, mostly making small products from nails to spurs and bits, also began to grow into something more substantial, but this seems never to have been studied.[10]

The metal industries of the 'Black Country' were mostly in the hands of small men, many of whom combined skilled metal-working with farming; but the ironworks of the Weald, what little we know about them, seem to have been from the first controlled by large capitalists, since they required much fixed capital and involved extensive excavations (e.g. for furnace and forge ponds) and a greater extent of land for their full development. What was possibly a typical example of the nature and scale of the development of ironworks in the Weald is cited in a petition dated 1548. Alexander Collyn had begun to make a hammer (forge) for iron-making in Kent on land granted to him by Sir John Gresham, knight, owner of the waste ground and common wood in and near Corselewood in Wadhurst. He had already cut down most of the oaks in the wood, and was beginning to fell the beeches also, to the great damage and 'utter undoing' of the inhabitants and tenants in these parts. There were already three hammers and four furnaces in Lamberhurst and Wadhurst, so that development had begun strongly in the 1540s.[11] A new industrial landscape was coming into being, including a great ditch some 1,300 yards long to cut out a big bend in the River Teise. Such works clearly required large capital, and a big landowner to initiate them. Other great landowners involved in the development of the Wealden ironworks in both Kent and Sussex by the 1540s were the Duke of Norfolk, Lord Seymour, and Lord Abergavenny.[12] It may be to such men as these that the Venetian ambassador referred in his report of 1551; but the feeding of armies of unprecedented size also created a class of large purveyors and victuallers and an official class to oversee them which presented many opportunities for corruption and quiet plunder.

---

[10] This section on warfare and weapons in Henry VIII's time is based mostly on Oman, *A History of the Art of War in the XVI Century*. Court, *The Rise of the Midland Industries*, has almost nothing to say about the early sixteenth century.
[11] Straker, *Wealden Iron*, p. 269.
[12] Stone, 'The nobility in business, 1540—1640' in *The Entrepreneur* (Cambridge, 1957).

TAXATION

The main basis of medieval taxation, that of fifteenths in the country areas and tenths from the boroughs, had broken down well back in the fifteenth century. It was still based on crude assessments of the early fourteenth century, finalized as fixed quotas from each town and village in 1334, quotas which had later been reduced more than once to take account of the poverty and depopulation that had followed the epidemics of the period. The original quotas had been rather haphazard in their incidence, with much local evasion; probably the greater part of the population escaped altogether and the rich made their usual token submission. In any event, by the time that Henry needed more money for his wars, the taxation system was about two hundred years out of date as regards assessments. Henry VII and earlier monarchs had tinkered with the old system but to little avail. The first large-scale revision of assessments was that of Henry VIII in 1515, which showed an average increase in the total assessment for England of well over threefold, and even this may have been an underestimate.[13]

Taking the 1515 figures as they stand, there were some remarkable upward revisions, indicating that a considerable part of the country had been wildly underassessed for generations. Thus in six counties the tax yield was more than five times that of the early fourteenth century, the highest being Devon with an 8.5 increase and Middlesex with 8.2 (or 12.6 if London is included).[14] At the other end of the scale, a few counties had less than doubled their yields. Even so, this was only the first squeeze. The total tax yields for all the counties between 1515 and 1545 are set out in Appendix I. They are not adjusted according to the area of the various counties since the Crown was only interested in the total yields and not in historians' averages; and further, we cannot compare the yield in each county as between the different years since the rate of the assessment was different in each levy. This again does not matter for our purpose. It was the total amount of money squeezed out of each county that mattered to the King. Thus, to take one example, the gross yield of fifteenths and tenths in Devon in 1334 was £953 15s; in 1515 the subsidy yielded £2,804; in 1524–25 it was no less than £9,139 though if we accept the fact that this was two separate instalments Devon yielded rather more than £4,500: still, the taxpayer

[13] Schofield, 'The geographical distribution of wealth'.
[14] The tax yields must not be confused with the basic assessments, since rates of tax could vary widely.

had to find well over £9,000 in two consecutive years, not to mention the fact that those over a certain level of assessment were further mulcted in 1527. The 'Benevolence' of 1545 — Henry VIII had some beautiful euphemisms for his extortions, such as the 'Amicable Grant' of 1525 and the 'Devotion Money' of 1543 (which was a total failure) — yielded £4,527 from Devon. Devon no doubt was an exceptional case, with the intervening growth of its textile industry, mining, and probably fishing also; but a study of any other county in the list would show that the country as a whole was vastly underassessed at the beginning of Henry's reign and to that extent the new and formidable tax assessments were fully justified.

There were loud howls over the proposals for the 1522 levy and Wolsey had a bitter struggle in forcing it through. The grant of 1515 had been paid 'unwillingly with extreme complaint' and in 1522, when he demanded a grant of £800,000 at four shillings in the pound, based on the new valuation of that year, he threatened to come down to the Commons in person. As it was, he had to be content with a smaller subsidy than he had hoped for. Nor did the Amicable Grant produce any amity: the London men, where Wolsey was chief tax commissioner, refused to pay even though Wolsey threatened that some might lose their heads over their refusal, and there were widespread troubles in the provinces. Archbishop Warham reported that it would be very difficult to raise the money and that people were 'cursedly saying that they shall never have rest of payments so long as some liveth'.

The subsidies and fifteenths and tenths of the 1540s were if anything more ferocious than those of the 1520s, culminating in the three-instalment levy of 1544—46 and the Benevolence of 1545. Ironically it was the so-called Benevolence that showed Henry at his most ruthless. A London alderman who refused to pay was immediately sent to the Scottish wars (the parallel with the Russian Front in the 1940s comes too readily to mind), where he duly perished. The example was noted by the rest of the taxpayers and the Benevolence was even more productive of money than the forced loan of three years earlier, a loan incidentally which was repudiated by statute the very next year. The finances of Henry's reign were as tangled and brutal as his matrimonial life.

Apart from the vast expenditure on wars and grand buildings, Henry's spending was of no great account, though there was a considerable increase in the expenditure on the royal household from 1538 to 1546. The chief financial officers, Wriothesley and Paget, were at their wits' end to raise the necessary funds to carry on despite the great debasement of the currency in 1544–46, which tried to meet some of the growing cost of yet another French war. Wolsey had first debased the silver currency in 1526, the first serious debasement since the Norman Conquest, though it had the respectable motive of bringing the English coinage into line with continental, so preventing an outflow of 'good' English silver; but the bad example was remembered without the good motives in the 1540s. The successive debasements of 1544–46 in particular were really intended to increase the supply of money in the country by reducing the fineness of the coinage. At the same time the Crown profited greatly: according to Dietz the profits of the Mint arising from the coinage of the debased money 'became the great "shot anchor" of the government, furnishing it with even more money than did the sale of monastic lands'.[15] Even so, the two financial officers were at odds with each other in the autumn of 1545, and with the Council through which the King's importunate demands came. Wriothesley wrote to the Council reminding them how much money had been raised already, lands consumed, and the precious plate of the realm melted down and coined. 'I lament', he said, 'the danger of the time to come.' And to Paget he wrote even more desperately, 'I would you felt a piece of the care and I wene you would not write so often as you do, knowing the state of things as I. . . . You bid me run as though I could make money.'[16] All expedients had been tried: the treasure was now exhausted.

PRICES AND POPULATION

Henry's financial problems may have been complicated to some extent by the major price inflation which is still the most controversial aspect of sixteenth-century economic history. In fact it did not become serious enough to be noticed as a national problem until the late 1540s, right at the end of Henry's reign. There is a whole literature, partly

---

[15] Dietz, op. cit., pp. 154–5.

[16] Ibid., pp. 155, 157, 176. When the English had been exhausted by taxation, Henry discovered the illusory beauties of borrowing money from the great financial centre of Antwerp. He began in 1544 and by the time of his death three years later he had run up a large debt and created further problems for his successors. See Outhwaite, 'Royal borrowing in the reign of Elizabeth' in *Eng. Hist. Rev.*, LXXXVI, 1971, 251–63.

contemporary and still being argued among modern economic historians, and if modern economists cannot agree about our own inflation
it can scarcely be wondered at that historians are just as much at odds
about sixteenth-century inflation. There is little hope as yet of
producing any answer that will be generally agreed.

Among the modern discussions of sixteenth-century inflation, the
most profitable seem to be Peter Ramsey's *The Price Revolution in
Sixteenth-Century England* and R. B. Outhwaite's *Inflation in Tudor
and Early Stuart England*. Ramsey's book has the merit of including a
selection of the major articles on the subject; Outhwaite's has the merit
of being a critical discussion of the main theories now holding the field.
Dr Ramsey wisely opens the whole discussion by saying that 'the great
price rise in Tudor and early Stuart England has been almost as puzzling
to modern economic historians as to worried contemporaries', and
observes almost at once that 'it is in the first place impossible to establish with any certainty how far prices did rise in England during the
sixteenth century'.

Among the varied graphs and statistics of the price-rise, which do we
choose on which to base an argument? 'For only a few commodities
have we reliable and continuous series, where we can be reasonably sure
that we are dealing with the same product over a long period of time.'
It is almost impossible to construct a viable cost of living index, though
the 'working-class budget' I attempt in Chapter Five perhaps takes the
complicated subject a step further. On the whole I prefer to use the
pioneer work of Phelps Brown and Sheila Hopkins, widely used by all
historians since it first appeared twenty years ago. Ramsey criticizes it
by saying that it is oversensitive to harvest fluctuations (but some 90
per cent of a working-class budget went on food and drink, both
dependent on the annual harvest); and that it does not reflect the
budget of the squire, the merchant and the peer (but these are a
minority of the population). Ramsey concedes that with all its defects
the Phelps Brown and Hopkins index can be used, though only with
great caution, as a general guide to the movements of prices in Tudor
England at large. The prices of industrial products present a particularly
difficult problem; yet though the data are few they entered to only a
fractional extent into the general cost of living in England.

The Phelps Brown and Hopkins price index of a composite unit of
consumables, using the period 1451–75 as a base (100) works out as
shown in Table 9.1 for the fifty years 1500–50, covering rather more
than Henry's reign:

217

Table 9.1 Price index for a composite
unit of consumables, 1500—50

1500	94	1526	133
1501	107	1527	147
1502	122	1528	179
1503	114	1529	159
1504	107		
1505	103	1530	169
1506	106	1531	154
1507	98	1532	179
1508	100	1533	169
1509	92	1534	145
		1535	131
1510	103	1536	164
1511	97	1537	155
1512	101	1538	138
1513	120	1539	147
1514	118		
1515	107	1540	158
1516	110	1541	165
1517	111	1542	172
1518	116	1543	171
1519	129	1544	178
		1545	191
1520	137	1546	248
1521	167	1547	231
1522	160	1548	193
1523	136	1549	214
1524	133		
1525	129	1550	262

Although the general trend of these prices is upwards, it is the extreme variations between one year and another which catch the eye; and these are due almost entirely to the rapid fluctuations in harvest prices and food prices in general, since a dearth of grain obviously tended to push up other food prices in sympathy. The pattern becomes a little clearer if we recalculate the annual prices of consumables by decades, beginning at 1450 in order to show the stability during the fifty years up to 1500 and the validity of using these fifty years as a base line for what was to follow:

	Composite unit of foodstuffs	*Sample of industrial products*
	(*average*)	(*average*)
1451—60	98	99
1461—70	105	103

	Composite unit of foodstuffs (average) — cont.	Sample of industrial products (average) — cont.
1471–80	93	100
1481–90	121	103
1491–1500	100	97
1501–10	106	98
1511–20	116	102
1521–30	159	110
1531–40	161	110
1541–50	217	127

It is true that figures calculated over a decade would be meaningless to the average household, in which even seasonal movements in any given year were of more relevance. For this reason the detailed figures for wheat prices given in Appendix III are, for all their deficiencies and qualifications, even more revealing, but they again mask what may have been important regional differences. Even so, the upward trend of food prices in the sixteenth century, expressed in decades, shows that they just about doubled between the first decade and the 1540s. Despite the runs of cheap years the general trend was upward.

The figures for industrial products show a much smaller rise over the same period, roughly about 30 per cent. They represent a small sample and 'raise almost insuperable problems of comparability' (Ramsey), yet they have been used in an important article to throw light on the major problem of when the population of England began to rise after the long depopulation of the fifteenth century.[17]

The problem of population and its rate of growth in England and Wales is an intractable one. The facts and documents are few, and the subject is riddled with myths, the most persistent being that women had naturally large numbers of children (and some indeed did: there are well-authenticated instances of a woman bearing twenty children and upwards) and that the great majority died in infancy. The facts and documents are few and not easy to handle. My own estimate of a population of 2.36 million for England in the 1520s plus 0.24 million for Wales gives a total of 2.60 million for the two countries at that date. The next record of any value is the returns, diocese by diocese, of 1603, which with all the usual faults are reasonably complete, and give a total for England of 3.45 million and of 0.355 million for Wales, a total of 3.80 million for the two countries. The chantry certificates of 1545, worked

[17] Y. S. Brenner, 'The inflation of prices in early sixteenth-century England', *Econ. H.R.*, XIV, no. 2, 1961, reprinted in Ramsey, *The Price Revolution*.

over by J. C. Russell in *British Medieval Population*, are so incomplete and deal so often in round numbers that they must be regarded as worthless for a national computation, valuable though they may be for a great number of individual parishes. So we are left with an increase of about 46 per cent in the eighty years between the early 1520s and 1603, equivalent to an average increase of 5.75 per cent over the whole period.

Such an average is meaningless. There is no doubt that population increased at a very varying rate during these eighty years: the problems are when did the rise begin, and how and why did it vary from time to time?

The only contemporary records that are of the slightest use are the parish registers of baptisms, marriages, and burials, which were ordered to be kept from the autumn of 1538 — one of the many minor yet valuable innovations introduced by Thomas Cromwell. Even allowing for the fact that a considerable proportion have failed to survive from the earliest years, they cannot be used effectively until some time after the starting date, that is until a new generation has appeared on the scene. From, say, the 1550s onwards one can begin to count the population and reconstruct families. We have to make what use we can of incidental evidence, and Brenner is inclined to see in the widening gap between the prices of foodstuffs and of industrial products a pressure of a rising population on a relatively static food supply, for most of the changes of the so-called Agricultural Revolution of the sixteenth century did not begin to operate until much later in the century. There was certainly a marked rise in population in the later years of the century, judging by the evidence of parish registers and of wills. The late Elizabethan family, and more so the Jacobean, resembled nothing more than the typical Victorian family in its bounty of children.[18]

Most of our information comes from the latter part of the century and does not help our immediate problem. But in the absence of any other records for the mass of the population it is only a plausible theory that the widening gap between food prices and industrial prices in the first half of the sixteenth century might be the result of population pressure on a relatively fixed supply of foodstuffs.

In theory a woman could produce some twenty to twenty-five children during her child-bearing life, and not a few heroic women did

[18] I set out some of this evidence in *The Midland Peasant*, in 'The population of Wigston Magna' (reprinted in *Provincial England*), and in 'The rebuilding of rural England' reprinted in the same volume. In my own yeoman family George Hoskins (1563–1625) produced ten children (five sons and five daughters) between 1584 and 1603. All survived into adulthood, and most of them married.

so (among the gentry, for whom the genealogical records are more reliable and copious), but for most women there were various contraceptive methods available. Even allowing for infant deaths, they did not produce half as many children as nature would have dictated. The various methods of contraception practised at this date, and probably long before, are made known to us from the Roman Catholic thunderings against all these practices, or we should be completely in the dark; they have been fully discussed by Professor Noonan in *Contraception* (1967). The Tudor wife was by no means the helpless victim of her husband. Some methods were by modern standards crude in their efficacy, but they worked for the greater part. Infant mortality played a considerable part in reducing even the number of infants that escaped the earlier net, but in all probability for all but the most ignorant element in the population some form of birth control was more important than the crude workings of infant deaths.

To return for a moment to Brenner's argument, he cites not only increased pressure of population on food supplies as a cause of the differential price rise, but also increasing urbanization. There is little doubt about this — the poor drifting to the towns for various reasons, enclosure being perhaps the major cause — but whether it was a major factor is doubtful. Yet it is true that increasing urbanization (though it can be exaggerated in the national picture) meant that town-dwellers ceased to be producers of food and became merely consumers. To that extent there was a pressure on food prices which is not directly attributable to population pressure. And it may be that the remarkable increase in markets, above all perhaps in food markets, as demonstrated by Professor Everitt, in the later sixteenth century may be indirectly due to the tilting of the old balance between country and town. It may not have been much of a tilt in national terms, but in every locality market towns increased in numbers and in importance, and especially the food markets. Thus was the balance between town and country redressed, but no doubt marketing increased the cost of urban living to a noticeable degree.

Whatever the degree of inflation of food prices, the well-to-do were protected by their ownership of tithes, and the larger landlords by the receipt of a portion of their rents in kind and the produce of the demesne. The economic value of tithes in kind, the great tithes especially, has been curiously neglected by economic historians, to whom the ownership of an advowson appears merely a useful piece of property for putting a younger son into the family living. But it was

221

much more than that. Let us look at a few examples of the real importance of tithes especially in a time of rising prices, beginning with the
simple case of William Farington, a Lancashire gentleman whose total
income varied from £700 to £800 a year in the 1570s. Of this total,
tithes in kind were worth £230 to £250 a year. Some were consumed in
the family and the remainder sold. The tithes in kind and his demesne
(kept 'in hand' naturally) supplied nearly all the domestic needs of the
Farington household, including foodstuffs, leather, wool, fruit, fuel and
salmon. In a time of rising prices, indeed, not only were such families
safely hedged against inflation, but their surpluses made the full market
prices and so enhanced the family income.

Though the Farington example comes from a somewhat later date
than Henry's time, this system of economics was centuries old.
Monasteries had been careful to keep several of their demesnes 'in hand'
for their own supplies, and to keep their tithes in kind in the huge stone
barns that still decorate the English countryside, as at Abbotsbury in
Dorset, Great Coxwell in Berkshire, or Bradford-on-Avon in Wiltshire.
Landed magnates did the same, more so when the Dissolution flooded
the market with tithes and advowsons, some of them worth more than
the manors in which they lay and which historians so assiduously
count. In Bedfordshire the Gostwicks rose to the ranks of the gentry
under Henry VIII and were knighted for their valuable administrative
services, which also brought some monastic plums to the family. Sir
John Gostwick (already cited) was a good example of a *nouveau riche*
who felt his way carefully into county society, leaving behind a book of
advice for his son and heir in which he says *inter alia* that he should not
levy enhanced fines on new tenants, nor should he raise his rents unless
his tenants were subletting at a profit. Among the practical advice he
gives is: 'I charge you to keape in your owne handes your parsonage,
the mill, the water and the warren, for these shall be veary necessary for
your howshold.' He was to have his own miller, who was not to be
married, a shepherd and a large flock of sheep, and sundry outdoor and
indoor servants. In addition the son was to keep a portion of the estate
in hand, with all the pastures about it, for cattle and sheep for his
household, and the rearing of young cattle. As a counterweight to the
overpopular myth of rapacious Tudor landlords, Sir John Gostwick lets
Henry Wild 'the keping of the pastures with certen milche kene, which
will helpe him, his wife & his children, for God knoweth he can make
but littell for him selfe'.[19]

[19] 'The Gostwicks of Willington', *Beds. Hist. Rec. Soc.*, XXXVI, 1956, 38–45.

Probably all landed families had similar rules involving the keeping in hand of the great tithes. In the Midlands the Spencers were assiduously buying up tithes over the whole period from 1544 to 1609, and in Essex Sir William Petre's household used rents in kind and the tithes from two lay rectories. Sir William Cecil grew most of his own grain and raised his own beef on his estate at Wimbledon. Grove, in his classic book *Alienated Tithes*, notes that the Duke of Somerset got grants from Edward VI of the tithes of ten country benefices and of sixteen in the city of Norwich. All these reverted to the Crown at the fall of Somerset, and were regranted to other laymen. The Duke of Norfolk had grants of the tithes of upwards of fifty parishes, and portions of the tithes in at least eighty others.

Farmers in general gained in a time of inflation, with enhanced prices for their foodstuffs at market, especially if they were freeholders and need not fear a rack-renting landlord. Such additional moneys served ultimately to supply the cash for the great rebuilding of rural England for which the evidence is abundant from the 1560s onwards.[20] With relatively fixed costs and rising selling-prices the yeoman class consolidated its position at the heart of English rural society during the second half of the sixteenth century. They enlarged their 'estates', adding farm to farm, and their personal estate as reflected in the remarkable rise in domestic comforts and belongings; and a higher proportion made the transition from yeoman to gentry than ever before. All this, it is true, takes place in the second half of the century, but the foundations had been well and truly laid a generation or so before. Probably the husbandman class, mostly copyholders and/or leaseholders, and farming on a smaller scale, also rose to a marked degree in the same period: but here much depended on the nature of their landlord and the precise nature of their tenure. The 'best' landlords did not worry overmuch, seeking rather to stand well with local society and the local community, until the galloping inflation of the later decades compelled them to face the facts of a new situation.

The wage-earning class bore the brunt of any inflation in this period, but even here the bare statistics do not give anything like a true picture. Thorold Rogers, for example, thought that a labourer's real wages might have fallen by as much as 50 per cent during the century. Rogers puts it realistically that a Rutland artisan would have to work forty-three weeks to earn the food in 1610 which his great-grandfather had

[20] See Hoskins, *Provincial England*, pp. 131–48, reprinted from *Past and Present*, no. 4, 1953.

earned in ten weeks in 1495. And a labourer could not earn in fifty-two weeks what his forebears had earned in fifteen weeks in the 1490s. Keynes thought this fall in real wages hardly credible: nor indeed is it.

Such a drastic reduction in the standard of living of the mass of the population is totally unrealistic, since even at the beginning of the century about a third of the population lived below the poverty line and another third on or just above it (see p. 99). Obviously the statistics of food prices and of wage rates tell far from the whole story. There were many mitigating factors.

The chief mitigating factor of the statistics (even for what they are worth for generalizations) is that a large proportion of the labouring class was fed by their employers. Even in towns, wage rates were quoted as 'with meat and drink' and 'without meat and drink'. A considerable proportion of the labouring class must have opted for the meat and drink, though wives and children may consequently have gone short. In the country, a considerable number of farm labourers 'lived in' and fed at the same table as the master and mistress. These again might be unmarried men in their early years, but since there has always been a chronic shortage of cottages in the English countryside, down to the present day, wives may have been employed on the same farm. What proportion of wage-earners opted for being paid partly in meat and drink we have not the slightest means of knowing: one may hazard the guess that the proportion grew in the latter part of the century when food prices were reaching a level beyond the memory of man. Whatever the proportion even earlier on, it must have been a considerable mitigation of any purely statistical conclusion about the rise in the cost of living.

In the enclosed regions, where farms were scattered and villages few, labourers lived in and received a low annual wage to cover outlay such as clothing; and in the open-field country of England the minute subdivision of the land into strips (often averaging as little as a quarter-acre) meant that a labourer could feed his family off what was virtually his allotment. His master might assist in various small ways, as contemporary wills show, by lending a plough or giving a sheep or the pasture for it. Again, the open-field country, because of its great subdivision of the land as opposed to the enclosed fields of the other parts of England, often provided a ladder of many rungs for the labourer: the keen man could get his foot on the first rung, and advance step by step. Some labourers' probate inventories in the second half of

the century show a proportion — admittedly small — of really prosperous labourers who have clearly got on by a slow stepping up the
open-field ladder. To such men, and to all those who managed to lease a
strip or two from the boss, the inflation of food prices was of little or
no account: the real danger was not inflation but hunger, the failure of
the crops, perhaps accompanied by disease among the animals.

There were other mitigating factors to be taken into account, without pretending that there were no disasters, shortages and sheer bad
luck. One of the major factors was the fact that outside the towns the
great majority of the population lived in an economy in which money
played only a marginal part, still basically a barter economy over the
greater part of England, in which the exchange of goods for services and
vice versa, was common. We hear little of it in records, of course,
because it was a way of life so accepted that it called for no record or
comment. But now and then we catch glimpses of it in a farmer's will.
The small amount of money mentioned in statutory wage assessments
at a somewhat later date was spent at the annual fair, and to a less
extent at the weekly market. Except in towns, shops and retail trading
were almost non-existent.

In addition to the universal survival, outside the towns, of a barter
economy, there was also the dual economy of which much has already
been said. It naturally took different forms in different parts of the
country, though farming was probably always the major element in the
system, but it did mean that the family had a double bastion against the
forces exerted by the money economy.

There were other factors, too. Any calculations about the impact of
inflation depend on an almost unknown factor — the regularity of
employment over a given week or a given year. If there was an increase
over the century in the average number of days worked, and that we do
not know, then all calculations about the money wage per week are
vitiated. And further, there is the intractable problem of substitution in
an age of rising prices. In our own age of inflation, ordinary foodstuffs
and other household necessities have a wide range of quality and prices,
and as the price pressure increases we turn to the lower qualities and to
some degree lessen the full impact of the general level of prices. In the
sixteenth century there were many different qualities of bread, ale and
meat, and this serves to cloak the real impact of general inflation, which
moreover, except under a very sophisticated and unreal system of
measurement, is not susceptible to statistical measurement. We are not
even sure what kind of food and drink the working-class family bought

225

with its money, and what adjustments they made to their customary diet as the pressure mounted.

These are more or less intractable problems of statistical measurement. I do not think they will ever be satisfactorily solved. Nor do I think the slow upward trend of food prices anything like as significant as the violent (at times) short-term fluctuations. One can adjust over a term of years to a long-term rise, but the short-term rises of Henrician England could be sudden, sharp, and at times catastrophic — even ending in death.

POVERTY

The rural poor suffered at times of bad harvests and epidemics, but the real burden fell on the special category of the poor in the towns. In times of bad trade or harvest failure the rural poor drifted into the nearest towns, where there was a greater variety of occupations, and became a growing burden on the town services and finances. Here they could not grow their own food and lived more fully in a money economy. Unemployment and a chronic shortage of housing became widespread in the towns. In the countryside, and to some extent in towns too, unemployment had been a family affair and was largely relieved by the family as a social group; but as towns slowly grew, and some industries became dependent on exports (as witness the Suffolk cloth industry) so unemployment developed from a family affair (age, sickness, ill-fortune) and gradually became institutionalized, that is to say an inherent element in the capitalist system and not so much a personal breakdown. In so doing it passed beyond the control of the family and became a problem of society.

The old order had dealt more or less satisfactorily with poverty and unemployment through the family and at times the parish; and in the wealthier towns through almshouses founded by pious benefactors, usually successful merchants. Such towns as Exeter had a considerable number of almshouses, but they were usually restricted to the sick and the old. Monastic houses also helped to some extent, but their contribution has been exaggerated and the Dissolution was not a major cause of the rising tide of vagrants during Henry's reign. Theoretically, one-third of the tithes paid to the Church was supposed to be allocated to the relief of the poor, but this had long ceased to be practised, even by the monastic orders, and with the vast transfer of tithes at the Dissolution to laymen this ancient obligation practically ceased to be of any value. There had always been a vagrant population in England: indeed it was necessary in certain seasonal occupations such as harvests. But it seems to have been growing from the 1520s onwards, and there was a tendency to overlook the true poverty arising from human causes such as old age and ill-health and to regard the whole merely as a problem of vagrancy which had nothing good to say for it. This failure to distinguish between true poverty and vagrancy vitiated much early legislation. The Act of 1531 was the first to attempt a distinction between the worthy poor and the true vagrant or itinerant beggar, though it made no provision for the former beyond a licence to beg in his or her own parish. It made no provision for the unemployable poor. The important Act of 1536 attempted to do so but also failed. It ordered the parish or municipal authority to assume full responsibility for the impotent poor and imposed a 'freeze' by pinning the poor down in the local area to which they belonged. A few exceptions were allowed — beggars with the appropriate certificate, mendicant friars, and servants seeking employment who carried letters setting out the facts of their case.

The Act of 1536 also introduced the notion that alms were to be raised by voluntary means for the helpless poor. The City of London had indeed already experimented with this method in 1533, but it had not worked: so in 1547 the principle of the compulsory poor-rate was introduced. Two years later the city of Norwich introduced the same principle: the foundations were slowly being laid for the great Poor Law Acts of Elizabeth's reign.[21] Yet for all this positive thinking, however slow, we must not forget that it was in the year 1547 that the most savage Act in the history of vagrancy legislation was passed by Parliament. Under certain conditions incorrigible vagrants were to be reduced to personal slavery. This Act was repealed two years later — the wonder is how it ever came to be passed. Clearly the authorities did not know which way to turn with the increasing numbers of 'masterless men' and wandering beggars, and vacillated wildly.

The pressure on the larger towns from the wandering poor in search of employment or better opportunities for begging produced serious housing problems as always, and shrewd landlords naturally took advantage of the situation. At Worcester and other Worcestershire towns an Act of 1534 virtually imposed a rent freeze. Landlords were not to let houses or cottages at any higher rent than was given within the previous twenty years. Although Worcester had experienced a

[21] This section is based on Jordan, *Philanthropy in England 1480—1660*, esp. pp. 83—6.

building boom in the later fifteenth century, very little new building was done between about 1520 and 1560.[22] Meanwhile the rural poor continued to tramp the roads that led to the city. Possibly the rent freeze of 1534 helped to account for this slowing-up of building, as there was still plenty of vacant land within the walls in the mid-sixteenth century. No doubt, too, working-class housing was a far from attractive proposition for wouldbe investors, despite the fact that the important cloth trade had fallen away from its earlier boom.

London, of course, suffered the most from the prolonged invasion of the masterless men. Robert Crowley published a savage attack on the urban landlords in 1550:[23]

> And to go to the cities we have no hope, for there we hear that these insatiable beasts have all in their hands. Some have purchased, and some taken by leases, whole alleys, whole rents [tenements], whole rows, yea whole streets and lanes, so that rents be raised, some double, some triple, and some four-fold to that they were within these xii years last past. .... Yea, there is not so much as a garden ground free from them. No remedy therefore, we must needs fight it out, or else be brought to the like slavery that the French men are in!

Not only had house rents risen under the pressure of population, but in a document of 1549 we catch a rare glimpse of the workings of inflation generally. Most of what we know about Tudor inflation, especially in its early impact, comes from the farming world, but here we are told that the artificers at first bought their food and clothing dear, now the rise had spread to 'his workinge toles and all other necessaries Derer and derer: and payinge also more rente for his howse then he was wonte to do'.[24]

The problem of rising prices among the poor, and the working class generally, was exacerbated, or thought to be, by the presence of aliens. They were thought to be stealing work that rightly belonged to Englishmen, and to be creating housing shortages locally: ill-informed complaints so familiar today. There had, it is true, been some aliens in the population in earlier centuries but they never amounted to a great number. They are not easy to trace as they anglicized their names as far as possible, but until the second half of the sixteenth century, when religious persecutions drove many aliens from their native lands, the

---

[22] Dyer, *The City of Worcester in the Sixteenth Century*, esp. pp. 162–3. For the Worcester Act, see *T.E.D.*, I, 175.

[23] Robert Crowley, *The Way to Wealth* (1550). Lever, in the same year, also refers to the many 'lesemongers' in London that raise the rents of empty houses, calling them 'the Marchauntes of myschyefe that go betwixt the barke and the tree'.

[24] *T.E.D.*, III, 320.

problem was not a national one. Cunningham[25] cites such cases as the dozen or so Frenchmen, shoe-makers for the most part, who settled in Dorset between 1496 and 1520, and a few others who followed later. Bretons probably crossed to Devon and Cornwall naturally, to settle in ports familiar to them from fishing in the same seas; and London attracted more from Flanders. But apart from London, one could have counted aliens by the dozen at the most in particular localities. The great London riot of Evil May Day in 1517 is about the only instance of violent reaction in Henry's reign, though no doubt there was a good deal of background grumbling at other times among the English artificers. In London especially, as one might expect, aliens tended to congregate together in such a huge and strange town. Thus the Middlesex subsidy of 1525 gives under East Smithfield 142 names, of whom no fewer than ninety-five were described as foreigners. Such a concentration was exceptional, and the general feeling against aliens was only fomented at times of bad trade, with local unemployment and a chronic housing shortage even amid the swarming and filthy alleys of London. Even in 1567 it has been calculated that there were probably only some 4,700 aliens in England — fewer than one in a thousand of the whole population, and at the maximum in 1593 they amounted only to just over 5,000. It was a highly emotional subject, as it is today, and aliens could easily be blamed for difficulties which were none of their making. On the credit side German experts could be called in to organize the Wealden ironworks, and the German miners had worked in England since at least the thirteenth century: they brought expertise to England well ahead of anything the native English knew; but it was the poor labourers and their families who bore the brunt of local disaffection and abuse in Henry's reign.

THE PEOPLE UNDER GOVERNMENT

One of the most curious features of the reign is the almost complete absence of any major rebellion by the people in general during the near-forty years of Henry's rule. As Fletcher observes, 'Tudor rebellions were essentially the responses of local communities to local grievances'.[26] Moreover, though the rebellions in Yorkshire (1489) and Cornwall (1497) were protests against increasingly heavy war taxation, and there were the local tax disturbances at various dates from 1513 to

[25] Cunningham, *Alien Immigrants to England.*
[26] Fletcher, *Tudor Rebellions*, p. 114.

1525, the major risings owed more to religious fears than to economic difficulties, notably the Pilgrimage of Grace (1536) and the Western Rebellion of 1549. The latter, it is true, contained the demand that in Devon and Cornwall the two largest monastic houses should be restored to use, but basically it was a purely religious uprising. Only Ket's Rebellion in 1549, two years after Henry's death in any event, was essentially an agrarian revolt, one in which, too, we have the first strong expression of class hatred since Jack Cade's time, a hundred years earlier.[27] The inflation of prices, of rents and fines by landlords, had sharpened greatly by the end of the 1540s, and could no longer be ignored or dealt with by *ad hoc* royal proclamations.

Enclosure and engrossing remained serious rural problems which various royal commissions had failed to solve; and there were also the relentless local pressures by landlords to encroach on the village commons, essential to peasant husbandry, either for their own increased sheep flocks and herds of cattle, or simply to enlarge the hunting parks that set off their new country houses. The French herald of 1549 had observed in the so-called Debate of the Heralds that a great part of England consisted of forests, chases, parks and enclosures for hunting, so that he surmised that we had as many deer in England as the French had people. Andrew Boorde, a widely travelled man, thought that England had more parks than all the rest of Europe put together. Harrison reckoned that Queen Elizabeth I alone had nearly two hundred parks and every county had scores: Harrison gave up counting them but considered that the counties of Kent and Essex had a hundred parks between them. Possibly the number of parks had increased slightly with the rapid building of country houses during the second half of the century, but it is quite likely there were as many in Henry's reign, mostly perhaps ragged survivals of the feudal age. At any rate, the pressure on the ancient commons by the landlords, new and old, was such that new courts had been set up to deal with small causes, the Court of Star Chamber and the Court of Requests. These were being used by the peasantry by the 1540s, but with all the usual difficulties when small men try to fight Mammon: in many cases the peasantry of a whole village clubbed together to fight such cases in

---

[27] Christopher Hill in his essay 'The many-headed monster', in Carter, ed., *From the Renaissance to the Counter-Reformation*, cites Norfolk in 1549 particularly as the region where 'all have conceived a wonderful hate against gentlemen and taketh them all as their enemies'. Also men were saying 'there are too many gentlemen by 500 . . .'.

London as encroachment on the local commons, or cases involving the undue raising of entry fines and other devices of greedy landlords, and sometimes they won. Often the difficulties were too great: for example the rising commercially-minded yeomen saw more eye-to-eye with the lord of the manor and might refuse to take part in such cases; but more than that, the peasants spoke a totally different language from that of London lawyers (familiar enough today when one tries to wrestle with the so-called Law) and must have often returned home dissatisfied with the course of justice. Even Commissions about enclosure faced such problems as juries packed by the local squire, and tenants afraid to come forward to give evidence that might lead to their eviction. Hence the agrarian passion roused in Ket's Rebellion, and the numerous specific demands.

There were other reasons why Henry's reign saw no serious rebellion of an economic nature. Apart from Henry's personal character, the Tudors were always conscious of the shaky foundations of their tenure of the throne and therefore quick and ruthless wherever there was the slightest potential threat to their rule. It has already been said that summary hanging was one of the major causes of death in Henry's reign. The governing class was nearly as ruthless as the monarch in stopping unrest in its tracts. But there were other ways of maintaining law and order. Much, if not most, of the unrest arose from harvest failures and the consequent effect on all food prices. The unrest was mainly urban because the urban poor represented a special class, unable to grow their own food and massed together in dangerous numbers. Action was therefore local and almost immediate, through the buying up of scarce foodstuffs and its distribution through the mayor and governing body of the affected towns. Mayors were chosen not least for the ability to sustain heavy expenditure of this kind, and aldermen and councillors likewise. Such swift action without reference to any central authority must have prevented the greater part of unrest from developing into open rebellion. Then, too, it is probably not farfetched to say that a revolution requires not only leaders but sufficient followers with continued energy to see the rebellion through; and the half-starved peasantry in times of dearth could not muster enough strength to fight a successful battle. Energy requires food and there was not enough of it. The governing class knew well the expression 'belly-cheer', and its importance in keeping the mass of people happy. Nef has observed the considerable growth of the brewing industry during Henry's reign (the London assessments for the Loan of 1522 show many wealthy brewers even then) and this may well have cheapened the price of beer as well as encouraging drunkenness. Contemporary writers comment not infrequently on the amount of drinking that went on. Alcoholism must have been a fairly common state, judging by such local chronicles as the history of Myddle in Shropshire. The English people as a whole were content with their cheap bread and beer, leaving the thinking about fundamental social and economic problems to others more learned.

Thus, though the reign of Henry VIII and its social structure and economy paint on the whole a harsh picture, there was arising as early as the 1530s a disparate group of writers and preachers who conceived such a thing as the 'commonwealth', a word which became a watchword in the 1540s and gave a collective name to the thinkers as 'Commonwealth Men'. They had their origins in the 1530s (if we exclude More's great *Utopia* as *sui generis*) and by the later 1540s constituted a group with some powerful figures in it, notably Hugh Latimer, Bishop of Worcester from 1535 onwards, and later a great sympathizer in the unlikely figure of Edward Seymour, Earl of Hertford, later Duke of Somerset. It was his great influence and favour that gave the group far more reputation than they might otherwise have got.[28] But their great days, in so far as they had any, came after Henry's death, and in the years that followed they too fell away when Seymour was executed. Their major writings belong to the dark age that followed Henry's death.

While Henry lived, men rightly feared his ferocity. His arbitrary executions, his 'state trials', remind one inevitably of Stalin's Russia: he was indeed the Stalin of Tudor England.[29] But until his second daughter, Elizabeth, died, and with her the last of the Tudors, men dared not speak freely about his loathsome character. It was left to Sir Walter Raleigh, himself under sentence of death in the Tower under James I, to sum him up in these words:

> Now for King Henry the Eight: if all the pictures and patterns of a merciless prince were lost in the world, they might all again be painted to the life, out of the story of this King. For how many servants did he advance in haste (but for what vertue no man could suspect) and with the change of his fancy ruined

---

[28] The best discussion of the Commonwealth group is probably to be found in Jones, *The Tudor Commonwealth 1529—59*, and to some extent in Elton, *England under the Tudors*, esp. p. 185 *et seq.*

[29] A significant sidelight on Henry's rule is cast by the fact that it saw an enormous increase in the number of penal statutes — 83 in all. Of these 44 were the product of the period 1529—39. See Elton, 'State Planning in early Tudor England', *Econ. H.R.*, sec. ser., XIII, no. 3, 1961, 436.

again, no man knowing for what offence? To how many others of more desert gave he abundant flowers, from whence to gather Hony, and in the end of Harvest burnt them in the Hive?

As Hurstfield, who quotes these words,[30] says, this was not the isolated opinion of an embittered man. King James I agreed with him, and so did Sir Robert Cecil whose father had profited so much by the almost unrestrained plunder of Henry's reign, and that of his son Edward the Sixth. It was Froude in the nineteenth century who produced the myth of a noble Henry 'the architect and saviour of the English nation'. One look at the Holbein portrait, with its ruthless and porcine face, should have made him think afresh; but even to the economic and social historian, not directly concerned with Henry's sadistic brutalities, he appears at the end to have been a disaster to his country, impoverishing its resources and stunting its growth for the sake of his futile wars, leaving it an empty treasury; and leaving its government in the hands of the most unprincipled gang of political adventurers and predators that England had seen for many centuries.

[30] Hurstfield, *Freedom, Corruption and Government in Elizabethan England*, p. 23.

Select Bibliography

The sources for the economic and social history of the reign of Henry VIII are enormous. Fortunately two bibliographies exist which break the back of listing most of them. Even so, the following list of books and articles is highly selective and inevitably at times rather arbitrary in allocating certain books, etc., to particular chapters, when in fact they have been used over and over again in different parts of the book.

The major sources are the *Bibliography of British History: Tudor Period: 1485–1603* ed. Conyers Read (rev. edn, Oxford U.P., 1959) and supplementing this, M. Levine, *Bibliographical Handbooks: Tudor England 1485–1603* (Cambridge U.P., 1968). I have not attempted to emulate these works, except in so far as I have made considerable use of particular books and articles.

Another work of general importance for the reign is *English Historical Documents*, vol. V, covering the period 1485 to 1558, ed. C. H. Williams (Eyre & Spottiswoode, 1967). Of cardinal importance for the subjects covered by my own book are, of course, the three volumes of *Tudor Economic Documents*, ed. R. H. Tawney and E. Power (Longmans, new impression 1951). Generations of students have profited by these source books, first published over fifty years ago and still standard works.

Then we have the colossal run of State Papers for the reign embedded in *Letters and Papers of Henry VIII*, and the *Calendar of State Papers Venetian*, perhaps the most useful of the foreign sources for the reign. At home, certain general surveys are useful, notably *Leland's Itinerary*, most recently republished in five volumes (Centaur Press, 1964); and Harrison's *Description of England*, ed. F. J. Furnivall (1877–81). Though it relates chiefly to the reign of Elizabeth I, Harrison contains many backward glances to earlier times. Wriothesley's *A Chronicle of England*, ed. W. D. Hamilton (2 vols., Camden Soc., new series, XI, XX, 1875–77) is also valuable for the reign of Henry VIII.

Among journals the long runs of *Past and Present*, the *Economic History Review*, and the *Agricultural History Review* (1953 onwards) contain scores of articles bearing directly or indirectly on the period 1500–50. I have listed a few of the more useful articles here, but reference should be made to the complete runs for further material. I have deliberately omitted from this select bibliography all works, however important in their own field, which are chiefly political, ecclesiastical, and so on, in order to keep rather a manageable length and also because I have only consulted them in so far as they threw light on the social and economic history of the reign.

CHAPTER ONE: *The Face of the Country*

Books

In addition to the general sources listed above, the principal sources used in this chapter are:

FISHER, F. J., ed. *Essays in the Economic and Social History of Tudor and Stuart England in Honour of R. H. Tawney.* Cambridge U.P., 1961.

HUGHES, P. L. and LARKIN, J. F., eds. *Tudor Royal Proclamations: I. The Early Tudors 1485–1553.* Yale U.P., 1964.

PEVSNER, N., ed. *The Buildings of England* (series). Penguin Books, 1951–74.

RICH, E. E. and WILSON, C. H., eds. *The Economy of Expanding Europe in the 16th and 17th Centuries. Cambridge Economic History of Europe,* IV. Cambridge U.P., 1967.

RUSSELL, J. C. *British Medieval Population.* U. of New Mexico P., 1948.

SLACK, P. 'Some Aspects of Epidemics in England 1485–1640.' Unpublished D.Phil. thesis, Oxford, 1972.

SUMMERSON, J. *Architecture in England, 1530–1830.* 5th edn. Penguin Books, 1969.

THIRSK, J., ed. *The Agrarian History of England and Wales: IV. 1500–1640.* Cambridge U.P., 1967.

WICKHAM, A. K. *Churches of Somerset.* New edn. David & Charles, 1965.

Articles

BEAN, J. M. W. 'Plague, population and economic decline in the later Middle Ages', *Econ. Hist. Rev.*, sec. ser., XV, no. 3, 1963.

CORNWALL, J. 'English population in the early sixteenth century', *Econ. Hist. Rev.*, sec. ser., XXIII, no. 1, 1970.

GORING, J. J. 'The general proscription of 1522', *Eng. Hist. Rev.*, LXXXVI, 1971.

HOSKINS, W. G. 'English provincial towns in the early sixteenth century', *Trans. R. Hist. Soc.*, fifth series, VI, 1956.

OWEN, L. 'The population of Wales in the 16th and 17th centuries', *Trans. Hon. Soc. Cymmrodorion*, 1959.

RICH, E. E. 'The population of Elizabethan England', *Econ. Hist. Rev.*, sec. ser., XI, no. 3, 1950.

SHEAILL, J. 'The distribution of taxable population and wealth in England during the early sixteenth century', *Trans. Inst. Brit. Geogr.*, Publ. no. 55, 1972.

TUCKER, G. S. L. 'English pre-industrial population trends', *Econ. Hist. Rev.*, sec. ser., XVI, no. 2, 1963.

WRIGLEY, E. A. 'Family limitation in pre-industrial England', *Econ. Hist. Rev.*, sec. ser., XIX, no. 1, 1966.

CHAPTER TWO: *The Shearers and the Shorn*

Books

GOUGH, R. *Human Nature Displayed in the History of Myddle (1700—1)*. London, privately printed, 1834.

HURSTFIELD, J. *Freedom, Corruption and Government in Elizabethan England*. Cape, 1973.

MOORE SMITH, G. C. *The Family of Withypoll*. Revised by P. H. Reaney. Walthamstow Antiquarian Soc., 1936.

MORE, Sir T. *Utopia*, ed., with Introduction and Notes by J. C. Collins. Oxford, Clarendon P., 1961.

STONE, L. *The Crisis of the Aristocracy, 1558—1641*. Oxford, Clarendon P., 1965.

Subsidy Rolls, Muster and Hearth Tax Rolls and Probate Calendars of the Parish of Constantine (Kerrier) Cornwall. Devon and Cornwall Rec. Soc., 1910.

TAWNEY, R. H. *The Acquisitive Society*. Bell, 1921.

TAWNEY, R. H. *Religion and the Rise of Capitalism*. Murray, 1926.

TAWNEY, R. H. *The Agrarian Problem in the Sixteenth Century*.

Articles

'Abstract of the original returns of the Commissioners for Musters and the Loan in Surrey', *Surrey Archaeol. Collections*, XXX, 1917.

CORNWALL, J. 'The people of Rutland in 1522', *Trans. Leics. Arch. and Hist. Soc.*, XXXVII, 1963.

HEY, D. G. 'A dual economy in south Yorkshire', *Agric. Hist. Rev.*, XVII, pt 2, 1969.

SCHOFIELD, R. S. 'The geographical distribution of wealth in England 1334—1649', *Econ. Hist. Rev.*, sec. ser., XVIII, no. 3, 1965.

CHAPTER THREE: *Rural Society and Agrarian Change*

Books

AULT, W. O. *Open-field Husbandry and the Village Community*. Trans. Amer. Phil. Soc., new ser., LV, pt 7, 1965.

AVERY, D. *The Irregular Common Fields of Edmonton*. Edmonton Hundred Hist. Soc., Occasional Papers, no. 9, 1964.

AVERY, D. *Manorial Systems in the Edmonton Hundred*. Edmonton Hundred Hist. Soc., Occasional Papers, no. 6, 1963.

BERESFORD, M. and HURST, J. G., eds. *Deserted Medieval Villages.*, Lutterworth. 1971.

BOURNE, G. *Change in the Village*. Duckworth, 1966. First published 1912.

CAMPBELL, M. *The English Yeoman under Elizabeth and the Early Stuarts*. Yale U.P., 1942.

CLIFFE, J. T. *The Yorkshire Gentry from the Reformation to the Civil War.* Athlone P., 1969.

ELTON, G. R. *England under the Tudors.* Reprinted with new bibliography. Methuen, 1962.

FINCH, M. E. *The Wealth of Five Northamptonshire Families, 1540–1640.* Northants Rec. Soc., 1956.

FUSSELL, G. E. *The Old English Farming Books from Fitzherbert to Tull, 1523–1730.* Crosby Lockwood, 1947.

GRAY, H. L. *English Field Systems.* Harvard U.P., 1915; London, Merlin P., 1959.

HEXTER, J. H. *Reappraisals in History.* Longmans, 1961.

HEY, D. *An English Rural Community: Myddle under the Tudors and Stuarts.* Leicester U.P., 1974.

HOSKINS, W. G. *The Midland Peasant.* Macmillan, 1957.

HOSKINS, W. G. *Essays in Leicestershire History.* Liverpool U.P., 1950.

KERRIDGE, E. *The Agricultural Revolution.* Allen & Unwin, 1967.

KERRIDGE, E. *Agrarian Problems in the Sixteenth Century and After.* Allen & Unwin, 1969.

ORWIN, C. S. *The Open Fields.* 2nd edn. Oxford, Clarendon P., 1954.

PAM, D. O. *The Fight for Common Rights in England and Edmonton, 1400–1600.* Edmonton Hundred Hist. Soc., Occasional Papers, no. 27, 1974.

Royal Commission on Common Land, 1955–58. Report, etc., H.M.S.O., 1958.

SIMPSON, A. *The Wealth of the Gentry, 1540–1660.* Cambridge U.P., 1961.

SMITH, R. B. *Land and Politics in the England of Henry VIII.* Oxford, Clarendon P., 1970.

TAWNEY, R. H. *The Agrarian Problem in the Sixteenth Century.* Longmans, 1912.

THIRSK, J. *English Peasant Farming.* Routledge, 1957.

THIRSK, J. *Tudor Enclosures.* London, Hist. Assoc., Pamph. 41, 1959.

THIRSK, J., ed. *The Agrarian History of England and Wales: IV. 1500–1640.* Cambridge U.P., 1967.

TROW-SMITH, R. *English Husbandry.* Faber, 1951.

TROW-SMITH, R. *A History of British Livestock Husbandry to 1700.* Routledge, 1957.

TUPLING, G. H. *The Economic History of Rossendale.* Manchester U.P., 1927.

Articles

ALLISON, K. J. 'Flock management in the sixteenth and seventeenth centuries', *Econ. Hist. Rev.*, sec. ser., XI, 1958.

BAKER, A. 'Field systems in the Vale of Holmesdale', *Agric. Hist. Rev.*, XIV, pt 1, 1966.

BAKER, A. 'Some terminological problems in studies of English field systems', *Agric. Hist. Rev.*, XVII, pt 2, 1969.

BECKINGSALE, B. W. 'The characteristics of the Tudor North', *Northern History*, IV, 1969.

BUTLIN, R. A. 'Enclosure and improvement in Northumberland in the sixteenth century', *Archaeol. Aeliana*, fourth ser., XLV, 1967.

COLEMAN, D. C. 'The 'gentry' controversy and the aristocracy in crisis, 1558–1641', *History*, LI, no. 172, 1966.

COOPER, J. P. 'Social distribution of land and men in England, 1436–1700', *Econ. Hist. Rev.*, sec. ser., XX, no. 3, 1967.

DICKENS, A. G. 'Estate and household management in Bedfordshire *c*. 1540', *Bedfordshire Hist. Rec. Soc.*, XXXVI, 1956.

FAITH, R. 'Peasant families and inheritance customs in medieval England', *Agric. Hist. Rev.*, XIV, pt 2, 1966.

HARRISON, C. J. 'Grain price analysis and harvest qualities, 1465–1634', *Agric. Hist. Rev.*, XIX, pt 2, 1971.

HOSKINS, W. G. 'Harvest fluctuations and English economic history 1480–1619', *Agric. Hist. Rev.*, XII, pt 1, 1964.

MacCAFFREY, W. T. 'The Crown and the new aristocracy', *Past and Present*, no. 30, 1965.

MILLER, H. 'The early Tudor peerage, 1485–1547', summary of thesis in *Bull. Inst. Hist. Res.*, XXIV.

MILLER, H. 'Subsidy assessments of the peerage in the sixteenth century', *Bull. Inst. Hist. Res.*, XXVIII, 1955.

PATTEN, J. H. C. 'Village and town: an occupational study', *Agric. Hist. Rev.*, XX, pt 1, 1972.

THIRSK, J. 'The common fields', *Past and Present*, no. 29, 1964.

CHAPTER FOUR: *Urban Life and Structure*

Books

A Calendar of the Freemen of Lynn, 1291–1836. Norfolk and Norwich Archaeological Soc., 1913.

CLARK, P. and SLACK, P., eds. *Crisis and Order in English Towns 1500–1700.* Routledge & Kegan Paul, 1972.

COZENS-HARDY, B. and KENT, E. A. *The Mayors of Norwich 1403–1835.* Jarrold, 1938.

DYER, A. D. *The City of Worcester in the Sixteenth Century.* Leicester U.P., 1973.

EVERITT, A., ed. *Perspectives in English Urban History.* Macmillan, 1973.

HOSKINS, W. G. *Provincial England.* Macmillan, 1963.

PALLISER, D. M. 'Some aspects of the social and economic history of York in the sixteenth century'. Unpublished D.Phil. thesis, Oxford, 1968.

PARKER, V. *The Making of King's Lynn.* London, Phillimore, 1971.

STOW, J. *A Survey of London.* Reprint of 1603 text with Introduction by C. L. Kingsford. 2 vols. Oxford, Clarendon P., 1908.

STRAUSS, G. *Nuremberg in the Sixteenth Century.* Wiley, 1966.

TAIT, J. *The Medieval English Borough*, First published 1936; repr. Manchester U.P., 1969.

WELFORD, R., ed. *History of Newcastle and Gateshead: II. Sixteenth Century.* London, Scott, 3 vols. 1884–87.

WILSON, C. H. *England's Apprenticeship 1603–1763.* Longmans, 1965.

Articles

BARTLETT, J. N. 'The expansion and decline of York in the later Middle Ages', *Econ. Hist. Rev.*, XII, no. 1, 1959.

CORNWALL, J. 'English country towns in the 1520s', *Econ. Hist. Rev.*, XV, no. 1, 1962.

DYER, A. D. 'The economy of Tudor Worcester', *Univ. Birmingham Hist. Jnl.*, X, no. 2, 1966.

HOSKINS, W. G. 'English provincial towns in the early sixteenth century', *Trans. R. Hist. Soc.*, fifth ser., VI, 1956.

HOSKINS, W. G. 'The Elizabethan merchants of Exeter' in *Elizabethan Government and Society* Athlone Press, 1961.

POUND, J. F. 'Social and trade structure of Norwich, 1525—75', *Past and Present*, no. 34, 1966.

CHAPTER FIVE: *The Condition of the People*

Books

ATKINSON, T. *Elizabethan Winchester*. Faber, 1963.

BEVERIDGE, W. H. *Prices and Wages in England from the Twelfth to the Nineteenth Century: I. Price Tables: Mercantile Era.* Longmans, 1939.

HARRIS, M. D., ed. *The Coventry Leet Book; or Mayor's Register, 1420—1555*. 4 vols. Early English Text Society, original ser., 134, 135, 138, 146, 1907—13.

SNEYD, C. A., ed. *A. Relation . . . of the Island of England.* Camden Society, old ser., XXXVII, 1847.

Yorkshire Chantry Surveys. 2 vols. Surtees Soc., XCI, XCII, 1892—93.

Articles

COLEMAN, D. C. 'Labour in the English economy of the seventeenth century', *Econ. Hist. Rev.*, sec. ser., VIII, no. 3, 1956.

DAVIES, C. S. L. 'Slavery and Protector Somerset', *Econ. Hist. Rev.*, sec. ser., XIX, no. 3, 1966.

POUND, J. F. 'An Elizabethan census of the poor', *Univ. Birmingham Hist. Jnl.*, VIII, no. 2, 1962.

CHAPTER SIX: *The Plunder of the Church*

Books

BASKERVILLE, G. *English Monks and the Suppression of the Monasteries.* Cape, 1937.

CALEY, J. and HUNTER, J., eds. *Valor Ecclesiasticus.* 6 vols. London, Records Commissioners, 1810—34.

DICKENS, A. G. *The English Reformation.* Batsford, 1964.

FINBERG, H. P. R. *Tavistock Abbey.* Cambridge U.P., 1951.

GAIRDNER, J. *The English Church in the Sixteenth Century from the Accession of Henry VIII to the Death of Mary.* (Vol. IV of *A History of the English Church* by Stephens and Hunt.) London, 1902.

HEMBRY, P. M. *The Bishops of Bath and Wells, 1540—1640.* Athlone P., 1967.

HILL, C. *Economic Problems of the Church.* Oxford, Clarendon P., 1956.

HURSTFIELD, J. *The Queen's Wards: wardship and marriage under Elizabeth I.* Longmans, 1958.

JORDAN, W. K. *Edward VI: the Young King.* Allen & Unwin, 1968.

JORDAN, W. K. *Edward VI: The Threshold of Power.* Allen & Unwin, 1970.

KNOWLES, D. *The Religious Orders in England: III. The Tudor Age.* Cambridge U.P., 1959.

MELLOWS, W. T., ed. *The Foundation of Peterborough Cathedral.* Northants Rec. Soc., XIII, 1941.

MELLOWS, W. T. and GIFFORD, D. H., eds. *Elizabethan Peterborough.* Northants Rec. Soc., XVIII, 1956.

OXLEY, J. E. *The Reformation in Essex.* Manchester U.P., 1965.

PALLISER, D. M. *The Reformation in York, 1534–1553.* Borthwick Papers, no. 40. York, St Anthony's P., 1971.

POLLARD, A. F. *England under the Protector Somerset.* Kegan Paul, 1900.

RICHARDSON, W. C. *A History of the Court of Augmentations, 1536–54.* Oxford U.P., 1961.

ROWSE, A. L. *Tudor Cornwall.* 2nd edn. Macmillan, 1969.

SPELMAN, Sir. H. *The History and Fate of Sacrilege (1698).* 4th edn, ed. C. F. S. Warren. London, Hodges, 1895.

WOODWARD, G. W. D. *The Dissolution of the Monasteries.* Blandford, 1966.

YOUINGS, J. A. *The Dissolution of the Monasteries.* Allen & Unwin, 1971.

YOUINGS, J. A., ed. *Devon Monastic Lands: Calendar of Particulars for Grants, 1536–58.* Devon and Cornwall Rec. Soc., new ser., 1, 1955.

Articles

DU BOULAY, F. R. H. 'Archbishop Cranmer and the Canterbury Temporalities', *Eng. Hist. Rev.*, LXVII, Jan. 1952.

CROSS, C. 'The economic problems of the See of York: decline and recovery in the sixteenth century', in *Land, Church and People*, ed. J. Thirsk. Brit. Agric. Hist. Soc., 1970.

HABAKKUK, H. J. 'The market for monastic property, 1599–1603', *Econ. Hist. Rev.*, sec. ser., X, no. 3, 1958.

SWALES, T. H. 'Opposition to the suppression of the Norfolk monasteries', *Norfolk Archaeology*, XXXIII, pt 3, 1964.

SWALES, T. H. 'The redistribution of the monastic lands in Norfolk at the Dissolution', *Norfolk Archaeology*, XXXIV, pt 1, 1966.

YOUINGS, J. A. 'The terms of the disposal of the Devon monastic lands, 1536–58', *Eng. Hist. Rev.*, LXIX, no. 270, 1954.

CHAPTER SEVEN: *Industry*

Books

CARUS-WILSON, E. M. *The Expansion of Exeter at the Close of the Middle Ages.* University of Exeter, 1963.

CLIFTON-TAYLOR, A. *The Pattern of English Building.* Rev. edn. Faber, 1972.

COURT, W. H. B. *The Rise of the Midland Industries, 1600–1838.* Oxford U.P., 1938.

CRUMP, W. B. and GHORBAL, G. *History of the Huddersfield Woollen Industry.* Huddersfield, Tolson Memorial Museum, 1935.

GOUGH, J. W. *The Mines of Mendip.* Rev. edn. David & Charles, 1967.

HATCHER, J. *Rural Economy and Society in the Duchy of Cornwall, 1300–1500.* Cambridge U.P., 1970.

HEATON, H. *The Yorkshire Woollen and Worsted Industries.* Oxford, Clarendon P., 1920.

LEWIS, G. R. *The Stannaries.* Harvard U.P., 1908; Truro, Bradford Barton, 1965.

McCLENAGHAN, B. *The Springs of Lavenham and the Suffolk Cloth Trade in the Fifteenth and Sixteenth Centuries,* Ipswich, Harrison, 1924.

NEF, J. U. *Industry and Government in France and England, 1540–1640.* Cornell U.P., 1940; repr. 1957.

PEVSNER, N., ed. *Buildings of England* (Series). Penguin Books, 1951–74.

RAMSAY, G. D. *The Wiltshire Woollen Industry.* Oxford U.P., 1943; 2nd edn, Cass, 1965.

SALZMANN, L. F. *Building in England down to 1540.* Oxford, Clarendon P., 1952.

STRAKER, E. *Wealden Iron.* Bell, 1931.

UNWIN, G. *Industrial Organization in the 16th and 17th Centuries.* Introduction by T. S. Ashton. Oxford, Clarendon P., 1904; repr. Cass, 1957.

Wills and Inventories . . . of the Northern Counties of England, from the Eleventh Century downwards, pt 1, ed. J. Raine. Surtees Soc., II, 1835.

Articles

ALLISON, K. J. 'The Norfolk worsted industry in the sixteenth and seventeenth centuries', *Yorks. Bull. Econ. Soc. Research,* XII, no. 2, 1960.

CLARKSON, L. A. 'The leather crafts in Tudor and Stuart England', *Agric. Hist. Rev.,* XIV, pt 1, 1966.

CLARKSON, L. A. 'The organization of the English leather industry in the late sixteenth and seventeenth centuries', *Econ. Hist. Rev.,* sec. ser., XIII, 1960.

CROSSLEY, W. 'The management of a sixteenth-century iron works', *Econ. Hist. Rev.,* sec. ser., XIX, no. 2, 1966.

HATCHER, J. 'A diversified economy: later medieval Cornwall', *Econ. Hist. Rev.,* sec. ser., XXII, no. 2, 1969.

HAY, D. 'The dissolution of the monasteries in the diocese of Durham', *Archaeol. Aeliana,* fourth ser., XV, 1938.

HOSKINS, W. G. 'The wealth of medieval Devon', in *Devonshire Studies* by W. G. Hoskins and H. P. R. Finberg. Cape, 1952.

NEF, J. U. 'A comparison of industrial growth in France and England from 1540–1640', *Jnl. Pol. Econ.,* XLIV, nos. 3, 4, 5, 1936.

RICHARDSON, W. C. 'Some financial expedients of Henry VIII', *Econ. Hist. Rev.,* sec. ser., VII, no. 1, 1954.

THIRSK, J. 'Industries in the countryside', in *Essays in the Economic and Social History of Tudor and Stuart England,* ed. F. J. Fisher. Cambridge, U.P., 1961.

CHAPTER EIGHT: *The Trade of England*

Books

BACON, N. *Annals of Ipswich* (1654), ed. W. H. Richardson. Ipswich, Cowell, 1884.

BOWDEN, P. J. *The Wool Trade in Tudor and Stuart England*. Macmillan, 1962.

BUNYARD, B. D. M., ed. *Brokage Book of Southampton 1439—40*. Southampton Rec. Soc., no. 40, 1941.

BURWASH, D. *English Merchant Shipping, 1460—1540*. Toronto U.P., 1947; repr. David & Charles, 1969.

CARUS-WILSON, E. M. and COLEMAN, O. *England's Export Trade, 1275—1547*. Oxford, Clarendon P., 1963.

COLEMAN, O., ed. *The Brokage Book of Southampton 1443—4*. 2 vols. Southampton Rec. Soc., vols. 4, 6, 1960—61.

CONNELL-SMITH, G. *Forerunners of Drake*. Longmans, 1954.

DAVIS, R. *The Rise of the English Shipping Industry*. Macmillan, 1962.

DUCKHAM, B. F. *Navigable Rivers of Yorkshire*. Clapham (Yorks), Dalesman, 1964.

GRAS, N. S. B. *The Evolution of the English Corn Market*. Harvard U.P., 1915.

HENDERSON, C. and COATES, H. *Old Cornish Bridges and Streams*. Simpkin Marshall, 1928.

HUNT, E. M. *The History of Ware*. Hertford, Austin, 1946.

MENDENHALL, T. C. *The Shrewsbury Drapers and the Wool Trade*. Oxford U.P., 1953.

PAM, D. O. *Tudor Enfield: the Maltmen and the Lea Navigation*. Edmonton Hundred Hist. Soc., Occasional Papers, new ser., no. 18.

RAMSAY, G. D. *English Overseas Trade during the Centuries of Emergence*. Macmillan, 1957.

SCHANZ, G. VON *Englische Handelspolitik gegen Ende des Mittelalters*. 2 vols. Leipzig, 1881.

SIMON, A. L. *History of the Wine Trade in England II. Sixteenth Century*. London, 1906—09.

WEBB, J. G. *Great Tooley of Ipswich*. Suffolk Rec. Soc., 1962.

WILLAN, T. S. *River Navigation in England, 1600—1750*. Oxford U.P., 1936; repr. Cass, 1964.

WILLAN, T. S., ed. *A Tudor Book of Rates*. Manchester U.P., 1962.

WILLIAMS, N. J. 'The maritime trade of the East Anglian ports, 1550—1590'. Unpublished D.Phil. thesis, Oxford, 1952.

WINCHESTER, B. *Tudor Family Portrait*. Cape, 1955.

Articles

EMMISON, F. G. 'Survey of the manor of Woodham Ferrers, 1582', *Trans. Essex Arch. Soc.* new ser., XXIV, 1951.

EVERITT, A. 'The marketing of agricultural produce', in *The Agrarian History of England and Wales*, ed. Thirsk, IV, 1967.

FISHER, F. J. 'Commercial trends and policy in sixteenth-century England', *Econ. Hist. Rev.*, X, 1940.

RAMSEY, P. 'Overseas trade in the reign of Henry VII: the evidence of customs accounts', *Econ. Hist. Rev.*, sec. ser., VI, no. 2, 1953.

RUDDOCK, A. 'London capitalists and the decline of Southampton in the early Tudor period', *Econ. Hist. Rev.* sec. ser., II, no. 2, 1949.

SCAMMELL, G. V. 'English merchant shipping at the end of the Middle Ages: some east coast evidence 1450–1550', *Econ. Hist. Rev.*, sec. ser., XIII, no. 3, 1961.

CHAPTER NINE: *The End of an Age*

Books

BINDOFF, S. T. *Ket's Rebellion, 1549.* Historical Association, Gen. ser., XII, 1949.

CROWLEY, R. *The Select Works.* ed. J. M. Cowper. Early English Text Society, Extra ser., XV, 1872.

CUNNINGHAM, W. *Alien Immigrants to England.* London, Swan Sonnenschein, 1897.

DIETZ, F. C. *English Government Finance 1485–1558.* First published 1921; 2nd edn., Cass, 1964.

A Discourse on the Common Weal of this Realm of England (1549). Edited from the MSS by E. Lamond, Cambridge U.P., 1893; repr. 1929.

FLETCHER, A. *Tudor Rebellions.* Longmans, 1968.

GOULD, J. D. *The Great Debasement: currency and the economy in mid-Tudor England.* Oxford, Clarendon P., 1970.

JONES, W. R. D. *The Tudor Commonwealth 1529–1559.* Athlone P., 1970.

JORDAN, W. K. *The Charities of London 1480–1660.* Allen & Unwin, 1960.

JORDAN, W. K. *The Charities of Rural England 1480–1660.* Allen & Unwin, 1961.

JORDAN, W. K. *Philanthropy in England 1480–1660.* Allen & Unwin, 1959.

NOONAN, J. T. *Contraception: a history of its treatment by the Catholic theologians and canonists.* Harvard U.P., 1965.

OUTHWAITE, R. B. *Inflation in Tudor and Early Stuart England.* Macmillan, 1969.

RAMSEY, P. H., ed. *The Price Revolution in Sixteenth-Century England.* Methuen, 1971.

RAMSEY, P. H., *Tudor Economic Problems.* Gollancz, 1963.

Articles

DAVIES, C. S. L. 'Provisions for armies, 1509–50', *Econ. Hist. Rev.*, sec. ser., XVII, no. 2, 1964.

ELTON, G. R. 'State planning in early Tudor England', *Econ. Hist. Rev.*, sec. ser., XIII, no. 3, 1961.

EVERITT, A. 'Social mobility in early modern England', *Past and Present*, no. 33, 1966.

FISHER, F. J. 'The sixteenth and seventeenth centuries: the dark ages in English economic history?', *Economica*, Feb. 1957.

PHELPS BROWN, E. H. and HOPKINS, S. V. 'Builders' wage-rates, prices and population: some further evidence', *Economica*, Feb. 1959.

PHELPS BROWN, E. H. and HOPKINS, S. V. 'Seven centuries of wages and prices: some earlier estimates', *Economica*, Feb. 1961.

PHELPS BROWN, E. H. and HOPKINS, S. V. 'Wage-rates and prices: evidence for population pressure in the sixteenth century', *Economica*, Nov. 1957.

STONE, L. 'Social mobility in England, 1500–1700', *Past and Present*, no. 33, 1966.

Appendix I Tax yields by counties (to nearest £) 1515—45

County	1515 subsidy	1524—25		Total subsidy 1524—25	1545 Benevolence
		1524 subsidy	*1525 subsidy*		
Bedfordshire	600	801	768	1,569	1,100
Berkshire	1,035	1,650	1,489	3,140	1,407
Buckinghamshire	837	1,054	1,000	2,054	1,262
Cambridgeshire	903	1,117	1,064	2,180	1,789
Cheshire	—	—	—	—	640
Cornwall	1,105	1,412	1,374	2,786	643
Cumberland	—	—	—	—	58
Derbyshire	308	561	543	1,104	438
Devonshire	2,804	4,677	4,463	9,139	4,527
Dorsetshire	1,139	1,882	1,782	3,664	1,418
Essex	2,518	3,654	3,348	7,001	5,252
Gloucestershire	1,841	2,557	2,293	4,851	2,529
Hampshire	1,748	2,385	2,227	4,612	1,443
Herefordshire	409	549	536	1,085	1,156
Hertfordshire	920	1,131	1,128	2,259	681
Huntingdonshire	526	821	845	1,666	651
Kent	2,502	4,549	4,175	8,723	6,471
Lancashire	114	298	297	596	660
Leicestershire	807	1,141	1,079	2,220	630
Lincolnshire	2,012	3,093	2,889	5,983	2,177
London	4,033	8,263	6,493	14,755	—
Middlesex	1,079	1,133	926	2,060	2,386
Monmouthshire	—	—	—	—	234
Norfolk	2,813	3,987	3,753	7,740	4,046
Northamptonshire	1,184	1,985	1,802	3,787	2,109
Nottinghamshire	434	544	512	1,056	432
Oxfordshire	879	1,264	1,140	2,404	2,412
Rutland	150	221	193	414	136
Shropshire	295	428	422	849	876
Somersetshire	2,734	3,168	3,046	6,213	7,174*
Staffordshire	409	661	539	1,201	464
Suffolk	2,154	3,812	3,383	7,195	4,512
Surrey	1,141	1,827	1,683	3,510	2,454
Sussex	1,300	2,368	2,278	4,647	2,379
Warwickshire	864	1,266	1,138	2,404	1,642
Wiltshire	1,903	3,277	2,886	6,163	1,769
Worcestershire	626	822	740	1,562	1,574
Yorkshire	1,249	2,183	1,949	4,131	—
King's, Queen's and cardinal's households	631	1,507	1,589	3,096	—
Personal payments of peers	—	1,670	766	2,436	—
Miscellaneous payments	—	26	21	47	—

* Including Bristol £366.

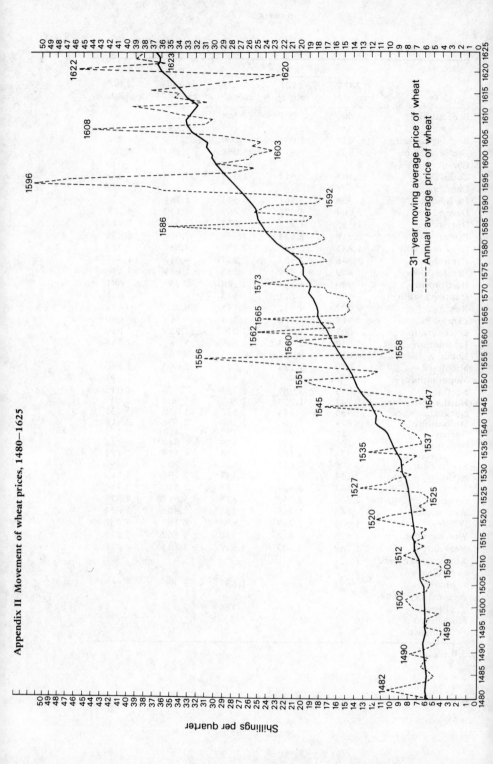

Appendix II Movement of wheat prices, 1480–1625

— 31-year moving average price of wheat
----- Annual average price of wheat

Shillings per quarter

Appendix III Annual prices (index numbers) of the grain and fodder crops, 1499–1558 (after Bowden)

Harvest year	Grains					Other arable crops				
	Wheat	Barley	Oats	Rye	Average – all grains	Hay	Straw	Peas	Beans	Average – all other arable crops
1499	72	100	97	74	86	96	95	103	115	102
1500	126	113	104	136	120	91	96	–	100	96
1501	128	113	119	135	124	95	94	119	101	102
1502	147	109	111	184	138	96	89	–	75	87
1503	130	117	105	141	123	115	118	121	98	113
1504	98	152	127	110	122	110	121	102	–	111
1505	99	116	104	149	117	57	94	115	82	87
1506	98	95	95	102	98	78	88	106	91	91
1507	113	88	104	121	107	93	96	112	102	101
1508	85	102	105	83	94	84	118	89	83	94
1509	69	77	94	67	77	115	85	86	97	96
1510	81	82	97	88	87	100	83	72	69	81
1511	111	99	103	112	106	112	91	95	83	95
1512	144	93	108	109	114	99	111	90	89	97
1513	121	104	101	100	107	123	104	117	–	115
1514	102	127	121	132	121	90	102	96	–	96
1515	127	112	115	96	113	102	103	105	107	104
1516	105	106	124	108	111	113	125	137	145	130
1517	109	132	178	97	129	117	152	151	176	149
1518	97	114	121	120	113	121	157	159	128	141
1519	140	154	127	156	144	160	138	188	279	191
1520	191	175	170	235	193	97	181	251	132	165
1521	166	176	153	236	183	88	126	162	132	127
1522	104	124	121	–	116	94	93	140	136	116
1523	109	77	135	118	110	96	99	97	–	97
1524	99	121	142	101	116	126	114	132	113	121
1525	95	116	129	101	110	115	80	157	156	127
1526	110	168	146	–	141	102	135	177	195	152
1527	227	121	207	236	198	125	174	239	231	192
1528	175	146	138	269	182	89	81	–	158	109

Appendix III continued on p. 248

Appendix III – *continued*

Harvest year	Grains					Hay	Straw	Other arable crops		Average – all other arable crops
	Wheat	Barley	Oats	Rye	Average – all grains			Peas	Beans	
1529	165	–	134	269	189	106	87	152	118	116
1530	130	160	129	172	148	85	124	115	127	113
1531	162	232	152	236	196	117	122	–	107	115
1532	150	162	173	267	188	97	173	173	146	147
1533	133	127	156	202	155	120	127	160	153	140
1534	116	106	145	225	148	113	99	150	122	121
1535	213	199	184	303	225	133	118	164	169	146
1536	156	124	182	154	154	121	124	149	133	132
1537	108	151	139	93	123	81	146	–	119	115
1538	113	136	144	102	124	95	144	112	163	129
1539	116	184	144	149	148	103	122	112	133	118
1540	122	201	140	–	154	111	111	–	143	122
1541	146	166	147	–	153	145	108	165	175	148
1542	139	239	147	–	175	126	105	–	140	124
1543	185	–	143	–	164	120	105	–	154	126
1544	192	–	192	–	192	138	119	–	178	145
1545	288	319	251	–	286	115	116	199	–	143
1546	139	142	200	–	160	131	119	–	166	139
1547	99	118	172	–	130	133	121	168	150	143
1548	138	–	186	–	162	197	133	–	–	165
1549	265	–	330	–	298	181	147	–	256	195
1550	294	–	411	–	353	259	212	–	469	313
1551	329	–	297	–	313	–	252	–	–	252
1552	204	302	337	–	281	277	255	–	332	288
1553	179	377	282	–	279	171	250	–	147	190
1554	267	–	413	–	340	328	304	–	171	268
1555	383	805	374	–	521	327	143	389	461	330
1556	528	582	564	–	558	164	184	454	469	318
1557	194	237	275	–	235	198	200	226	–	208
1558	179	402	270	–	284	160	168	–	256	195

Appendix IV Annual prices of livestock (index number) 1500—58 (after Bowden)

Harvest year	Sheep	Cattle	Horses	Pigs	Poultry and rabbits	Average – all livestock
1500	92	85	83	92	110	92
1501	84	91	107	114	84	96
1502	88	92	99	99	95	95
1503	81	99	78	80	140	96
1504	82	102	89	125	225	125
1505	88	109	109	149	161	123
1506	107	102	139	142	143	127
1507	108	100	127	118	106	112
1508	111	141	148	99	—	125
1509	108	105	162	96	125	119
1510	111	90	94	91	91	95
1511	122	102	70	122	72	98
1512	150	105	117	128	94	119
1513	108	87	101	153	87	107
1514	144	107	100	158	94	121
1515	126	118	138	121	87	118
1516	146	146	144	113	94	128
1517	128	147	110	163	92	128
1518	124	135	101	144	90	119
1519	123	156	111	161	108	132
1520	174	158	151	127	101	142
1521	144	126	138	178	109	139
1522	143	163	153	197	109	153
1523	130	154	150	118	—	138
1524	125	116	103	121	—	116
1525	121	116	133	142	—	128
1526	136	126	142	146	—	138
1527	131	151	110	138	—	133
1528	137	161	—	157	—	152
1529	134	161	153	114	131	139
1530	169	137	105	126	112	130
1531	184	169	157	117	107	147
1532	149	153	121	140	153	143
1533	151	119	97	134	138	128
1534	179	151	197	127	—	164
1535	148	139	118	133	103	128
1536	160	157	—	144	—	154
1537	167	155	174	103	—	150
1538	141	153	148	94	—	134
1539	133	140	154	126	180	147
1540	190	152	88	130	195	151
1541	165	163	196	139	188	170

Appendix IV – *continued*

Harvest year	Sheep	Cattle	Horses	Pigs	Poultry and rabbits	Average – all livestock
1542	201	156	180	141	157	167
1543	195	171	154	144	153	163
1544	198	160	–	–	244	201
1545	196	175	169	146	196	176
1546	240	143	167	138	192	176
1547	244	204	196	164	216	205
1548	239	215	293	164	239	230
1549	228	198	209	169	263	213
1550	315	259	280	184	250	258
1551	279	264	307	292	235	275
1552	222	244	206	352	–	256
1553	227	223	193	219	209	214
1554	204	212	258	243	326	249
1555	258	258	225	228	288	251
1556	293	339	216	447	192	297
1557	285	277	293	220	299	275
1558	255	282	271	256	220	257

Index

251